# An Introduction to Using Computers in the Law

# An Introduction to Using Computers in the Law

By

**MARY ANN MASON**

Professor St. Mary's College of California

ST. PAUL, MINN.

**WEST PUBLISHING CO.**

1984

## ABOUT THE AUTHOR

Mary Ann Mason teaches courses in Using Computers in the Law and in Legal Research and Writing. As the Director of the Paralegal Program at St. Mary's College in Moraga, California, she has been a pioneer in computer education for legal professionals.

Ms. Mason holds both a Ph.D. and a J.D. She has practiced law in San Francisco, California, and is currently a member of the California State Bar, The San Francisco Bar Association, and the Alameda and Contra Costa County Bar Associations. She lives in Berkeley, California with her husband, two children, and NORTHSTAR computer.


50 West Kellogg Boulevard
P.O. Box 43526
St. Paul, Minnesota 55164



**Library of Congress Cataloging in Publication Data**
Mason, Mary Ann.
An introduction to using computers in law.

Includes index.

1. Law offices—United States—Automation. 2. Information storage and retrieval systems—Law—United States. 3. Legal research—United States—Data processing.
I. Title.
KF320.A9M3 1984 340'.028'54 83-27443
**ISBN** 0-314-80352-1

Mason Computers in Law

For My Dad

*

# PREFACE

Learning to use computers as an adult is something like learning to ski at mid-life. First, one must be convinced that it is worth the effort, possibly overcoming years of fear and dismissing horror stories about unfortunate skiers. Then a thorough investigation of the potential ski resorts and necessary hardware must be undertaken. It is only with the first trips down the slope, however, that the new skier can finally evaluate the worth of his brave new venture.

Using computers to assist in the practice of law is definitely worth the effort, but it does require a good deal of preparation. This book will help the potential user become familiar with the possible applications of the computer in law offices of different sizes, and provide a general introduction to the rapidly changing varieties of hardware and software available. It is written for the computer novice, which may include everyone from the senior partner to the bookkeeper. It will take the novice to the edge of the slopes, but only using the computer itself will convince him of the value of the venture.

MARY ANN MASON
March, 1984

*

# ACKNOWLEDGMENTS

I am most grateful to my NORTHSTAR computer, which made the writing a speedy and pleasurable process, and to my husband Paul, who brought it home and first instructed me in the wonders of word processing. My son Tom, with his steady hand, took some of my very obscure sketches and turned them into comprehensible line drawings.

As a technical reader, Bruce Phillips, an attorney and currently marketing director of new products for CORVUS, verified the accuracy of the technical descriptions and provided some very sound stylistic observations as well. Clark Moscrip and Joyce Ellenberg were kind enough to read and comment on an early draft. Bev Hildenbrand and Pat Lapin provided some important clerical assistance.

*

# TABLE OF CONTENTS


| | Page |
|---|---|
| Preface | V |
| Acknowledgements | VI |

**PART I. ALL ABOUT COMPUTERS**

| | |
|---|---|
| Introduction: Practicing Law Tomorrow | 1 |
| **CHAPTER 1. BASICS** | **5** |
| Why Computers? | 5 |
| How Do Computers Work? | 6 |
| Hardware | 6 |
| A. Central Processing Unit | 7 |
| B. Auxiliary Mass Storage or Memory | 10 |
| C. Input/Output Devices | 13 |
| Software | 18 |
| A. Operating Systems | 19 |
| B. Language Assemblers, Compilers and Interpreters | 20 |
| C. Utility Programs | 20 |
| D. Application Programs | 20 |
| E. Communications Programs | 21 |
| **CHAPTER 2. COMMUNICATING** | **22** |
| Telecommunications | 23 |
| Telecommunications and the Practice of Law | 26 |
| A. Electronic Mail | 26 |
| B. Intra-Office Networks | 26 |
| C. Out-of-House Computers | 27 |
| Future Communications | 28 |
| **CHAPTER 3. WHAT SIZE IS YOUR COMPUTER?** | **30** |
| Microcomputers | 30 |
| A. Hardware | 30 |
| B. Software | 33 |
| Word Processors | 39 |
| Minicomputers | 40 |
| A. Hardware | 41 |
| B. Software | 41 |
| C. Personnel | 42 |

Page

Mainframes ---- 42
A. Computer Service Bureaus ---- 42
B. Time Sharing ---- 43

**CHAPTER 4. COMBINATIONS AND CONFIGURATIONS: THREE CASE STUDIES ---- 45**

More Hardware ---- 45
More Software ---- 45
Better Communications ---- 46
Fewer Employees ---- 46
Case Study # 1: Mr. Solo, Esq. ---- 46
Case Study # 2: Up and Coming ---- 49
Case Study # 3: Rich, Big and Old ---- 50

**PART II. COMPUTERS AND MANAGEMENT**

INTRODUCTION: Computers and the Organization of Documents and Financial Matters ---- 53

**CHAPTER 5. MANAGING DOCUMENTS: COMPUTERIZED LITIGATION SUPPORT SYSTEMS ---- 55**

Advantages of Computer-Assisted Litigation Support ---- 57
A. Speed and Thoroughness ---- 57
B. Simultaneous Access From Separate Locations ---- 57
C. Production of Indices and Reports ---- 57
D. Statistical and Financial Analysis ---- 58
When to Computerize? ---- 58
Creating a System ---- 59
A. System Design ---- 59
B. Choosing Hardware and Software ---- 59
Creating a Database ---- 62
A. Collecting Documents ---- 62
B. Document Analysis ---- 62
Searching and Retrieving ---- 68
Using the Information ---- 70
A. Discovery ---- 70
B. Witness Preparation ---- 70
C. Trial ---- 70
The Future of Computer Assisted Litigation Support ---- 70

**CHAPTER 6. MANAGING WORDS: WORD PROCESSING 71**

Functions ---- 73
A. Text Editing ---- 73
B. Merging ---- 73
C. Storage ---- 73

Page

D. Spelling Checks ---- 73
E. Records Management ---- 73
F. Global Search and Replace ---- 74
G. Repagination ---- 74
H. Math Functions ---- 74
I. Docket/Calendar Control ---- 74
J. Communications ---- 74
K. Photocomposition Interfaces ---- 74

Applications ---- 74
A. Memoranda, Briefs, Pleadings ---- 75
B. Litigation ---- 75
C. Corporate Practice ---- 75
D. Family Law, Probate, Bankruptcy, Immigration ---- 75
E. Real Estate and Estate Planning ---- 75
F. Tax ---- 75

Savings ---- 76

Hardware for Word Processing ---- 77
A. Microcomputers as Word Processors ---- 77
B. Stand-Alone Dedicated Word Processors ---- 78
C. Combinations and Permutations ---- 79

Optical Character Recognition Units ---- 80

The Computer Marriage of Word Processors and Data Processors ---- 81
A. Data Base Management ---- 81
B. Sophistication ---- 81
C. Cost ---- 81
D. Disadvantages ---- 82
E. Offspring of the Marriage of Word Processing and Data Processing ---- 82

Restructuring the Law Office ---- 83
A. The Secretary ---- 83
B. The Paralegal ---- 83
C. The Attorney ---- 84
D. Law Office Managers ---- 84

**CHAPTER 7. CASE MANAGEMENT: DOCKET/CALENDAR AND CONFLICT-OF-INTEREST SYSTEMS 85**

Docket Control/Calendar Systems ---- 86
A. Manual Systems ---- 86
B. Computer-Based Docket Control Management ---- 86
C. Word-Processor-Based Docket-Control System ---- 88

Conflict-of-Interest Systems ---- 88
A. Manual Systems ---- 89
B. Computer-Assisted Conflict Systems ---- 89
C. The Human Factor ---- 90

Page

**CHAPTER 8. FINANCIAL MANAGEMENT** ---- **91**

Time Is Money ---- 91

Computers as Timekeepers ---- 93

More Money Managers ---- 94

A. Accounting—Keeping Track ---- 94

Computer Options ---- 96

A. Service Bureaus ---- 96

B. Minicomputers ---- 97

C. Microcomputers ---- 97

**PART III. COMPUTERS AND RESEARCH**

An Introduction to Computer-Assisted Legal Research ---- 99

A. Public and Private Data Bases ---- 99

B. Information Storage: The World on Your Desk ---- 100

C. Information Retrieval: Lightning Access ---- 100

**CHAPTER 9. PUBLIC LEGAL DATA BASES** ---- **103**

The Pros and Cons of Using a Legal Data Base ---- 103

The Data Bases ---- 104

WESTLAW and LEXIS ---- 104

A. Operation ---- 104

WESTLAW ---- 106

A. Equipment ---- 106

B. Operation ---- 107

C. WESTLAW Data Bases ---- 107

D. WESTLAW as a Litigation Support System ---- 109

E. Costs for WESTLAW ---- 110

LEXIS ---- 110

A. Equipment ---- 110

B. Operation ---- 110

C. LEXIS Data Bases ---- 111

D. LEXIS as a Litigation-Support System ---- 114

E. Costs for LEXIS ---- 114

Legislative Tracking Systems ---- 115

Governmental Data Bases ---- 116

A. JURIS ---- 116

B. FLITE ---- 117

C. RIRA ---- 118

D. LAWNET ---- 118

**CHAPTER 10. A USER'S GUIDE TO WESTLAW AND LEXIS** **119**

Using WESTLAW ---- 120

A. Step 1. Formulating the Search Query ---- 120

B. Step 2. Entering the Computer ---- 122

C. Step 3. Changing the Search Query ---- 122

Page

D. Step 4. Changing the Data Base 123
E. Step 5. Shepardizing 124
F. State Statutes 125
G. Evaluation 125
H. Further Research Techniques 126
I. Specialized Searches 128

Using LEXIS 129
A. Step 1. Formulating the Search Query 129
B. Step 2. Entering the Computer 131
C. Step 3. Changing the Search Query 132
D. Step 4. Changing the Data Base 133
E. Step 5. Auto-Cite and Shepard's 134
F. Further Research Techniques 134
G. Specialized Libraries 135
H. Nonlegal Data Bases 136

Conclusion 136

**CHAPTER 11. PUBLIC NONLEGAL DATA BASES 137**

Legal vs. Nonlegal Data Bases 138

Pros and Cons of Nonlegal Data Bases 138

Specialized Data Bases 139
A. Legally Related Information 139
B. Congressional and Legislative Information 140
C. Business and Finance 140
D. Medical and Technical 141
E. General News and Information 143

Access to Nonlegal Data Bases 144
A. Single Data Base 144
B. Multiple Data Bases 144

Using Dialog 145
A. Data Bases 145
B. Operation 146
C. Following Through 147

NEXIS 147

Retailers 147

**CHAPTER 12. THE FUTURE OF PUBLIC DATA BASES 149**

Computer Typesetting 149

Data-Base Publishing 150

Electronic Publishing 150
A. Cost 151
B. Desktop Terminals 151

Disk Publication 152

## PART IV. COMPUTERS AS REASONERS, PREDICTORS, AND TEACHERS

Page
Introduction ---------- 153

**CHAPTER 13. FROM DOCUMENT PREPARATION TO LEGAL CONSULTATION ---------- 155**
Automated Documentation-Preparation Systems ---------- 155
A. Automated Word Processing Substantive Systems ---------- 155
B. Automated Computer Document-Preparation Systems ---------- 156
Computers as Consultation Machines ---------- 159

**CHAPTER 14. COMPUTERS AS PREDICTORS AND EDUCATORS ---------- 161**
Computers as Predictors ---------- 161
A. Judicial Decisions ---------- 161
B. Jury Selection ---------- 162
Computers as Educators ---------- 164
A. Law School Education ---------- 164

## APPENDICES

App.
A. Glossary ---------- 167
B. Selected Bibliography ---------- 172
C. WESTLAW Data Base ---------- 176
D. WESTLAW—Certified Compatible Equipment List ---------- 189
E. LEXIS Data Base ---------- 193
F. Dialog Database (File Number(s)) Dates of Coverage ---------- 208
INDEX ---------- 217

# PART ONE

# All About Computers

## INTRODUCTION: PRACTICING LAW TOMORROW

The product that a lawyer offers is information. A legal practice is set up to: take in information from many sources (clients, courts, and legislatures); organize it; store it; analyze it; and produce specific information in response to a specific problem. Because computers have almost limitless memories and nearly instantaneous retrieval powers, they are a wonderful time-saving tool for attorneys and legal support staff. However, they cannot replace human brains. Their memories are superb for storage and retrieval but at present they are very limited for analysis.

Because they are so efficient, computers are rapidly transforming the everyday work habits of lawyers and their legal support staffs. This is what a day in the life of an attorney in a medium-sized law firm in the not-too-distant future may be like.

The attorney arrives at his desk. The only object on it is a computer terminal, consisting of a keyboard and video screen. Calling forth his calendar on the video screen, he is informed that he must file a trial brief three days from today in a suit involving a breach of contract in a shopping center under construction. The video screen calendar also notifies him that he has a luncheon engagement with a new client from Fast Foods Inc. at noon, and that he is scheduled to take the deposition of a witness in a personal-injury suit at 2:00 this afternoon. The computer serves as a nearly infallible calendaring device: it projects all possible filing deadlines and automatically reschedules deadlines when there is a continuance.

Next, the attorney checks his electronic mail. His video screen reveals that a client for whom he is drafting an inter vivos trust has transmitted a copy of all his stock holdings. The electronic mail also tells him that one of his law partners, who specializes in tax, has forwarded a memorandum on inter vivos transfers that the attorney requested yesterday.

The attorney decides to work on the trial brief this morning. He commands the computer to retrieve the client's file, and reviews on the screen those portions that interest him—in this instance, the pleadings and all memoranda relating to that suit. Client files are organized so that individual documents or generic documents, like all pleadings, can be reviewed separately.

He recalls that there was a previous suit handled by his firm regarding a breach of contract during construction. Therefore he accesses the data base that contains all the firm's memoranda and briefs. Using key words based on this legal problem, he retrieves two memoranda that have similar fact situations. Skimming them quickly on the screen, he commands the high-speed printer next to his desk to print five pages of relevant text.

With the printed text at hand, he now begins to draft a trial brief on the keyboard of his terminal. Using the computer's split-screen capability, the attorney transfers many of the arguments and legal authority that have already been researched in the previous memoranda from one part of the video screen to the new document on the other part of the screen. Realizing that he must refer back to the client file for particular facts, the attorney again uses the computer's split-screen capability, reviewing the client file on the left-hand side of the screen and drafting the brief on the right.

Since he requires research on current case law in order to complete the brief, the attorney places the draft of the trial brief into memory. He then accesses the WESTLAW data base in St. Paul, Minnesota, via the telephone modem attached to his terminal, and TELENET, a private telecommunications network. Within a few minutes he has located the most recent case law in this area, has printed relevant sections of the opinion on the high-speed printer, and has "Shepardized" the pertinent cases through WESTLAW.

The conglomerate corporation that is developing the shopping center and suing his client (one of the contractors) for breach of contract is on the American Stock Exchange. In order to assess his opponent's strength, the attorney makes contact with DIALOG, the huge information-retrieval service in Menlo Park, California, via the same telephone modem, which is still connected to TELENET. Selecting from among the 170 data bases offered by DIALOG, the attorney chooses DISCLOSURE II, which provides extracts of reports filed with the U.S. Securities and Exchange Commission. The attorney quickly determines his opponent's economic standing—an important factor in developing his trial strategy.

He now recalls his brief, revises it at the keyboard, and merges it with the proper court form, which is in the computer memory. He prints a draft copy and sends the electronic copy to his secretary's terminal for final production and filing.

It is not yet lunch time, and already he has completed a complicated trial brief without even leaving his desk.

The computer will facilitate the afternoon's deposition as well. It is possible to enter the entire text of the reporter's transcription directly into the computer if it is prepared on machine-readable tape (which is now customary). Any portion of the transcript can then be retrieved with the appropriate search terms. This is an enormous aid in sifting through the mountains of evidence often required to present a case at trial. All the other documents in this personal-injury litigation can be entered into the computer data base, either in full-text form or in abstracted form for easy organization and retrieval when preparing for trial.

Before the attorney leaves the office, he will enter his billable hours into the computer. These will be recorded directly in each client's account. The attorney also will bill the client for such technical services as time spent on WESTLAW and DIALOG. However, the client is well served: the attorney's total time is greatly shortened by these technological aids.

That evening, after dinner, the attorney suddenly recalls that his firm may have represented one of the subsidiaries of the firm that Fast Foods is about to sue. Since he is catching a plane very early the next morning to meet with the general counsel of Fast Foods, he needs to find out quickly whether there is a possible conflict of interest. He connects his portable home microcomputer to a telephone modem and makes contact with the data base at his law office to determine whether there is indeed a conflict. Since the computer cannot locate a conflict, the attorney is satisfied. He catches the early morning plane carrying his portable computer, which will allow him (by means of the telephone) complete access to all the information in the law office. It will also allow him to relay information back to the office in the form of electronic mail.

## COMPUTERS AND LEGAL SUPPORT STAFF

The use of the computer is by no means restricted to the attorney. Its efficiency reaches into all aspects of the law office—in fact, it restructures the entire operation. Until the day (perhaps not so far off) when both courts and clients will accept documents electronically transferred from computer to computer, a human still has to prepare final documents for mailing, to open and sort incoming mail, and to answer the telephones. Logically, this same person would also enter important dates for each attorney's calendar on his own terminal, and would enter appropriate information into each client file as it arrived in the mail. The computer will eliminate nearly all the labor-intensive typing and retyping of drafts and forms, since word-processing capacities make revisions simple, and computerized forms require only a few insertions. The traditional role of the legal secretary will shrink.

On the other hand, the role of the paralegal (which was already established in the precomputer era) will expand greatly in the computer age. With easy access to computerized forms of all kinds, trained paralegals can be used to draft pleadings, divorce proceedings, simple wills, probate proceedings, and so forth on their own terminals. In a well-developed system, computers that receive the appropriate information can even suggest which forms or clauses to use. Attorneys can easily review and revise this electronic draft into final form on their own terminals. Much time and paper will be saved. All interoffice communications will take place between computers. In the area of litigation support, paralegals will continue to organize documents for trial; however, they will use the computer, rather than time-consuming manual methods, to store and retrieve.

The remaining sphere of a law office—the so-called "back-office," where the not-so-glamorous but essential functions of billing and accounting take place—are the first to be transformed by the computer. Almost all large firms and most smaller firms already have some kind of computerized billing system, often using an outside service. The task of billing becomes simple if good timekeeping records are kept, and the computer makes this much easier. Electronic accounting programs make accounting faster and more accurate. The computer can also be put to good use in developing models of future income and of tax planning for better firm management.

This description of the computerized law office is by no means visionary. All the technology already exists and is actually being used by some of the largest firms as well as by some innovative smaller firms. The cost of implementing law-office automation no longer is restricted to only the largest firms. Hardware—the machine and its peripherals—seems to grow less expensive, smaller, and more efficient by the day. Software—the programs that make the machines work—is becoming more available for all varieties of law practice.

# CHAPTER 1

# Basics

## WHY COMPUTERS?

Computers are useful because they perform two functions at incredible speed, and with almost total accuracy: the storage and retrieval of vast amounts of information, and the computation of numbers. Almost all the tasks performed by the attorney in "Practicing Law Tomorrow" required the creation, storage, and retrieval of information. Most of the functions performed in his law firm's back office involved storage, retrieval, and computation. Broken down into these two categories, attorneys and legal workers are called upon to perform the following tasks daily:

1. Storage and retrieval of information
   - Legal research
   - Factual research
   - Storage and retrieval of litigation documents
   - Creation, storage, and retrieval of memoranda, pleadings, forms, and other office work products
   - Calendaring and docketing
   - Conflict-of-interest checks
   - Client mailing lists
   - Personnel records
   - Legal education
   - Tracking legislation
   - Electronic mail

2. Computation
   - Time-keeping
   - Billing
   - Accounts receivable
   - General ledger
   - Financial management reports
   - Tax preparation
   - Amortization schedules
   - Estate planning
   - Financial modeling

A combination of these two skills is applied in the newly developing area of decision making or artificial intelligence. This can be put to use in law practice to predict the outcome of litigation, to choose juries, and potentially to make decisions regarding legal strategy.

## HOW DO COMPUTERS WORK?

Fortunately, lawyers or legal workers do not have to deeply understand how computers actually perform their functions of storage and retrieval or computation in order to apply these functions to daily legal tasks. Nor do they need to know how to program a computer—there are trained programmers who can put together sophisticated, ready-to-use packages for legal use, or who can design a custom package for individual needs. In fact, since a new program can take months of a professional programmer's time to produce, it does not make sense for an attorney to put billable hours to this use.

What an attorney or legal worker does need to know is which time-saving tasks computers can perform for him, and what kinds or configurations of computers can best accomplish these tasks. In order to make these assessments, however, some understanding of the actual technology is useful.

## HARDWARE

The term *computer* really describes the entire system. This includes both the machinery—called "hardware'"—and the instructional programs that operate the machinery—called "software." The hardware of different computer systems may look like members of entirely different species, but computer systems operate on common principles, whether they are designed to read the prices on cans at the supermarkets, monitor a spacecraft to Mars, or edit a standard contract.

In all computer systems, the machinery—hardware—can conceptually be divided into three parts: the central processing unit, the auxiliary mass storage devices, and the input and output apparatus.

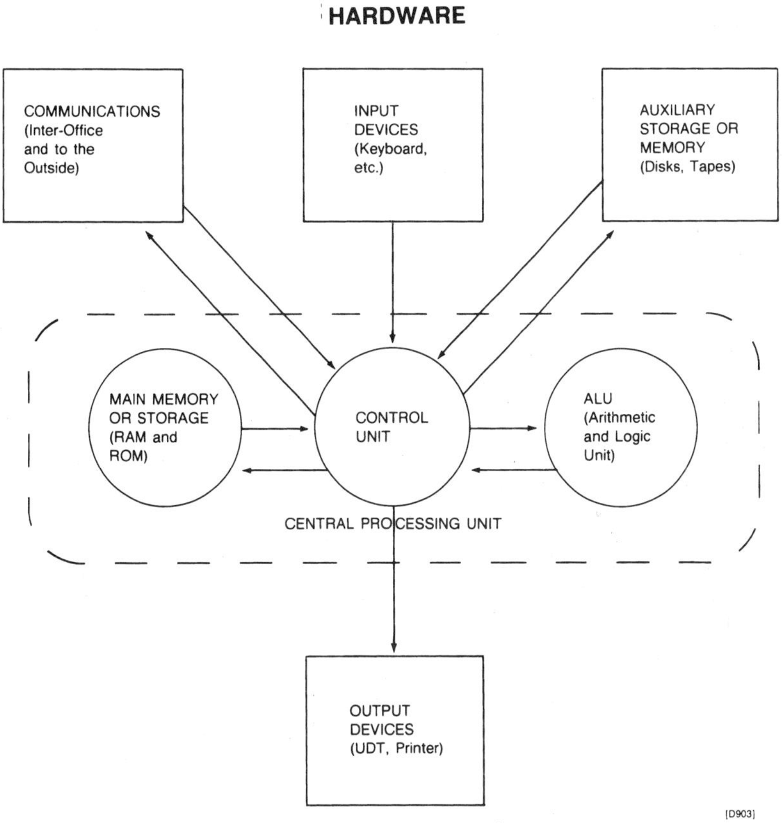


## A. Central Processing Unit

The central processing unit (CPU) is truly the brain of the computer. In modern computers it is made up of silicon chips that are about 1/4 inch square in size. Each chip is a complex semiconductor containing thousands of transistors and other parts commonly referred to as large-scale integrated circuits, or LSIs. The CPU performs all the arithmetic and logical functions of the computer; it has a memory to retain information for instantaneous retrieval; and it provides the control mechanism to regulate all the other functions of the computer. The operational divisions of the CPU are the arithmetic/logic unit, the main memory, and the control unit.

### 1. *Arithmetic/Logic Unit (ALU)*

The ALU of the central processing unit performs arithmetic functions and makes logical decisions, based on the instructions given to it by a program. It carries out these instructions by breaking a task down into logical operations that can be carried out on binary numbers—strings of 0s and 1s—and by doing hundreds of thousands or millions of such operations each second.

### 2. *Main Memory, or Storage*

#### a. *Bits and Bytes*

Information is stored in the main memory or storage of the CPU in binary format. This means that the smallest element of computer memory can be in only one of two electronic states: "on" or "off," which corresponds to the binary numbers 0 or 1. This smallest element is called a binary information digit, commonly abbreviated as "bit." In most microcomputers it takes eight bits to represent a single character, such as the letter "q" or the number "8." Data is stored and transmitted between main storage and the ALU for mathematical and logical operation in multiples of eight bits, or "bytes."

A computer's power is often described by the terms "8 bit" and "16 bit." These designations represent the amount of information that can be processed in one machine cycle. The more bits that can be processed in one machine cycle, the faster—and therefore more powerful—the machine. The amount of information a computer can hold in main memory is also determined by "bit" size. (See RAM and ROM, below.) Computers used for scientific purposes are often "32 bit."

Computers operate with superhuman speed. Machine cycles are measured in nanoseconds, or billionths of a second. For instance, an "8-bit" computer accomplishes approximately two million cycles per second, while a "16-bit" machine performs four million cycles per second. The speed at which a computer operates is the most important factor in determining the number of user terminals that can be connected to it. WESTLAW's computer can handle thousands of user terminals, while most microcomputers give reduced performance with more than two or three terminals.

#### b. *RAM and ROM*

Bits of information are stored in main memory or storage in one of two forms: RAM (random access memory) and ROM (read-only memory). The information bits that are stored in RAM memory can be accessed in any random order, without having to search the memory serially, or bit by bit. This makes access almost instantaneous. The time needed to get a bit out of memory can be as little as ten millionths of a second. RAM is used to store data and programs that may change. For instance, if a legal worker uses the computer for word processing on Monday morning and for timekeeping functions on Monday afternoon, he will be using different programs and different data. This information will be stored in RAM memory so that it can be removed when programs and data are changed. All information in RAM memory is extinguished when the computer is turned off.

Since many programs take a great deal of RAM memory, this is a number you will see advertised when looking at computers. RAM memory is measured in thousands of bytes, or kilobytes, normally referred to as K. Therefore, when a computer manufacturer advertises that its product has 64K RAM, it is saying that the computer has 64,000 [redacted]bytes of random access memory in main storage. In general, computers with larger memories can handle more sophisticated programs. Some of the largest computers measure their main memory in millions of bytes, or megabytes (MB). The huge computers owned by WESTLAW and LEXIS run programs that must retrieve information from millions of documents. These have main memories that are measured in megabytes, while a dedicated word processor with only one function may have a main memory of only a few kilobytes.

The relationship of "bit" size to RAM memory size is as follows: 8-bit microcomputers generally can directly access 64K RAM; 16-bit computers can directly access up to 1 MB RAM; and 32-bit computers can directly access up to 16 MB RAM.

ROM, or read-only memory, is electronically similar to RAM. The only differences are that the information stored in ROM does not change, and it is not extinguished when the machine is turned off. The information is written in at the factory; it cannot be altered. Some computers such as dedicated word-processors, or pocket calculators, perform only one function. The programs for these computers are kept in ROM memory and cannot be changed or taken out. They also cannot be updated, which can be a serious disadvantage. These machines normally have little or no RAM memory.

There are also unchanging functions that control the operation of a computer. These functions, which are stored in ROM memory in all computers, might include at least some of the most fundamental "systems programs," such as those that get a computer going when it is turned on, or those that interpret a keystroke.

Most modern computers have what is called MOS memory—"metal-oxide semiconductor" memory. Information stored on MOS chips is volatile, which means that data is lost when the power to the computer fails. In the future, computers may contain "bubble memory," in which the memory chip is made from synthetic garnet and is nonvolatile. Information can be stored more compactly on bubble chips in the form of magnetic fields. Therefore, larger main memories will become the norm. Unfortunately, the access time to the information stored in "bubble memory" is somewhat slower than with MOS memory.

*3. Control Unit*

The control unit of the CPU monitors and supervises the operation of the entire system. It includes a cycle clock, counters, and decoding circuits, which enable the unit to direct and schedule movement of data within the CPU as well as between the CPU and the various peripheral devices (for example, the printer, or terminal). How fast information can be processed is determined by the speed at which the cycle clock operates, as well as the "bit" size. A faster clock and a larger "bit" make a more powerful computer.

## B. Auxiliary Mass Storage or Memory

After the CPU, the next most important component of computer hardware is auxiliary mass storage, also referred to as auxiliary memory. Main storage in the CPU is extremely expensive, in terms of both the initial investment and power used. Although the programs or part of programs that give instructions to the CPU must be stored in main memory, you don't usually have to store more than a fraction of the data you are processing there at any given moment. For instance, if you are using a word-processing program to draft Points and Authorities on a small multi-use computer, the computer may take only the specific part of the program you are using (for example, the editing function) into RAM memory and only a few hundred words of the text you are editing. The remainder of the program and the text will remain in an auxiliary storage medium, probably a floppy. Access time to main memory is from about 25,000 to 75,000 times faster than access to auxiliary storage. For many functions, however, such as editing a document, the access time to auxiliary storage is still so fast that this does not present a practical impediment. For other functions—such as searching a hard disk containing several hundred documents to find a specific piece of information in preparation for trial—a small computer's lack of speed may cause problems.

There are several existing varieties of auxiliary storage, and more in the development stages. The larger the amount of data storage that is "on-line" (that can be accessed by the CPU), the larger the variety of functions that can be performed. For instance, while you would not need access to a large amount of data when editing a will or drafting a pleading, you would need a large "on-line" data base for storing and retrieving hundreds of documents in preparation for litigation.

### *1. Disks*

A disk is a device that stores large amounts of data in a manner that allows fast access. The disk is the medium of storage, and a disk drive is the machine that makes it work. Data is stored on disks similar to the manner in which music is stored on records. The surface of the disk is coated with magnetic compound, and electric signals representing the data are fed onto the surface using a read/write head. The disk is divided into concentric rings called tracks, like the tracks on an LP record. Each track is divided into sectors. Each track and sector has an address so that individual pieces of information can be readily retrieved, just as a particular song can be picked out on a phonograph record.

The amount of data that can be stored on disks is measured in bytes, as it is in main memory. Disk storage is usually expressed in thousands of bytes (K) or millions of bytes (MB). The capacity of disk storage is far greater than that of main storage; even microcomputers may have many hundred megabytes of disk auxiliary storage. At this time, disks usually come in two varieties: floppy disks, which are exchangeable, and hard disks, which are usually fixed.

#### *a. Floppy Disks*

The reason these disks are called "floppies" is because they appear as a flexible plastic disk contained in a square envelope. They may be either $5^1/4$ or 8 inches in diameter. The total storage of a floppy disk varies according to (1) the density of the data stored along a track, and (2) the number of segments into which each track is divided. Most floppy disks now have a capacity of from 125 to 500 K; some new varieties can store more than 1 MB. 500 K represents about 140 printed pages. The access time for retrieval on floppy disks is relatively slow, since the disk drive generally is not very fast. Floppies usually are found on microcomputers and larger machines such as dedicated word processors, where the ability to store and retrieve a large amount of data for any single task is not needed. Because floppies are easily removed for off-line storage, hundreds of forms and old client files can conveniently be stored on floppy disks.

#### *b. Hard Disks*

Hard disks are used in applications that require large data-storage and fast retrieval facilities—for example, searching and retrieving hundreds of documents for litigation. Most very large computers today use hard disks. A single disk can have a storage capacity of from five to several hundred megabytes. The single disk can be joined with others in one disk drive to produce millions more bytes of memory storage. It can also be joined with still other disk drive configurations to produce billions of bytes of storage. While most everyday tasks in a legal practice do not require billions of bytes or storage, the huge data bases maintained by WESTLAW and LEXIS do.

The disk drives that run hard disks are far more powerful than those that propel the floppies. Therefore the rate at which the information can be retrieved ranges from hundreds of thousands of bits per second for floppy-disk systems to 10 million bits per second for hard disks.

Hard disks normally are called Winchester disks. This was the code name for the first hard-disk memory system, which was introduced by IBM in 1973. A Winchester disk is usually permanently sealed in the disk drive (there are some exchangeable varieties). Winchester disks have their disadvantages too: they are considerably more expensive than floppies; and since they contain so much data and cannot be removed, they must normally be backed up (copied) by some other medium, such as floppies or tape.

Recently, there have been great advances in developing hard disks for smaller and smaller computers at a reasonable price. Most microcomputers now advertise that they can be equipped with a hard disk as well as floppy disks. This greatly expands their versatility by allowing for storage of larger amounts of information. Networking several small computers around one or more commonly shared hard disks is also increasingly popular.

### c. *Optical Disks*

The technology of auxiliary storage has advanced dramatically in the past decade with the widespread adoption and improvement of the Winchester disk, and it continues to progress. In the near future, an optical disk system—in which information is stored and retrieved by laser—may enable the contents of a library of several thousand books to be stored on a single disk.[1] Unlike microfilm, where print is simply made smaller, with optical disks all the powers of instant retrieval by key words or phrases would be possible. The implications for the legal profession are staggering. The case files for an entire courthouse could be kept on a single disk, not to mention all the inactive client files in a law office.

**1.** White, "Disk Storage Technology," 243 *Scientific American*, no. 2, August, 1980, 138–148.

In many ways the technology of the magnetic and optical systems are alike. Both require disks; both require a head to "write" and "read" the data onto and off of the surface of the disk. In the one case, the head is an electromagnetic device that resembles a tape-recorder head; in the other, the head is a laser and its associated optics.

The main disadvantage of the optical system at this time is that the laser burns a hole into the metal disk medium. This makes it impossible to erase or alter the information burned into the disk. Therefore, unless the technology that allows alteration can be developed, the main use for optical disks will be for archival material (such as old client files or reference libraries) that can be updated by some other medium.

### 2. *Magnetic Tape*

Magnetic tape is both the least expensive and the slowest medium for retrieval. While information on disks can be accessed at random, information on magnetic tape is stored and accessed sequentially. In that sense, disks are like LP phonograph records in that the needle arm can be placed at any point, whereas tapes are like audio cassettes in that you must play through the whole tape in order to locate a particular song.

Because of the slow nature of the retrieval, tapes are most commonly used in law offices for back-up, off-line storage of large data bases (for example, financial records), or outdated material that probably will never be needed again.

### 3. *Future Auxiliary Mass Storage Applications*

The law office of the future is likely to use a variety of storage media. Optical disks will be used for archival storage, including reference libraries; hard disk storage will be used for projects requiring large data bases that must be updated continually (for example, litigation documents); and floppies will continue to be used for routine text editing. The same computer system will be capable of handling all media.

## C. Input/Output Devices

The third category of hardware—input and output devices—come in many different forms. The machine that reads prices on cans at the supermarket is an input device, while the machine that prints your airline ticket is an output device. Sometimes a device serves as both an input and an output device. An example is a terminal on which you both enter and retrieve information.

### 1. *Terminals*

A keyboard is the most common type of input device in a law office. Often a combined video screen and keyboard are attached to a computer as a single unit. A video screen is sometimes called a cathode ray tube (CRT), or a video display terminal (VDT). The whole unit is referred to as a terminal.

#### a. *Dumb Terminals*

A "dumb terminal" is a terminal that must rely on the CPU of a central computer; it has no memory or logic of its own. When several terminals share the same central computer, the configuration is called a "shared-logic" system. This configuration is currently popular in law offices that have a large central dedicated word processor with several "dumb terminals."

#### b. *Intelligent Terminals*

An intelligent terminal has some memory and can perform many functions without relying on the central computer. A system that uses both intelligent terminals and a central large computer is called a "distributed-logic" system.

#### c. *Microcomputers as Terminals*

Microcomputers are certainly intelligent terminals and they offer increasingly more memory. They can be attached to one another, or "networked" to share data bases and to communicate. This configuration is sometimes referred to as a "shared-resources" systems or a "network" system. The network may include printers and duplicating machines as well. Each of these may have a very small memory of its own.

### 2. *Optical Character Recognition Unit (OCR)*

An optical character recognization unit is an input device that converts printed characters into computer machine-language for storage on magnetic medium, or for entry into the CPU for processing. The main mechanism of the OCR is an optical character reader, or scanner, which "reads" hard copy (a printed page), then converts it into an electronic impulse for entry into the computer or for storage on a magnetic tape. Scanners work via laser and photocell technology. Currently, they can "read" data or text at a speed of approximately two pages per minute.

Although potential applications are dramatic, current applications in law offices are limited, for the most part, to "reading" documents that have already been typed in the office into a word processor or data processor. This circumvents the labor-consuming step of rekeying the document. For instance, a secretary types the first draft of a brief in the proper format, then gives it to the word-processor operator, who "reads" it (rather than typing it) into the word processor, where it will be available on a floppy disk for easy editing. Since the OCR does not "read" red or blue felt-tipped pens, the attorney can make corrections even before the draft is sent to the OCR. A similar procedure is followed by "reading" typed time sheets into a data processor for computation. In some offices the OCR's repertoire has been expanded to include the "reading" of full-text deposition tapes into the computer.

The possible applications of OCRs are almost unlimited. Full text of client files, office memoranda, and litigation documents could be "read" into a central data base. In short, all the documents that comprise the practice of law could be placed in a computerized data base for rapid access and editing. Unfortunately, the technology has not yet lived up to these expectations. There are limitations: the hard copy that can be "read" by a scanner is limited to certain fonts (type faces), and the copy must be on appropriate paper, with appropriate formats. Almost everyone who has worked with an OCR has experienced the frustration of losing whole lines, or having the machine arbitrarily substitute characters throughout the document. OCRs are also very expensive thus far, ranging from about $10,000 to $40,000.

Since there is a potentially enormous market for OCRs in business as well as law, much engineering activity is focused on perfecting these devices. There is hope that technological developments will proceed with OCRs as they have with other areas of computer hardware: vastly improving the quality and lowering the cost.

### *3. Automatic Speech Recognition*

The ultimate fantasy of almost every attorney who has worked or who hopes to work with computers is to speak directly to the computer in ordinary language. The attorney might simply say to the computer, "Find me all the cases in the federal court system since 1975 that have dealt with the issue of the pirating of computer software." The computer then would dutifully search its data base and produce the relevant cases on the screen; or it might respond by asking, "Do you mean all forms of software, or would you like to limit your request to application programs?" Whether the computer responds in a humanlike voice or in a printed response on the video screen probably does not make that much difference. The important points are that (1) the attorney does not need to touch the keyboard, and (2) the computer will make leaps in logic, which will allow it to conceptually limit a very broad request.

Of course, the applications of such a capability are almost limitless. The labor-intensive task of typing or entering words and numbers would disappear. An attorney could dictate the document into the computer, which would print it on the video screen. Alterations could then be made by simple voice commands. Bookkeepers would enter the numbers with their voices, and make their corrections that way too.

Unfortunately, the technology to accomplish this fantasy is not just around the corner. After 40 years of research in this area by governmental and private organizations, the automatic recognition of natural or conversational speech remains a utopian goal. Current speech-recognition devices have small vocabularies and little ability to deal with fluent sequences of words; usually they must be trained to recognize only one speaker's voice. Even so, the advantages are so great that devices capable of recognizing a vocabulary of from 10 to 30 words are commercially available, and are economically practical in some applications.

The core of the problem of speech recognition is the complex and variable way in which linguistic messages are encoded in speech. Computers do not live in the world of people, nor do they learn from everyday experience. Therefore, for a computer to "know" a natural language, it must be provided with an explicit and precise characterization of the language. At the present stage of understanding of language, this is possible only to a very limited degree.

A second major difficulty is that human voices are remarkably different. Anyone who has attempted to learn a foreign language from one teacher and who then visits the country where that language is spoken is always dismayed to learn that the same words sound very different when spoken by different people.[2]

For attorneys and legal professionals, however, even very limited voice-communication capabilities may be useful. It might not be possible to draft a trial brief by voice, but it would be a dramatic advance if key words could be used to call up cases from a data base. Unfortunately, the keyboard itself often keeps attorneys away from computers. Many attorneys learned touch typing quite proficiently at some point in their adolescence, but as adults are unwilling to ever approach a keyboard again. This means that they must depend upon others to perform the simplest computer tasks. Even limited voice recognition could break this keyboard barrier.

**2.** Levinsa and Liberman, "Speech Recognition by Computers," 244 *Scientific American*, no. 4, April, 1981, 64–76.

### 4. *Handwriting Recognition*

Technology is progressing more rapidly with the problem of handwriting recognition than it is with voice recognition. The written word is obviously a less complex phenomenon than the spoken word, although there is still the problem of individual differences. Both hardware and software are expected to be available to conquer this problem in the '80s. Currently, a particular system (DATASYSTEMS, from England) is being used by some law firms to facilitate the coding of documents in litigation support. This eliminates the step of typing the codes into the computer, and it is particularly handy for the coding of documents at sites away from the law office. The existing system, however, demands a stylized block print; it will not accept normal handwriting.

The capability of reading handwriting and putting it into machine-readable form is a useful one, but obviously a far less significant capability than voice recognition. For experienced typists, it takes much longer to handwrite a document than to type it. However, handwriting recognition may be most useful for those attorneys who either cannot or will not use a keyboard.

### 5. *Printers*

The two major output devices used in a law office are the video display terminal and the printer. Until paper is eliminated in the practice of law, the printer is an essential ingredient of computer hardware. Since law practice generally demands a very polished finished product, the quality of the printer is an important issue.

Printers are generally classified as either impact or nonimpact. An impact printer creates a printed character by striking the paper with some device. A nonimpact printer creates a character by some other means—for instance, spraying with an ink jet or burning the paper with a laser. The major considerations in choosing a printer have to do with speed, quality of print, noise level, reliability, and cost.

#### a. *Impact Printers*

Impact printers are generally less expensive and more reliable than nonimpact printers. They also have multicopy capacities. However, they are also slower and noisier. For letter-quality output, most law offices use either selectric printers, which are very slow (15 characters per second), or daisy wheel printers, which are speedier (30 to 55 characters per second). For a product that does not require letter-quality printing (such as first drafts or in-house financial reports), matrix printers or line printers are used. Matrix printers deliver up to 340 characters per second. while line printers can accomplish 600 lines per minute.

*b. Nonimpact Printers*

The future probably belongs to nonimpact printers. Improved technology and lowered costs will make these very fast, quiet printers the preferred choice. Currently, the ink-jet printer, which offers letter quality at 92 characters per second, is the most common nonimpact choice for legal professionals. Laser printers, with their good quality and incredible speeds of up to 200 pages per minute, will become widely used when their cost is lowered; at $30,000 plus, they are out of the range of most firms. Other technologies, which include thermal printers and electrosensitive printers, are also likely to become more popular. However, most require specially treated paper.

## SOFTWARE

Although dramatic advances have been made in virtually all areas of hardware over the past ten years, the machinery is useless without the proper instructions to run it. Good software that is "debugged" (well tested) is extremely difficult and time-consuming to produce. Programs to perform complicated tasks may take months or even years of a talented programmer's time. Unfortunately, some law offices have had the experience of buying the hardware first and then hiring a programmer to produce customized software. Several years and many thousands of dollars later, the programs may still be filled with "bugs."

Software, or program instructions, come in several forms, each providing different functions. These are called: operating systems; language assemblers, compilers, or interpreters; utility programs; communications programs; and application programs. The attorney really needs to become familiar only with application programs. These instruct the computer to perform specific tasks, such as word processing or accounting. All the other programs usually come with the computer and are "transparent" (not visible to the user).

**SOFTWARE**

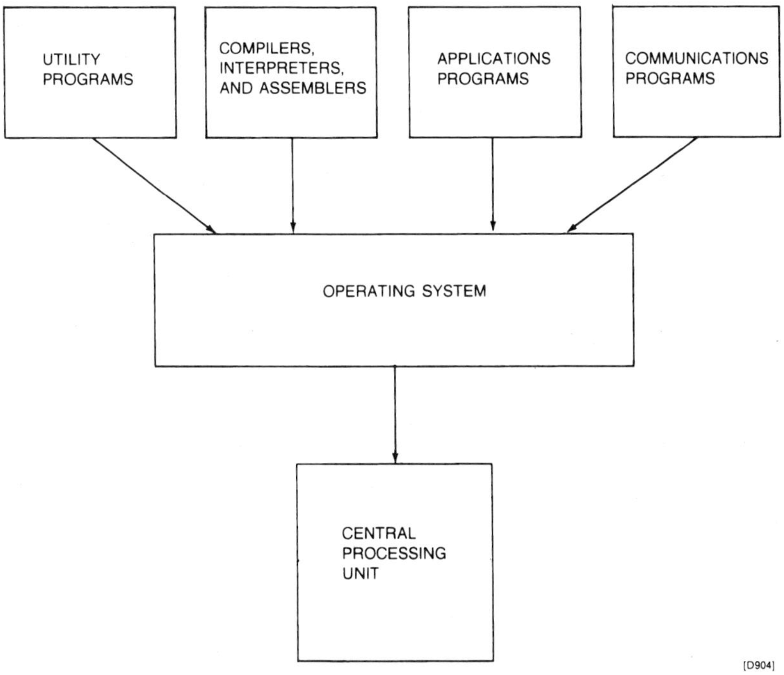


## A. Operating Systems

The operating-system software serves as the traffic director of the computer system: it controls the flow of data entering and exiting the entire system. The flow of its instructions may be seen in the following sequence: it relays information from input devices to auxiliary storage devices; it transfers the information from the auxiliary storage devices into the main memory; it orders the execution of arithmetic and logic functions; it orders the processed information to be outputted (usually to a printer); and, if communication to another terminal or by telecommunications is desired, it gives the necessary command.

For large computers, a specific operating system is usually designed by the manufacturer for that specific hardware. Among the microcomputers, however, there has been a distinct trend to use the same operating system—currently, CP/M or MS–DOS—in order to make use of the same application programs.

## B. Language Assemblers, Compilers, and Interpreters

Programs must be in "machine language" (a string of binary digits) in order to be executed. The translation from a higher-level language, such as BASIC, FORTRAN, or COBOL, to machine language is done by programs called assemblers, compilers, and interpreters. Assemblers and compilers translate the entire program before it is run; interpreters translate each instruction in turn as it is being run.

## C. Utility Programs

Utility programs are routine programs that are used to perform system-related maintenance functions and tasks. An example of a utility program is the "bootstrap" program, which supplies the initial instructions when the program is first turned on. A utility program may also enable the user to sort data files alphabetically or numerically.

## D. Application Programs

Application programs are what make the computer useful. These are the programs that the user deals with directly. Instructions on different application programs allow the same computer to perform such diverse functions as drafting a pleading and computing a time sheet. All the other programs merely prepare the computer for these complex applications. Often, application programs that give instructions for sophisticated tasks can be more expensive than the hardware that performs them.

Some computers, such as dedicated word processors, perform only one appliction, and have a program that is permanently written into their ROM memory. The trend in law offices, however, is toward multi-use computers. Their use may be limited only by the available application programs. For instance, the same computer may be able to perform word-processing activities, time-keeping functions, and billing functions, but unable to perform the calendaring functions because the appropriate application program for calendaring has not been written for that computer system. Some computers can accept more than one application program at the same time. In such a system, one terminal can be performing editing functions and another can be performing accounting functions, or both can be performed on the same terminal with a split screen.

Currently, application programs for law offices can be obtained from the hardware manufacturers, from software houses (which provide either packaged or customized programs) from computer retail stores (packaged programs), or from an individual progammer who is hired to develop customized programs in-house. For microcomputers, there is a tremendous cottage industry of individual entrepreneurs who develop application programs and market them through the computer trade journals or legal periodicals. Because of the tremendous growth and increasing competition in the area of packaged application programs, the choices are confusing and often expensive for the consumer.

## E. Communications Programs

Communications programs enable one computer to talk to another computer or to another terminal, whether it is in the next room or the next state. (See Chapter 2, "Communicating"). This can be done via in-house wiring or via a hookup to a telecommunications network. Communication among computers or terminals is commonly termed "networking." The programs for this are usually supplied by the computer manufacturer and are specific for each computer. Recently, however, software houses have been developing communications programs that allow communication among different brands of computers. Programs to accomplish networking have been especially susceptible to faulty "debugging." This is an area in which the software has not successfully kept up with the hardware.

# CHAPTER 2

# Communicating

The attorney in "Practicing Law Tomorrow" communicated on an interactive basis (talked back and forth) with a WESTLAW computer in Saint Paul, Minnesota. He also communicated interactively with the DIALOG computer in Menlo Park, California, which contains over 170 nonlegal data bases. The attorney used this same computer to transmit and receive information from other computer terminals in his law office. When he left the office he used his portable computer to contact the computers there in order to receive and send information, both from home and from out of town. He also received information from the computer of one of his clients. Currently this is quite feasible, providing that the client has the appropriate hardware and software to communicate with the attorney's computer. Short messages, whole documents, or 30-page memoranda could be transmitted between client and attorney at electronic speed. The attorney could send long documents to clients in major cities in Europe and some parts of Asia in only a few minutes rather than several days, by way of TYMNET [1] or one of the growing number of international private telecommunications networks, providing that the European client possessed the correct hardware and software with which to receive it.

If physical space becomes no limit to communication, will the walls of the law office come tumbling down? It is already possible for an attorney to work at home, or almost any place in the country and have nearly complete access to all the services he would have while sitting at his office desk. There are still psychological, and perhaps practical, reasons for centralizing work in a traditional office atmosphere; but the technical necessity for doing so is fast disappearing.

**1.** TYMNET, the largest private telecommunications network, currently advertises 400 continental access locations, and 29 international access locations.

When computers were first introduced into the business scene, they were primarily used to store, retrieve, and compute information at a single site. Increasingly, however, the communication of information between and among computers has become a major focus in itself, helping to expand the office and shrink the world. We have grown accustomed to national and international telephone and television communication via satellite. Now this is being expanded to national and international data-communication of all kinds, serving the needs of even the smallest business, such as the law office of a sole practitioner.

## TELECOMMUNICATIONS

Telecommunications is the basic term used to describe the process of transmitting information electronically from one location to another. This definition encompasses not just the transmitting of computer data but also other well-established media used in the law, such as telephones, telex machines, and facsimile equipment. Computer data is the latest entry in this media family, and it shares the same networks of transmission. These networks are normally "transparent" to the users (users don't know if the telephone call they are receiving has been transmitted through transatlantic cable or bounced from a satellite). In fact, many forms of communication may use more than one network in a single communication.

Within the United States, communications networks may use copper coaxial cable (used in telephone lines), and microwave and satellite channels. Internationally, undersea cable and more satel-

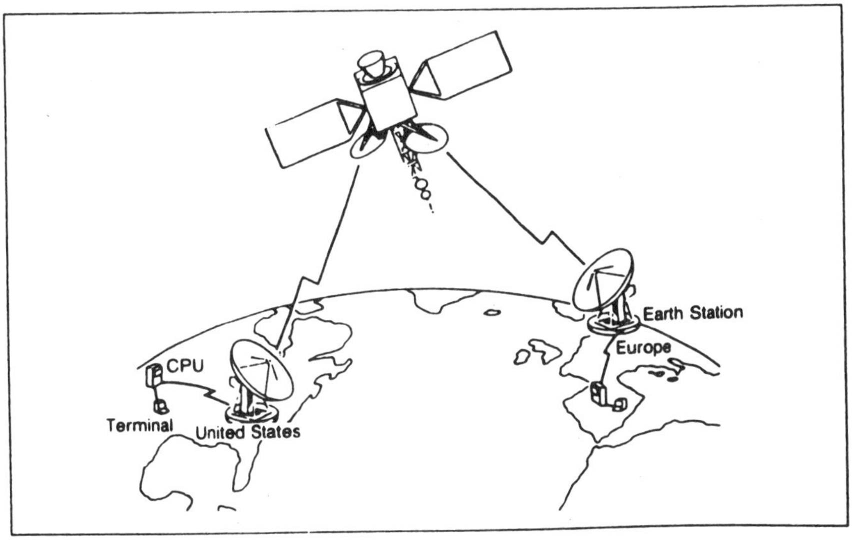


**SATELLITE COMMUNICATIONS**

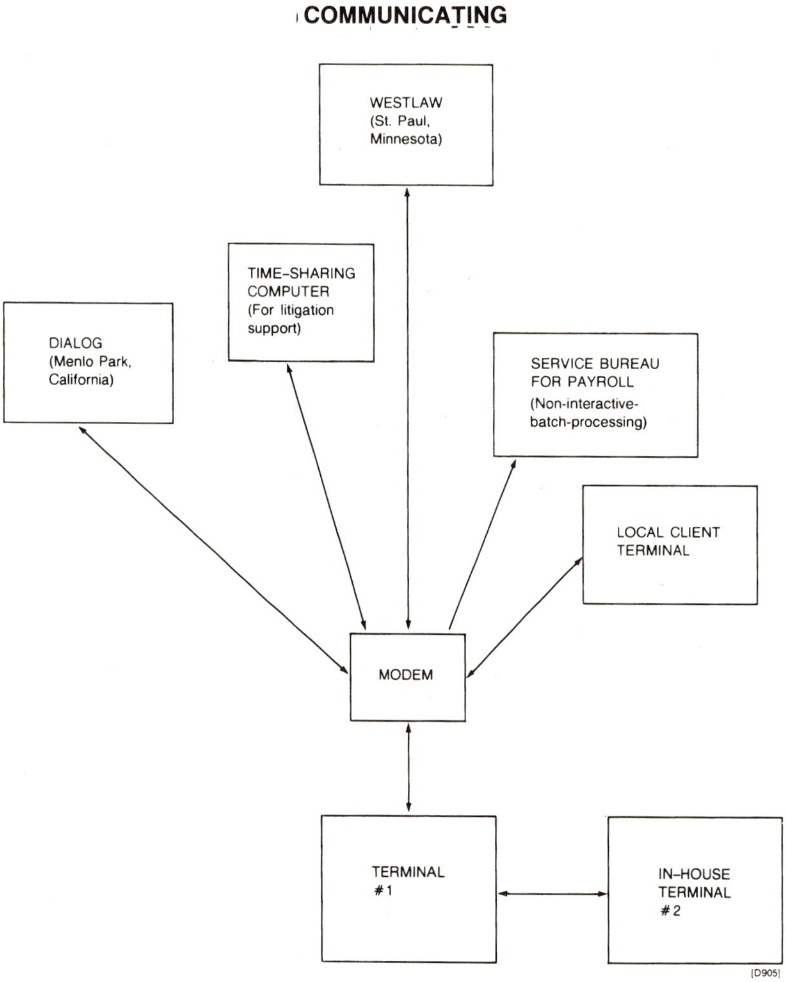


lites are used. Fiber optic and infrared transmissions are being actively researched. Those offer promise for the future, since they can carry many more messages on the same channel without interference from one another, and at greater speed than is possible with copper coaxial cable.

Currently, most national data transmission is carried through coaxial cable, including public telephone lines, private dedicated lines, and private package-switching systems. More than 60 percent of the telephone lines are designed for analog transmission, which means that electronic impulses are transmitted in a continuous range. This kind of transmission is particularly suited for the voice. In contrast, a digital signal is a stream of on/off electrical pulses that are sent in a coded format down the communications channel. These on/off pulses are what make up binary digits or "bits," which are the signals generated by the central processing unit of computers. Therefore, digital transmission is quite suited to the transmission of computer data; analog transmission is not.

An analog transmission line (most cable lines are still in this form), requires a piece of hardware called a "modem" to change the computer digital signals into analog signals so that they can be transmitted along the telecommunications wires. The modem is attached to or placed near a computer terminal. Sometimes it is installed inside the computer, and thus is not visible. Computer terminals require a modem at each end to convert the digital signal into an analog signal for transmission along the line, and then to reconvert the analog signal back into digital form to be understood by the second computer. Most new telecommunications lines are being established as digital lines to better accommodate computer transmissions. However, telephone companies have a massive investment in the existing analog lines, and it will be a long time before the modem becomes just a piece of antique computer memorabilia.

Most attorneys use ordinary public telephone lines for communication between computers outside the office. This is partly because telephone lines may be less expensive, and also because they reach virtually everyone in the country. However, they have their disadvantages: they transmit large amounts of data relatively slowly, and the interference on these crowded wires can be substantial. A private dedicated leased line is frequently used between organizations or between branches of organizations with a lot of internal business. Law offices generally don't use a private line unless branch offices are involved, since the cost is competitive only where there is larger volume.

Private packet-switching lines, however, are becoming increasingly popular because of their very fast transmission rate. TYMNET and TELENET are the most well known of these private lines. A packet-switching network is significantly different from an ordinary telephone line. Packet-switching computers capture the communication from the sender and reformat it into a packet, or predefined block of data. This predefined block of data makes use of wide band communications and is sent over the wires at an extraordinarily high speed. At the other end another computer translates the signal back to its original form for reception by the second computer. This service is more expensive than transmission over ordinary telephone lines, but is essential for tasks where a large amount of data must be transmitted at fantastic speeds, such as the transmission of very long court opinions by WESTLAW. All the major data base services, such as LEXIS, WESTLAW, DIALOG, BRS, and ORBIT, use either a packet-switching, or a dedicated leased line, to insure clear transmission at high speeds.

# TELECOMMUNICATIONS AND THE PRACTICE OF LAW

## A. Electronic Mail

The term "electronic mail" has become a popular "computerese" term to describe a variety of different functions. Some home computer information services, like The Source, use it to advertise what is basically an electronic message board, where subscribers can leave notes for other subscribers in The Source computer for retrieval. Alternatively, there are sophisticated software packages, which allow not just messages, but whole files of information, to be sent between computers within the same office, or over a telecommunications line (with a modem) to computers at the farthest point reached by the telecommunications line. This electronic mail service even allows certain computers of different manufacture to exchange "mail", as long as they are both equipped with the same software. It is also possible, though considerably more expensive to use software which will allow interactive communication between computers (a back-and-forth exchange).

Unfortunately, the U.S. Post Office is not threatened with imminent extinction. Although a great deal is possible and new software breakthroughs occur every day in the communications field, progress is made very difficult by the way in which computer industry has grown up—with no standardized regulations for storage or communications functions. It's as if there were hundreds of varieties of telephone receivers, and special extra equipment had to be added to enable one telephone to communicate with another. Or it's as if every record-player company made its own LPs with specifications that could be used only by certain record players.

Data transmission from a computer is a technically complex phenomenon in which there are many varieties and possibilities. For instance, computers may be in a serial or parallel mode; they may send data in a synchronous or an asynchronous fashion; or they may use 6-bit, 7-bit, or 8-bit codes. Although a user doesn't have to understand all these technical variations, he must be certain that technically the computers can actually communicate with each other, even with software adjustments. Unfortunately, this is not always possible.

## B. Intra-Office Networks

Lawyers use "electronic mail" mainly to transmit data to other computers or terminals in the same law office (at least as of this writing). A computer network may consist of a fairly large central computer with several nonintelligent terminals connected to it, or to several free-standing computers wired to one another, or to any combination of the above. The network may also include word processors, printers, duplicating machines, and facsimile devices.

The main purpose of a computer network is to make maximal use of the available computing and storage capacities, and to share and exchange information within the office. Accomplishing this requires some kind of telecommunication, which usually takes the form of a coaxial cable that physically links all the hardware together and allows data transmission, either one-way or two-way. This telecommunication network usually does not require modems, since it can transmit digital signals. An intra-office telecommunication system is relatively simple when the user is connecting hardware from the same manufacturer, designed for this sort of communication. However, the system may become difficult or impossible when the user tries to link computers of different manufacture, or even of the same manufacture but of different vintages. Many older word processors, for instance, were not designed to communicate at all.

## C. Out-of-House Computers

Many attorneys use the services of large computers outside the office for a variety of essential tasks. It is often more economical to use computer capabilities in this manner, and sometimes it is the only choice, as in the case of large research data bases.

One fast-growing area is computer-assisted research, using the computers that house enormous legal data bases (such as WESTLAW and LEXIS) or nonlegal data bases (such as those provided by DIALOG or BRS). In terms of communication, each of the legal and nonlegal data bases is located in a large mainframe computer somewhere in the country (St. Paul, Minnesota, for WESTLAW; Dayton, Ohio, for LEXIS; and Palo Alto, California, for DIALOG), and must be accessed by telecommunications. The company will either provide its own terminal, with appropriate communications software and modem (when necessary) or it will become compatible with some but not all microcomputers or word processors by adding appropriate software. Many of these database services use packet-switching systems such as TELENET or TYMNET, which allow much faster transmission of information. If they are relatively close by, the regular telephone lines may sometimes be used less expensively.

Service bureaus, which provide a large computer to perform such tasks as billing, payroll, accounting, and management reports, are increasingly popular with all sizes of law practices. Information can be sent to these services either in a batched form by mail, or by telecommunications, using an in-house terminal, appropriate software for communications, a modem (if transmitted on an analog line), and the telephone lines. Usually the service is close enough to use the telephone line rather than a private network such as TELENET. (These services are discussed at length in other chapters.)

Other service bureaus offer the use of large computers on a time-sharing basis, or offer a full staff in addition to the computer to handle the sometimes gargantuan task of organizing documents in preparation for litigation. Some of these services are national in scope and have a single central computer. Communication with this computer may take place by mail or by means of an in-house computer with proper software and modem. The telephone lines or (with very large cases) the private packet-switching lines may be used. (The use of computers in litigation support will be fully explored in Chapter 5.)

## FUTURE COMMUNICATIONS

It is obvious that the need for computers to communicate with one another will grow as the use of computers grows. There have been dramatic advances in the area of telecommunications, most notably with increased use of satellites. The trend in telecommunications transmission systems is to offer mixed and merged voice, video, and data communications at the choice of the individual or business. This means that in the not-too-distant future, an attorney in San Francisco could have a face-to-face video conference with a client in New York, and exchange documents during the course of the conference.

Telecommunications are rapidly becoming faster and cheaper. Telecommunications costs to the user have been dropping 10 to 12 percent each year. While this is a very respectable drop, it is not as dramatic as the 20 percent per year decrease in the price/performance curve of computing. For most legal tasks, it is still probably too expensive to send long documents by telecommunications rather than mail, if time is not a critical factor. However, this may change in the near future. When the cost of telecommunications becomes much cheaper than the cost of gas required for commuting, the concept of the central office may be challenged.

To create a truly effective communications network among computers, however, what's needed to assure compatibility is not just improved telecommunications transmission but also more standardized hardware and software in the manufacture of computers. Organizations such as the Institute for Computer Science and Technology of the National Bureau of Standards are promoting uniform communications standards. Market demand will probably determine this within the next decade.[2]

**2.** Branscomb, "Moving Data Between Computers", in Bigelow, ed. *Computers and the Law,* 3d ed., A.B.A. Section of Science and Technology, 1981, 33.

# CHAPTER 3

# What Size Is Your Computer?

Once a lawyer or legal worker has decided that a computer will indeed make him more productive and, he hopes, wealthier, he faces his most difficult choice: which hardware or configuration of hardware and which software will do the job best. The kind of hardware he chooses may determine the software possibilities. Often, it is necessary to reverse the order of choice, since the most sophisticated hardware in the world will not edit a will if the appropriate software has not yet been developed to accomplish this.

Computers basically come in three sizes: micro, mini, and mainframe. (However, rapidly advancing technology has blurred these distinctions.) There is a fourth category—home computers. These have small memories (usually less than 50 K) but good graphics and simulated sound capacities. Although the distinction between a home and a business computer is not always so clear, home computers are usually reserved for fun and games, and would not be a likely choice for a law practice. Micros, minis, and mainframe computers can stand alone or form limitless configurations by hooking up to dumb or intelligent terminals, or to each other.

## MICROCOMPUTERS

### A. Hardware

Since 47 percent of all practicing attorneys are solo practitioners and another 17 percent are in law firms of from two to three employees,[1] the microcomputer (which was designed for small

1. *Report of the A.B.A. Annual Meeting*, August 8, 1981.

**COMPUTER CHIP**

businesses) may prove to be the most significant piece of equipment introduced into law practice since the typewriter. Its greatest attraction is that it can do most of the tasks performed by large computers at a cost affordable to most solo or small law practices.

Microcomputers, or personal computers as they are often called, have presented themselves to the public in the most dramatic manner in the past few years. Because of their rapidly increasing powers, the only clear way to distinguish them from the larger minis is price. Currently a microcomputer can be purchased for under $5,000 (this does include a letter-quality printer). This fact makes it possible to introduce computers into small law practices where only a few years ago the idea of a computer was merely an expensive fantasy.

Microcomputers can be distinguished from the more limited home computers, which are normally hooked up to the home television, in the following ways: the system can support a main memory of 64 K or more (this means about 10,000 words of English text); auxiliary storage memory, in the form of floppy disks, hard disks, or tapes, are included or can be added; the computer can handle at least one high-level language, such as BASIC; and the operating system allows an interactive dialogue (it responds to the user's continuing requests). A final but critical characteristic is that the system is designed to use a wide range of application programs performing varied tasks, and is not designed for a single purpose (for example, playing Donkey Kong).

In a microcomputer the CPU consists of the following: a microprocessor, which performs the arithmetic and logical functions and is contained within a single integrated circuit on a chip of silicon; several silicon memory chips, which contain the computer's main memory; and still other chips, which carry out the control functions. (See the discussion of the central processing unit in Chapter 1.) The chips are mounted on a heavy plastic circuit board; a printed pattern of conductors interconnects the chips and supplies them with power. The input devices that normally accompany the CPU of a microcomputer include: auxiliary mass storage devices in the form of disks or tape; a keyboard; ~~and a video screen~~. Output devices usually include a printer and perhaps a modem, which can convert the computer's signals for transmission over the telephone lines, or receive signals from other computers by means of the telephone lines.

The microcomputer is the result of the fantastic decrease in the cost of computer processing units and the increasing tread toward miniaturization. The cost of computer logic devices is falling at the rate of 25 percent per year, and the cost of computer memory is falling at the rate of 40 percent per year. Computational speed has increased by a factor of 200 in 25 years. In the same period the cost, the energy consumption, and the size of computers of comparable power have decreased by a factor of 10,000. The result is that the microcomputer can deliver the same basic computing power as a mainframe in the early 1960s, and as a minicomputer in the early 1970s.

It is difficult to characterize the power of a microcomputer, since its capabilities change almost daily. The two major determinants of the microcomputer's power are (as with any computer) its "bit" size and its electronic clock. The bit size represents the amount of information that can be processed in one machine cycle. As the bit size increases, an operation can be completed in fewer machine cycles; as the electronic clock increases in frequency, more cycles occur per second. With a larger bit size, there is usually access to a larger volume of main memory, or RAM. (See bits and bytes in Chapter 1.) The first generation of computers all had 8-bit word sizes. In 1982, 16 bit and 32-bit computers were available, and the trend is definitely toward larger bit sizes.

Since the larger bit size usually allows faster access to main memory and auxiliary memory, these volumes have also expanded. Currently, the 64 K RAM chip of main memory is common; but it is predicted that by 1988 256 K will be the norm. This will allow for increasingly sophisticated application programs. Although most microcomputers use floppy disks, there is a strong trend toward hard Winchester disks. This means that many megabytes of auxiliary storage (which are necessary for large data bases) of the size required for litigation support in medium-sized cases are possible even now with micros. For instance, a 10 MB hard disk can hold 10,240,000 characters—about 5,120 double-spaced letter-sized pages of text.

## B. Software

Microcomputers are really aiming toward the small business market, and the vast majority of law offices are small businesses. In addition to being low in cost, microcomputers also cater to this species of business by offering packaged, relatively inexpensive application programs that can be operated by any user. Many manufacturers have adopted a standardized operating system—primarily CP/M for 8-bit micros and MS–DOS for 16-bit micros (with a smaller trend toward XENIX for 16-bit machines as well). This has encouraged mass-market development of these programs. The simplicity of using these packaged programs supposedly eliminates the high overhead of specialized computer operators.

The first generation of microcomputer application programs could, in fact, be operated by any user, but they generally took a fair number of hours to master. The second generation, which began to appear with the advent of 16-bit microcomputers, are more user friendly and offer integrated systems with a single menu. This means that the user can choose from the menu to create a document or to balance the accounts, and that each of these application programs can make use of a common data base of information. Some programs also make it possible to use a split-screen technique to perform more than one task at a time. The most highly publicized of this new genre, Apple's "Lisa," advertises a split screen on which a user can review information on one side while creating a new document on the other. While Lisa software represents the trend in microcomputer software, it is geared toward general business use and does not address specific legal needs. It is also, at the moment, out of the $5,000 range defining a microcomputer.

Another 16-bit microcomputer, Alpha Micro, which can support hard disks, also advertises many of same integrated features offered by Lisa, as well as a special integrated software package for law practice. Called PROMIS, and provided by Western Computer Systems, Inc., this system offers multiple functions on a single menu: word processing, billing and accounting, management reporting, a tickler file, and an automatic conflicts file. Although this system, when fully configured with a printer, currently costs somewhat more than $10,000, it is within reach of some small offices.

### 1. *Legal Application Software*

At this time, microcomputer software for legal needs lags somewhat behind the capabilities of the hardware available. However, new software is introduced every month. It is confusing and frustrating for a small firm that cannot afford a consultant (and most cannot) to have to evaluate all the possible choices. Probably the best strategy is to routinely read some of the journals that regularly evaluate legal software, such as *Law Office Economics and Management* (Callaghan and Co., 3201 Old Glenview Road, Wilamette, IL 60091); *Legal Economics Automation and Management* (575 Madison Avenue, New York, NY); and *Legal Automation News* (Communications Exchange Inc., 1730 North Lynn Street, Arlington, VA). General computer magazines, such as *Infoworld,* are useful for ascertaining trends and new software of a general-business nature, but they do not often deal with specific legal software. It is also useful to talk with other attorneys who have made software purchases, and to join local Bar Association sections that focus on computers or technology. Visiting computer stores may be helpful, but the sales staff is usually not very knowledgeable about legal applications. The following list suggests some of the currently available software. Hopefully, this is just the beginning of a great flowering of legal application programs.

#### a. *Word Processing*

Since each law office is virtually a private publishing house, producing long and short documents in great abundance, the single most universal need for computer assistance is in the area of word processing. Fortunately, the general word-processing packages offered for business and personal use are adaptable to legal needs as well. Those manufacturers that have adopted a CP/M operating system offer the following word-processing packages: WordStar, Select, Perfect Writer, Spellbinder, and others. WordStar and Perfect Writer are also available for the IBM PC and Apple II and IIe. WordStar is currently the most popular. It offers almost all of the features available on dedicated word processors.

The 16-bit IBM PC (which can use the standard operating system, MS–DOS) has its own word-processing package, Easywriter. Apple II, Apple IIe, and Radio Shack's TRS Model II provide their own operating systems and their own word processing packages, although these can be converted to CP/M with additional software.

### b. *Time Keeping, Billing, and Accounting*

The second greatest demand for computer assistance is in these so-called "back-office" functions, which provide the fuel to run the machine. Unfortunately, a law firm's billing system is different from that of other professionals. With many attorneys, time keeping is complex, and billing arrangements can include complicated retainers, contingent fees, fees awarded by court, minimum fees set by statutes, and so on. The trend is toward very detailed billing accounts, and the generally available business software packages that deal with billing and accounting are usually inadequate.

For CP/M-operated microcomputers, the available packages for legal applications are quite expensive: from $2,500 to $8,000. These include software packages from the Business Group, DataLaw Co., and Lawtomation. Less expensive but less sophisticated programs are offered by Microcraft, Micro Information Systems, and Advanced Legal Software.

Apple II, Apple IIe, TRS–80, and other manufacturers offer their own billing packages, but these are not considered entirely adequate for legal billing needs even though they are advertised for legal use.

For law-office accounting, the general-business software packages are quite appropriate. There are no lack of these for CP/M, MS–DOS, and individual operating systems.

Electronic spreadsheets, such as SuperCalc and VisiCalc, are available for a wide variety of microcomputers. They are suited to long-term financial modeling, for such projects as predicting the financial status of the firm in five years.

### c. *Data-Base Management*

A powerful data-base management system (DBMS) can perform many tasks. Its basic function is to store and retrieve information with amazing rapidity. In a law firm the uses of DBMS are almost limitless. The same software can be used for time keeping and billing, litigation support, docket control, calendaring, and storing and retrieving work products. DBMS is perhaps the least developed but most promising area of computer application in the law office. Currently, the best DBMS software packages are not designed primarily for law offices; however, they can be adapted for this use. These packages include Aston-Tate's dBASE II and Condor, both for CP/M systems. dBASE II is also available for the IBM PC.

Lotus I, II, and III combination electronic spreadsheets, database managers, and graphics packages are available only for IBM

PCs, but they are scheduled to expand their compatability to other systems.

A major difficulty in using DBMS with microcomputers is the limited capacity of the auxiliary storage. A microcomputer that is equipped only with floppy disks can really only manage a data base that has a maximum of 150 pages of text. This would certainly not be very useful for gathering documents in a personal-injury suit, where the documents (even in indexed form), might run for several hundred pages, and the full-text depositions for several hundred more. For this kind of application, at least one hard disk (Winchester disk) would be required to boost the auxiliary storage capacity by a factor of ten or more. Many microcomputers can be expanded to include Winchester disks, although the power of the CPU will not allow an indefinite expansion of hard disks that are on-line. For really large data bases, a larger CPU is necessary.

The 10 MB hard disk now available to some microcomputers holds over 5,000 pages of text. This allows for the storage of large numbers of documents; however, the available search-and-retrieval software cannot compare with that developed for larger computers.

*d. Research*

Some microcomputers can already connect to WESTLAW, one of the major legal data bases. This gives them almost instant access to the full text of all court decisions within the last 20 years, as well as to an enormous offering of tax, corporate, administrative, energy, and other areas of specialized law. (The list of compatible microcomputers appears in Appendix D.) LEXIS, has just begun to move away from requiring its own equipment and may be accessed by a few non-dedicated terminals.

Most microcomputers, accompanied by a telephone modem, can access huge nonlegal data bases through DIALOG or ORBIT. (See Chapter 11, on nonlegal data bases.) The user then has the power to retrieve on his video screen literally hundreds of data bases in all conceivable areas of knowledge.

*e. Automated Substantive Systems*

An automated substantive system is a complete automated package containing all the information necessary to handle a particular kind of legal transaction such as a divorce proceeding or an estate plan. It contains checklists that elicit information about the client and the fact situation, and then presents legal forms with variable names and paragraphs. The more sophisticated a substantive system is, the more it will perform a level of legal analysis. In essence, with the most advanced substantive program, by requesting routine factual and legal information the computer is interviewing the attorney or paralegal. The program then prepares drafts of necessary documents. Based on the information it is given, the computer makes many choices for the attorney or paralegal.

The implications for the practice of law are overwhelming. Potentially, a well-conceived program could suggest litigation strategies, as well as indicate the appropriate form in a probate proceeding.* The packaged software in this area is just beginning to appear. Most of it is appropriate for microcomputers or word processors. General tax packages, such as Aardvark and Shortax, have a mass market, but they are useful for law practice as well. Estate planning packages are available for major word processors through Matthew Bender, with plans to expand offerings to microcomputers. Matthew Bender and other publishers of form books are rapidly working to transform these books into software packages.*

Since so much of what attorneys do is individualized, there is also a major commercial effort to develop a program that will allow them to create their own systems. The American Bar Foundation has sponsored a project to develop a special programming language, called ABF, for legal transactions.* Still in its experimental stages, this program may, in the near future, be offered to CP/M microcomputer users.

### *f. Artificial Intelligence*

This is a term that is abused in the computer world, but usually it refers to a program that will make choices and/or predictions.* At this point there is a great deal of experimentation and very little usable software available for the microcomputer. Predicting judicial decisions and making computerized jury selections have received a great deal of attention, but have produced no packaged software. Other experiments * are on-going in the area of legal reasoning, but are nowhere near producing usable software.

Even though the subject area is still experimental, imaginative entrepreneurs have been creating some software for microcomputers in the general area of artificial intelligence. One of the more interesting, but as yet untested programs is EXPROB. Developed for Apple II Plus, EXPROB is designed to estimate the probability of success in a product-liability case on a scale of one to ten, based on the attorney's responses to how he rates various elements of the case. An attorney can use EXPROB in combination with another program called INVAL—which predicts the cost involved in preparation, negotiation, and trial of the proposed product liability case—to make some sophisticated judgments regarding

* See Chapter 13.

settlement offers and other negotiations. An artificial intelligence research firm called General Robotics, in California, is offering a free verdict prediction with the use of CP/M software not yet for sale, to anyone who currently has a criminal case pending in federal court or on appeal.

## HOW TO CHOOSE A MICROCOMPUTER FOR LAW OFFICE USE

1. Which applications would you use immediately, or within the next two years? (Always try to plan at least two years ahead)

___ a. word processing

___ b. time-keeping and billing

___ c. general ledger

___ d. financial planning (electronic spreadsheet)

___ e. client records

___ f. calendaring

___ g. conflict of interest check

___ h. electronic mail

___ i. research in non-legal data bases

___ j. storing, searching, and retrieving documents in preparation for litigation

___ k. research in legal data bases

2. If you checked any, or all applications from a-i, almost any 8 or 16 bit microcomputer would be able to handle the task mechanically, (providing there was available software). It is always wise, however, to choose a system that has flexibility in terms of expansion or up-dating. If you checked j it would be necessary to investigate a microcomputer that could be configured with a hard disk for additional storage. If you checked k you must look at Appendix D to discover which microcomputers are able to access the WESTLAW data base.

3. Determine your price range and choose several microcomputers to investigate that meet the criteria established in 2.

4. Visit several computer stores and discover whether there is software written for the microcomputers you are investigating which will perform the applications you have chosen in 1. See as many demonstrations of the appropriate hardware and software as possible. Ask a million questions.

5. Once you have narrowed down the microcomputer and software to a few choices try to read reviews in computer magazines or law office computer journals. Talk to other attorneys who have used the product.

6. Having reached a decision on hardware and software decide upon the vendor (wholesale or retail) by considering the following criteria:

   a. Is this the best price?

   b. Are there on-going training and service arrangements?

   c. Are they likely to be in business in two years?

**WORD PROCESSING SYSTEM**

## WORD PROCESSORS

Word processing is one of the application programs that can be used by a microcomputer or larger computer; or an entire computer system can be dedicated only to word processing. In the case of a dedicated word processor, the application program is permanently written into the ROM memory of the CPU. This means that no other programs can be used on that computer, whereas the microcomputer can perform many functions.

Stand-alone dedicated word processors, which currently are very popular in law offices, generally have a memory capacity of under 32K, and auxiliary storage in the form of floppy disks. A larger version of a dedicated word processor uses a more powerful CPU with hard-disk storage and can support many terminals. However, it still is programmed to do only one task. The trend in recent years has been away from dedicated word processors, and toward multifunction computers. Here, word processing, data processing, and other application programs can all be handled by a large CPU with several terminals. The rapidly increasing use of microcomputers for word processing tasks is still another trend away from dedicated units, but they are still very commonly used in law practices. (See Chapter 6, "Word Management".)

A MINICOMPUTER SYSTEM

## MINICOMPUTERS

In light of the rapid changes made in the size and power of central processing units, the definition of a minicomputer is a slippery one. Some insiders define a mini as being bigger than a bread box and costing more than $10,000 (usually considerably more). Since the purchase is so large, however, the buyer can count on a great deal more vendor support and advice than he can with the micro, where the pieces of hardware and software are often literally dropped on his doorstep. There are also consultants who specialize in law-office computers of this size so that the buyer will not have to depend upon reviews in computer journals.

For such a large investment, a great deal of planning must take place. Even if a consultant is hired, the members of the law firm, attorneys, and support staff must first decide what their actual needs are. It is common practice, then, for a consultant or firm member to draft a Request for Proposal, which asks for price bids from several possible vendors. In *Planning for Computers,*[2] the American Bar Association's Section of Economics of Law Practice provides excellent advice and models for drafting this proposal. This Section offers another monograph, *Locate,*[3] which surveys 200 vendors and service bureaus nationally.

**2.** Landsburg, Laventhal, Howarth, *Planning for Computers,* Section of Economics of Law Practice, American Bar Association, 1981.

**3.** Heintz and Dill, eds., *LOCATE,* Section of Economics of Law Practice, American Bar Association, 1980.

## A. Hardware

Generally, minis have 256K or more RAM memory and use hard-disk auxiliary storage that can support between 20 and 100 MB of on-line auxiliary memory. Their main advantage over micros, at least for the present, is that their more powerful CPUs can support more terminals and more sophisticated programs.

Before the advent of the relatively inexpensive micro, most law offices that used computers at all, rather than just dedicated word processors, were likely to use some form of minicomputer, often with more than one terminal. Because the initial investment (including two or more terminals and software) typically cost over $50,000 and could well cost several hundred thousand, only a small percentage of medium and large law offices had used any in-house computers.

## B. Software

Software for minicomputers is usually very expensive, since it is often custom designed (in whole or in part) and since, unlike microcomputers, it is not sold as an off-the-shelf package to a mass market. It is not uncommon for the software to cost considerably more than the hardware. The operating system and utility programs are usually supplied by the manufacturer, but the specific application programs (for example, data base management, accounting, and so on) are commonly obtained in one of the following ways.

### *1. OEM or Systems Company*

An OEM (this stands for "original equipment manufacturer," but actually is an independent dealer) will install both the hardware and application software as a completed, or "turnkey," system. The OEM may assemble the parts of the system from several different systems but place a common brand name on the completed configuration. The application software may be part of a standard package, or it may be specifically designed for the customer.

### *2. Software Houses*

Software houses do not deal with the hardware. Rather, they provide programs on a customized basis, or they find appropriate ready-made packages. They will also make later changes, on a fee-for-service basis.

*3. In-House Programmer*

Some firms (usually, larger firms with larger computers) hire full-time in-house programmers to design and maintain application software. Developing the original software is usually a long and expensive process, but having a programmer in-house may provide a system that is most tailored to the firm's specific needs.

### C. Personnel

Firms that purchase minicomputers usually hire personnel specially trained to use them. This can be very costly, and it often segregates a law office. Attorneys, paralegals, and legal secretaries already on board may never go near a terminal. This kind of specialization, rather than being efficient, may severely restrict the possible uses of the computer while raising the level of operating expenses. It is better to train all in-house personnel, although initially this is very time consuming.

## MAINFRAMES

Mainframe computers are much larger, much faster, and much more expensive than minicomputers. Mainframes can have a main memory capacity of several megabytes, and an auxiliary memory capacity (usually on huge hard disks) of thousands of megabytes. Because of their enormous speed and main memory capacity, mainframes can support hundreds of users simultaneously (some can support thousands of simultaneous users—for example, the mainframes of WESTLAW and LEXIS) and can provide on-line access to literally millions of pages of court opinions and other legal documents. Usually, more than one application can be performed at the same time as well.

Since most law firms are small businesses, they do not need the power and expense of having a mainframe in-house. Only the very largest law firms or the legal counsel of a corporation could justify such a purchase. Many firms, however, do make use of the services of a mainframe outside their office.

### A. Computer Service Bureaus

Service bureaus provide the capabilities of a computer, usually a mainframe, to many clients. These bureaus currently are used by some attorneys for payroll, billing, accounting, word processing, litigation support, calendaring, legal research, microfilming, and printing. The relationship with the computer is noninteractive: the law office will gather the information (for instance, time keeping sheets) and send it to the service bureau by mail, by telecommunications,

**MAINFRAME COMPUTER**

or on a floppy disk. The bureau will enter the information into the computer for processing, and the bills will be produced and sent out. The employees in the law office itself will have no involvement with the computer, and therefore no opportunity to make changes or corrections once the information has been sent out. Because computer hardware is declining in price, and because working with a noninteractive system can be both frustrating and expensive, the trend is to move many of these tasks—particularly word processing and billing and accounting—back into the office, via an in-house computer.

## B. Time Sharing

In this arrangement, the user is utilizing an in-house terminal to share time on an outside mainframe with many other users (perhaps thousands). The connection is made through telecommunications, and the relationship with the computer is interactive (the user can ask questions and receive responses from the computer). Perhaps the most common use of time sharing is to gain access to the public legal data bases, WESTLAW and LEXIS. With each of these companies, the data is maintained on a single large mainframe in the Midwest (St. Paul, Minnesota, and Dayton, Ohio), and user terminals all over the country are connected by telecommunications. Nonlegal data bases, such as ORBIT, BRS, and DIALOG, are accessed in a similar fashion.

Time sharing is sometimes used to store and retrieve the masses of information gathered in preparation for a very large trial, as well. In this situation, the user can enter or alter data as well as retrieve it.

Time sharing is also available for financial accounting and for word processing. However, it is quite an expensive method for accomplishing these tasks.

Although the user pays only for the time he is actually communicating with the computer (on-line), telecommunications are very expensive; and, depending on the size of the computer and the number of users, the interactive process can be expensively slow.

# CHAPTER 4

# Combinations and Configurations: Three Case Studies

All attorneys and legal workers do not wear the same size shoe, nor will they use the same size computer or computer configuration. There are some general trends, however, that should affect the entire legal community within the next decade.

## MORE HARDWARE

"A terminal on every desk and maybe one at home" could be the slogan of the computer revolution in the law office. As the price of terminals, and of microcomputers (which can serve as intelligent terminals in a network as well as stand on their own) continues to deflate, it becomes economically sensible for all lawyers and legal workers to make use of the time-saving virtues of computers. Keyboard phobia (a disease particularly acute among attorneys) will provide some obstacles to this goal, but it may be conquered through gentle training and friendlier computers.

## MORE SOFTWARE

A virtual explosion of new applications programs, particularly in the areas of automated substantive systems, will shower the legal market. Most of the new programs will be written for microcomputers and will provide better, easier to use, and less expensive packages in the established areas of word processing, time keeping, billing, financial accounting, and data base management. Integrated, multitask programs that can make use of a common data base will become available for minis and micros.

## BETTER COMMUNICATIONS

Computers will all be talking to each other and sharing information and programs, both inside and outside the office. Increasingly standardized hardware and software will make it simple for computers from different manufacturers to communicate. Print on paper mail will be reduced, and will be replaced by the more efficient form of electronic mail.

## FEWER EMPLOYEES

The computerized law office should be able to handle more work with fewer people. All tasks should be accomplished more quickly, and in particular the labor-consuming tasks of research, production typing, and bookkeeping should be greatly reduced. The use of paralegals as support personnel should increase, and the use of legal secretaries and bookkeepers should decline.

## CASE STUDY # 1: MR. SOLO, ESQ.[1]

Sidney Solo represents the 47 percent of all practicing attorneys who practice alone. Ten years after being admitted to the bar, he had developed a strong general practice with an emphasis on personal injury. He had a large number of clients for whom he performed a wide variety of services—from drafting their wills to defending them in an occasional drunk-driving criminal action.

Solo employed one full-time secretary, who did the billing, and retained an accountant to organize his books once each month. The secretary used a conventional electric typewriter.

Solo liked the independence of practicing on his own, but he felt overworked and underpaid. He billed out as many hours as he could, and often had to turn away work because he was overloaded. However, he spent a great deal of time performing routine tasks that he felt he could not bill to his client, such as finding appropriate forms, or figuring out his time sheets. He also seemed to have more trouble collecting than ever before.

**1.** These case studies are based on the actual experiences of three law practices, but the time frame has been projected forward. The first study, Sidney Solo, is based on the experience of a sole practitioner in Oakland, California. He did increase his income by 30%, and is currently in the process of specializing in tax. The second study is based on the experience of an innovative new company which offered the integrated microcomputer-based system offered by NOVALAW, creating all of their own software. The third study is based on the experience of a fairly large San Francisco law firm which did combine its word processing and data processing functions two years ago and is reporting good results.

For Christmas Solo bought his son a home computer that hooked up to the television set. The whole family had a wonderful time playing games and they picked up some programming skills. This introduction to computers gave Solo the courage to think about purchasing a microcomputer for his law office. He began to ask his lawyer friends about their experiences and to read all appropriate articles in the bar journals. Soon he began reading computer magazines and stopping by at the computer store after work.

Within three months he had made his choice of a well-known microcomputer brand with 64K RAM memory, dual floppy disk drive, and a CP/M operating system. He also chose a letter-quality printer. This initial hardware purchase cost a little more than $5,000. To save money he went through a dealer, rather than a retailer, which meant that he received no training and hooked it up himself.

Solo's first software purchase was a highly recommended word processing program that ran on CP/M. It took Solo several hours to become accustomed to it, but he was immediately fascinated by its ability to edit and to merge different paragraphs into any standard document (e.g., a will or a marital-settlement agreement). His secretary was not so fascinated; she quit, refusing to work on this new-fangled machine. Solo hired a new secretary who had no previous word-processing experience but who was willing to learn.

Within a year, Solo had all his forms on floppy disks for easy editing and merging of parts. He also invested in packaged substantive systems—one for setting up a corporation and one for doing federal income tax. Writing with a word-processing program was so easy that he started to draft his own trial briefs directly on the microcomputer keyboard, rather than scribbling them on his old yellow pad. He could turn out a revised, completed version in approximately one-third the time he previously had taken with revisions, requiring little secretarial support. By mutual agreement it was decided that his secretary could complete her work in half a day. Solo also decided he needed his own terminal, and he purchased a second microcomputer for his own desk. Although it cost more than a nonintelligent terminal, he believed the extra power and memory justified its extra cost. He hooked it up to the first computer so that they could communicate with each other and share information.

In the second year, Solo bought a standard data base management software package and worked with his secretary to set up a docket control and calendaring system. In order to take maximum advantage of this system he bought a hard disk for additional storage, and he began to develop an index of documents for each of his personal-injury cases so that they could be easily searched and retrieved. He also entered all his in-house work products: memoranda, points and authorities, trial briefs, and so on into a data base as they were produced. This enabled him to easily retrieve them when working on a similar legal problem.

At the end of the second year, Solo was beginning to feel well organized and decided that he could take on more clients if he had a little more support. He hired a paralegal half-time who used his secretary's microcomputer terminal in the afternoon. Once the paralegal was trained to his computer system and its data base of forms, she could perform many of the routine tasks that Solo had been performing. So Solo expanded his practice and his income by 25 percent within one year.

During the third year, Solo bought yet another microcomputer, this time a portable that he could use at home or take to court with him. With the use of a telephone modem Solo could communicate with his computer in the office and gain access to information on his data bases, such as documents relating to a personal-injury suit, correspondence, or pleadings. He could also work effectively at home rather than the office if he chose. That same year Solo bought a software package for legal timekeeping and billing that allowed him to produce complicated billing statements, involving contingency arrangements, disbursements, and court costs. He found that the rate of return on his billing was better with a more accurate and detailed system. His accountant continued to come once a month, but now the accountant used a computerized general ledger that allowed Solo and the other legal workers to make additions and corrections during the month.

Solo was doing so well and was so enthusiastic about the advantages of the computer that in the fourth year he decided to shift his focus and concentrate on a tax specialty. He believed that in the long run, even for a sole practitioner, specialization was the way to go, and that he could handle many difficult computations and projections with his computer. He had been an accounting major in college, and now he prepared himself for the transition by taking several tax-specialty courses in the evening. His next step was to subscribe to WESTLAW, which offered a complete legal data base and could provide completely up-to-date tax information, including private letter rulings and I.R.S. rulings. Since WESTLAW was compatible with his microcomputer, he did not need to buy or lease new hardware. He also subscribed to DIALOG, a nonlegal data base, to have easy access to technical and general information to suit his growing new business clientele.

Altogether, over four years Solo spent less than $20,000 on a system that included three microcomputers, a letter-quality printer and a great deal of software. His net income had increased by 50 percent and would probably increase further with his new specialty. He had, however, put a great deal of thought, time, and attention into choosing and learning to use his computer system efficiently, and into restructuring administrative and legal tasks.

## CASE STUDY # 2: UP AND COMING

Up and Coming, a nine-attorney law firm, had been together for four years. Most of the attorneys were under 35, and only two were over 50. They already had two stand-alone, dedicated word processors, and a terminal that accessed LEXIS, the legal data base system. They were eager to be modern and efficient. They had developed a reputation as a strong litigation firm that specialized in real estate litigation. Their ratio of attorneys to secretaries was one to one, and they employed two litigation paralegals whose sole duties were to organize documents in preparation for trial. Billing and payroll activities were sent out to a computerized service bureau, and one full-time bookkeeper was employed in-house.

After several months of discussion and investigation (the investigation being undertaken largely by partner John Up, a computer enthusiast), the firm decided to make a significant capital investment and to purchase a new concept in computer design. For an initial outlay of a little over $200,000, the firm hired a new corporation, called NovaLaw, which provided a unique, integrated legal system designed around microcomputers. The initial system included nine 16-bit microcomputers, each with 256 K of RAM memory and a combination of hard-disk and floppy-disk storage. Any single computer had a capacity of 10 MB of auxiliary storage on a single hard disk; and, linked together in a network, they shared a common hard-disk storage facility of 120 MB. This arrangement gave each computer a great deal of independence and flexibility, but allowed access to a common data base of information as well. The nine micros also shared a state-of-the-art laser printer for final production, while each micro had an inexpensive but fast dot-matrix printer as well. With this system, any individual terminal had the capacity to perform as many as four functions at one time, and could make use of a split screen to see all the tasks in operation. For instance, the user could review the appropriate client file while continuing to work on editing a sale of property agreement. The software application programs were integrated so that the user could order any task, such as editing, from a single menu which also included calendaring, time keeping, accounting, storage and retrieval of documents, and so on. The same data bases could be put to use for any of the different functions on the integrated program.

The software was specially designed for this firm by NovaLaw, which also carefully selected the hardware. NovaLaw representatives set up the system and trained everyone in the law office. They were on call for troubleshooting during the first year.

During the first six months there was indeed a lot of trouble. The customized software had a number of "bugs" in it, which impeded work and caused the attorneys and legal workers to lose confidence in the system. Several secretaries pleaded to have their word processors back and for two full months no bills were sent out at all. Two attorneys and two secretaries quit during the confusion. This time of troubles proved very expensive to the firm.

NovaLaw was responsive to the problems, however, and by the beginning of the second half of the year all the system problems had been solved. However, major personnel problems persisted: four of the remaining attorneys refused to go near the terminals, and three of the remaining secretaries and one of the paralegals expressed the same reluctance. Also, it was still cheaper in terms of employee time to send out the payroll to a service where it could be batch processed. The firm subscribed to the nonlegal data base service, BRS, which could be accessed by a telephone modem from any of the nine computers.

Sometime during the second year, the system began to display its advantages. It was not necessary to rehire the two secretaries who had left; instead, another paralegal was hired to help enter documents into the computer in preparation for litigation. Litigation support had been handled manually in the past. Three new attorneys were hired who were enthusiastic about computers, and three new terminals were purchased for their own use. Two portable terminals also were purchased specifically to take on-site when gathering documents for litigation. The attorney or paralegal could sort through a warehouse of documents and enter into the computer abstracts of those that were relevant. The relevant documents were then sent out for microfilming.

The reputation of the firm for efficiency and organization in trial preparation grew, and the firm received many referrals from other attorneys. Within three years, half the attorneys and all the other legal workers had their own terminals, and the initial investment had almost been totally recaptured by higher income.

## CASE STUDY # 3: RICH, BIG, AND OLD

Rich, Big, and Old was a venerable law firm of 73 attorneys, 25 paralegals, 73 legal secretaries, and 11 back-office financial-management personnel. The firm was representative of the 8 percent of law firms of between 25 and 99 lawyers. It had been in existence for 75 years, and several of the senior partners had been with the firm for over 25 years. A generally conservative attitude prevailed regarding new technology (several of the partners refused to use a dictating machine); however, there were a few younger partners who were interested in computers, and the firm was financially solid.

Most of the clients were large businesses or corporations. The firm handled a large variety of corporate concerns and sometimes got involved with very large-scale litigation: one antitrust case went on for six years and generated two million documents in preparation for trial.

The support functions of the firm were already quite specialized by the beginning of the '80s. In 1975, the firm had purchased a very large dedicated word processor with six terminals and two high-speed printers, on which all the major (production) typing was performed by word-processing specialists. In 1980, a large minicomputer with a main memory of 256 K of RAM and hard-disk storage capacity of 20 MB was purchased. The system could be expanded to include eight CPUs on the same control system and additional hard disks up to 96 MB of auxiliary memory storage. Initially, software was purchased to perform only time keeping and billing functions, and data-processing operators were hired to operate the computer. The payroll was sent to an outside service bureau; calendaring and docket control were handled manually; and most litigation support functions were handled manually by the paralegals. For the very largest cases, a litigation support service was used to organize the documents for entry into a computer data base on a large mainframe in a distant city. There were two terminals in the library on which researchers could access WESTLAW and ORBIT (one of the nonlegal data base services).

Since the partners had a difficult time agreeing on their computer needs and little time to spend investigating the options, a computer consultant was brought in to make recommendations. He advised that the new minicomputer could handle many more tasks, and with his help software packages for calendaring, docket control, and litigation support were introduced over the next two years. The very largest cases were still sent out to a large mainframe, but now it was strictly on a time-sharing basis; the documents were entered on the in-house terminals and transmitted via telecommunications to the shared mainframe.

The consultant also recommended that the word-processing functions be handled by the minicomputer connected to a network of microcomputers, and that decentralization would be more efficient. Microcomputers were given to 25 secretaries. These computers performed all basic word-processing tasks, and also were hooked up to the minicomputer in order to share data bases and other programs (e.g., time keeping and calendaring). The ratio of secretary to attorney changed from one-to-one to one-to-two. Ten more paralegals were hired and given terminals in order to handle the increased load of in-house litigation support tasks, and also to perform some basic document creation and editing functions (e.g., drafting pleadings, trust agreements, and incorporations). These tasks had become much less complicated with the gradual development of in-house substantive systems. The last recommendation of the consultant was that every attorney should also have a desktop microcomputer, which could be connected with the mini in order to perform research, writing, and time keeping functions at the desk. Each of the desktop computers would have access to WESTLAW with a telephone modem and to all in-house work-products and current client-files. At the end of three years, half of all the attorneys had such a desktop computer.

The firm had always done well, and it did even better over the next five years. The computer supporters claimed it was a result of more efficient organization; the computer skeptics said it was coincidence.

# PART TWO

# Computers and Management

## INTRODUCTION: COMPUTERS AND THE ORGANIZATION OF DOCUMENTS AND FINANCIAL MATTERS

Good management is one of the essential ingredients of a successful law practice. The most expert attorneys can handle their clients' problems with great finesse, but if the documents do not get filed on time or if the bills are not sent out correctly, the practice will ultimately fail. One of the goals of every practitioner is to have an office-support system so well organized that he can completely devote himself to thorny legal problems, not to mundane management problems.

A well-chosen computer system can certainly provide a giant step forward toward maximum organization and efficiency in law-office management. It is in this area that most law practices have already begun to experiment with computerization. Word processing, and time keeping and billing—the two most labor-intensive support functions in a law office—are usually the first candidates for a computer. Computerized litigation support systems, previously limited to only the very largest cases, are now becoming possible even for very small cases. Common data bases, serving a multi-user, multitask office network, are at least appearing on the horizon, while computerized docket control and conflict-of-interest systems are commanding attention.

*

# CHAPTER 5

## Managing Documents: Computerized Litigation Support Systems

*All Steel* v. *Mighty Tough* was a gargantuan price-fixing suit that involved five defendants and six years of trial preparation. The documents gathered by Rich, Big, and Old, the law firm representing Mighty Tough, numbered in the hundreds of thousands; the depositions alone produced over 30,000 pages of text. Rich, Big and Old combined their documents with the other four defendants into a common data base.

During the third day of trial, All Steel produced a witness, Mr. Slick, one of its corporate vice presidents, who claimed that he had lunched with Mighty Tough's chief sales vice president, Mr. Jones, in Pittsburgh, on May 3, 1975, and that the vice president suggested to him that they might consider a mutually advantageous collaboration on the price of steel girders.

Immediately, the trial team of Rich, Big, and Old went to work on their computer terminals. They entered the search term, "Slick," and the time-frame, "May, 1975." The computer searched the hundreds of thousands of documents that were stored on a major mainframe computer in a shared data base with the five other defendants. All the documents that satisfied this search query were called up: there were 132 such documents, including depositions, employee expense accounts, payroll records, and assorted memos. A quick perusal of the abstracts of the documents indicated that most of them would be useless in determining whether such a meeting had actually occurred. A deposition taken of another vice president and Mr. Slick's own expense account, however, clearly indicated that Slick was, in fact, in New York on the day of the alleged meeting.

This evidence was presented the next day in trial to impeach Slick's testimony. Although Slick was only one witness among many in this mammoth trial, his testimony was a critical element in All Steel's case, and the contrary evidence retrieved by the computer seriously discredited it. All Steel lost its suit against all five defendants.

The impeachment of Slick's testimony was a very dramatic use of "computer-assisted litigation support," and could probably not have been achieved without it. Less dramatic but equally important applications had occurred throughout the very lengthy period of trial preparation and in the presentation of witnesses and evidence at trial. For example, all the price data of all the defendants over the ten-year period in question were entered into the computer. Charts were produced by the computer that illustrated graphically how the prices of each of the defendants compared with one another over the entire period in question. These charts indicated that there was extraordinary diversity in pricing, with no evidence of collusion. Chronological lists of persons and events generated by the computer allowed the attorneys to better understand the logical sequence of events, and therefore to ask more appropriate questions at depositions and to seek facts through discovery—facts that filled the holes in this sequence. Each of the witneses in this cast of hundreds was prepared for trial by a review of all the documents in which the witness was mentioned. Sometimes these documents numbered in the thousands.

Meanwhile, at the county courthouse, Sidney Solo was representing a plaintiff who had been hit by a truck while riding a bicycle, sustaining multiple severe injuries. The patient spent two years in and out of hospitals and was examined by 24 different specialists. There was disagreement about his ability to work again and the attorney representing the truck driver refused to settle at the sum demanded by Solo. Six months before trial, Solo collected all the 143 medical and hospital reports; coded them by injury, doctor, date, prognosis, as well as by six other relevant categories; and entered them into his microcomputer, using a hard disk for storage. With a data base management software package, he then requested the computer to create reports that organized the documents chronologically, by doctor, by injury, and so on. He used these reports to interrogate opposing medical witnesses in depositions and to prepare his own witnesses for trial.

Solo also entered the data regarding his client's lost wages, projected lost wages, and other special and general damages into his microcomputer. With a financial management software package, he was able to calculate the projected damages and to present polished reports for determination of damages at trial.

# ADVANTAGES OF COMPUTER-ASSISTED LITIGATION SUPPORT

## A. Speed and Thoroughness

Some of the same advantages that WESTLAW and LEXIS offer to the researcher of public legal data bases are available to the researcher of privately developed data bases. Retrieval of information requested by key words or phrases is stunningly fast, compared with manual research. Even if the information in the data base is in abstract or bibliographic form rather than full-text form, the retrieval of the source document is still a speedy matter.

Perhaps even more important is the computer's ability to expand the search net. A conventional document-indexing system allows the researcher to cross-reference a document in perhaps only four or five different ways. But a computer can keep track of an almost unlimited number of reference terms; and with full text on a large computer, every word becomes a reference term. This feature made it possible for Rich, Big, and Old to find a specific needle of information in a veritable haystack of evidence.

## B. Simultaneous Access From Separate Locations

Think of the attorney bending over his portable terminal in the courtroom to call up evidence that will impeach a witness's testimony. This is the most dramatic image of remote access to a computerized data base of information imaginable. Yet this scenario was actually enacted during the recent sensational murder retrial of Juan Corona, an alleged mass murderer in California. This kind of situation is still a rare scene, however. A more likely use of remote-site terminals is in multiparty lawsuits, such as *All Steel* v. *Mighty Tough*, where all five defendants shared the same data base, connected by telecommunications to the separate offices of defense counsels in five different cities. It would not have been possible to keep a manual system up-to-date for all five sites.

## C. Production of Indices and Reports

Once the data has been placed into the computer data base, indices and reports of all kinds can be generated immediately. For instance, all documents can be arranged in chronological order, by type of document, author, or by any other criteria that might be useful in getting ready for a particular trial. Witness Jones could be prepared for her testimony at trial by generating an index that listed, in chronological order, all the documents that mentioned her name.

### D. Statistical and Financial Analysis

In both the enormous price-fixing case and relatively small personal-injury case, the computational powers of the computer were put to good use. In fact, it is possible to perform certain kinds of analyses that are nearly impossible to perform manually (no matter how much labor is expended), such as the comparative pricing graphs of all the defendants in the *All Steel* case.

The fantastic graphic abilities of many computers are best displayed by lawyers in a trial setting. The results of a complicated statistical analysis are most persuasive when presented in clear and striking graphs to juries who have little or no statistical or technical background.

Of course, computational functions can be separated from the functions of search and retrieval. The pricing graphs in the *All Steel* case could be produced by entering only the price data into the computer. The rest of the hundreds of thousands of documents could conceivably be handled by manual procedures (although this would drastically reduce the search-and-retrieval capabilities).

## WHEN TO COMPUTERIZE?

Since there are so many dramatic examples of the virtues of computerization, this may seem a foolish question. Unfortunately, however, it costs an average of about $8 or $9 *per document* to create a fully computerized data base in a large case. These costs include all personnel costs at every stage in the process. If there were 300,000 documents in the *All Steel* case, the cost of creating and using the computerized data base (aside from attorney fees and other costs) could be as much as $270,000. A totally manual system, although only a fraction as effective, could cost 25 to 50 percent less. So when is the greater cost considered justified?

a. When the volume of evidentiary materials is so great that a manual system would founder under the weight. The cut-off number that is traditionally used is 10,000, but this is only one factor among many in making the decision.

b. When the facts are so complex that only a computer can sort them out. This would be true in any large price-fixing or class-action employment-discrimination suit, where thousands of price or payroll figures are analyzed in order to establish a statistical trend. It would also be true in any case where there were multiple parties, offering the possibility of combinations and permutations of facts.

c. When the amount of money at stake is very high. If the suit has potential damages of $400,000,000, then spending $270,000 on computerized support may not seem so outrageous.

Of course, it is possible—and increasingly likely—to use a computer for only part of a case (perhaps only the financial analysis), or to use an in-house computer in a much smaller case (such as Sidney Solo's personal-injury suit) with less sophisticated search-and-retrieval software but at a greatly reduced cost.

# CREATING A SYSTEM

Whether a case has 200,000 documents or 200, the procedure for successfully preparing for litigation is similar, although with smaller cases some steps may be skipped.

## A. System Design

Once the decision to computerize fully or partially has been made, it is important for the entire litigation team of attorneys and paralegals to decide what they need from a system. In doing so, they must make some long-range estimates on: what evidence they will need to gather, both from the party they are representing and from the opposing party; which witnesses they will call on for testimony; and what the general trial strategy will be. Only then can they decide on an intelligent and economical system. In the best of all possible worlds, this decision would include all the attorneys representing all the defendants or plaintiffs in a multiparty suit. In the real world, one hopes for as much coordination as possible. It is also important for the attorneys and legal personnel to stay in touch with the computer's activities throughout the suit and not leave decisions to the computer "specialists," who may not have a clue about which facts are important.

## B. Choosing Hardware and Software

### 1. *Full-Service Vendors*

Rich, Big, and Old would probably have begun their computerization process by hiring a consultant. Since their task was so immense, they could consider it a well-justified expenditure to plan the overall design and strategy themselves, and then let an expert decide on the mechanics. The consultant would carefully analyze the design presented by the firm and, working with the attorneys assigned to the suit, develop a proposal (usually called a request for proposal, or RFP), which he would send out to full-service vendors for competitive bidding.

A full-service litigation-support vendor can handle all aspects of a litigation-support project. This includes (1) providing the hardware, software, all the support personnel to gather the information and enter it into the data base, and (2) assisting in search and retrieval. Some of the largest full-service vendors that specialize in litigation include Aspen, Control Data, Informatics, Matsco, and Mellonics. For smaller cases, Atlis Systems and American Legal Systems are new and vying for the market.

Like a good caterer, a full-service vendor will take care of all the details, even providing out-of-the-office sites for the personnel they hire. Usually these vendors have their own large mainframe computer and their own software, although they may custom design or modify software for special client needs. Because of the full range of service they provide, this is by far the most expensive way to develop a computerized data base. The cost goes down proportionately with the number of documents, however; and with a really enormous case, such as *All Steel,* the firm may not have the personnel or expertise to manage it in-house and must seek outside help.

### 2. *Public Information Data Bases*

A few of the major public data base services—specifically, WESTLAW, LEXIS, DIALOG, and BRS (Bibiliographic Retrieval Services)—offer subscribers the option of creating their own private data base on the service's large computer, and searching and retrieving the information they store with the same software used to search and retrieve information in the public data bases. This is very powerful software, of course, and allows the subscriber to search the full text of any document he chooses to enter.

These public data base vendors supply the hardware and the software, but they do not provide any trained personnel to handle the collection of data, entry into the data base, or search and retrieval. The same terminal and telephone connection that the subscriber uses to access the public data base are used to create and search the private data base. Since the subscriber must pay for storage and for on-line retrieval time, this can be quite an expensive undertaking. Generally, however, it costs less than full-service vendors with personnel included.

### 3. *In-House Computers*

#### a. *Minis*

There is a major, enthusiastic trend toward the creation of data bases for litigation support on in-house minicomputers. It can be a much less expensive undertaking than using outside computer services, and it makes it possible to use computers for smallish cases of 3,000 to 10,000 documents. Several of the "turnkey" vendors that supply all the hardware and software as a complete system offer a data-base management system suitable for litigation support. This is a competitive and fast-moving field; therefore, this partial list of vendors may already be a victim of instant obsolescence: Barrister Information Management System (formerly Comptek Research, Inc.), Mini-Computer Systems, Professional Software System, and Systems and Software Associates, Inc.

It is also possible to purchase litigation-support packages from software companies, although they are generally produced for a specific manufacturer. For instance, IBM produces a data base management program called STAIRS, which is used on its own equipment; and Unicorn Systems markets a package called DOCKET, which can be used on any system that uses COBOL.

Minicomputers, however, have a much smaller main memory and far less auxiliary memory than a large mainframe. They can neither store nor search-and-retrieve a data base of the size necessary for *All Steel.* Depending upon their size, however, they can adequately handle smaller cases, and most of the turnkey vendors will offer training for in-house personnel. It can be cheaper than using a full-service vendor, or a public data base retrieval system, providing it does not tie up too much computer time and storage space or too many employees.

### *b. Microcomputers*

It is still a relatively rare phenomenon for an attorney to use the office microcomputer(s) for litigation support. Perhaps attorneys still think of computers only in terms of 10,000-plus document cases. It is just as easy for a sole practitioner to get confused by 300 documents, however, as it is for a large firm to get confused by 30,000. There are obviously limits to the size of the data base with microcomputers, even with hard disks, and the available software probably would not allow full-text retrieval. Nevertheless, a good general data base management program, such as dBASE II or CONDOR, can provide a super-indexing and referral system, permitting documents to be retrieved by up to 40 different reference terms. Sidney Solo handled complicated medical documents pertaining to a not-uncommon personal-injury suit in a far more efficient manner than would be possible with manual indexing methods.

Since microcomputers and their software are relatively cheap, vendors are not eager to spend much time training their purchasers in their various applications. A whole new industry of books and training disks is growing up to meet this need. It is hoped that computer-assisted litigation support on microcomputers will become a subject for this industry.

# CREATING A DATABASE

## A. Collecting Documents

Whether or not the litigation team plans to create a computerized data base, the first step in organizing documents for trial is to collect and number them. These documents might include:

- Attorneys' work product (pleadings, briefs, memoranda)
- Deposition and/or trial transcripts
- Produced documents (your side), which might take any form, ranging from payroll accounts to psychiatric reports
- Discovered documents (their side), which also could include almost any imaginable document
- Physical exhibits
- Relevant materials from other cases

Sometimes the discovered or produced documents are available only in warehouses, offices, or factories across town, or across the country. Litigation teams must be sent into the field, often for weeks, to gather the necessary evidence. Facing a warehouse full of invoices can be an overwhelming and discouraging experience, and at that point the computer cannot be much help. The members of the trial team must painstakingly search through each document, making decisions as to which documents are relevant, then numbering them sequentially for identification and control.

When the numbers of documents are in five or six figures they usually are not brought into the law office (they would bury several rooms). Instead, the normal procedure is to produce a xeroxed copy of each document and also to micrograph it, then to set up an archive, possibly at the original site. The micrograph is what gets carried around the country in a suitcase, and what often becomes the working version of the document (since parts or all of it can be xeroxed again at will).

For a small case, archives and micrographing are not necessary. However, 300 documents can get easily confused, and clear numbering and storage are essential.

## B. Document Analysis

By far the most labor-intensive (and therefore most expensive) aspect of creating a data base is analyzing the documents and deciding what to put into the computer. There is a sliding scale of labor expenditure, depending on how much of the document the analyst wishes to place in the computer.

### *1. Coding*

Most documents are not entered word-for-word into the computer. Rather, an extensive description of the document is created and entered into the data base. In the retrieval process the researcher searches the descriptive terms to locate appropriate documents, which he then retrieves and works with in hard copy or microfilmed form.

There are many ways of describing the documents, but the thoroughness of searching the data base depends on the accuracy and completeness of these descriptive terms. The development of accurate descriptive terms—or a "controlled vocabulary," as it is commonly referred to—is a critical step. Even the smallest case needs some uniformity in proper names, places, and so on.

**TYPICAL COMPUTER DIALOGUE**

```
BEGIN SEARCH

                      RETRIEVED
 SET                  DOCUMENTS                DESCRIPTION

NAME/SMITH J AND JONES W                       SEARCH THE DATA BASE FOR ALL DOCUMENTS WHICH
   1                     120                   WERE AUTHORED BY, ADDRESSED TO, COPIED TO, OR
                                               MENTIONED J. SMITH AND W. JONES

DATE/760701-760930                             SEARCH FOR ALL DOCUMENTS WHICH WERE CREATED
   2                     253                   BETWEEN JULY 1, 1976 AND SEPTEMBER 30, 1976

CONTRACT(S) NEGOTIAT:                          SEARCH FOR ALL DOCUMENTS WHOSE TEXT CONTAINS
   3                     342                   THE WORD "CONTRACT" WITHIN THE SAME SENTENCE
   4                     513                   AS THE ROOT WORD "NEGOTIAT," WITH ALL OF ITS
   5                     257                   SPELLING VARIATIONS (NEGOTIATE, NEGOTIATION,
                                               NEGOTIATING)

1 AND 2 AND 5                                  COMBINE THE RESULTS OF THE FIRST THREE SEARCHES
   6                      48

SORT 6, DATE                                   SORT THE RESULTING SET OF DOCUMENTS INTO
   7                      48                   CHRONOLOGICAL ORDER BY DATE

TYPE 7/ALL                                     TYPE OUT ALL OF THE DOCUMENTS

AUTHOR:  SMITH J DATE:  76/07/05

TITLE:  MEMO TO W. JONES ON STATUS OF CONTRACT NEGOTIATIONS

.
.
.

BYE                                            SIGN-OFF FROM THE COMPUTER

END SEARCH
```

[D749]

#### *a. Authority Lists*

The simplest form of "controlled vocabulary" is to develop a standardized list of personal names, organizations, places, products, etc., so that every time a document is indexed by one of these names, the exact same term is used. For instance, if Sidney Solo were entering several medical reports from the same doctor, he would always refer to that doctor as "White, Robert, M.D.," not

"Bob White," or "Dr. White." Since the computer is very literal, it would recognize these variations as entirely different persons and not retrieve all the reports written by that doctor.

### *b. Taxonomies*

In very large cases, an expert lexicographer is usually hired whose sole duty is to develop a controlled vocabulary code, usually a taxonomy, specifically designed for the factual issues involved in that case. A taxonomy is usually used in addition to the authority lists, and it describes the subject content of a document. It can be very simple. For instance, all parts of the body can be coded:

| CODE | SUBJECT |
|---|---|
| N | Neck |
| C | Chest |
| A | Abdomen |

In reading detailed medical reports, a coder—the paralegal, attorney, or other specialist who analyzes the document—will assign these code letters, describing the contents of the report.

Or a taxonomy may be very detailed and hierarchical. It may allow the coder to become very specific in his descriptions:

| CODE | SUBJECT |
|---|---|
| N | Neck |
| NV | Neck Vertebra |
| NV1 | Neck Vertebra # 1 |
| NV2 | Neck Vertebra # 2 |

When searching hierarchical taxonomies, it is possible to call up documents either by the more general term (all documents containing Ns) or by the subset; (only documents containing NV1). The only problem with really complicated taxonomies is that many different coders work on the documents, and they may have different ways of interpreting the nuances of complicated hierarchies. With fewer and broader categories, however, there is less likelihood of miscoding and losing the document.

## *2. Data Entry*

### *a. Full Text*

Many litigation-support vendors promote entry of the full text of every document into the computer. This would require very little analysis or coding, since the document could conceivably be located by any word or search term in the text, as with WESTLAW or LEXIS. It would also eliminate a step in the retrieval procedure, since it probably would not be necessary to fetch the hard copy;

instead, the researcher could view the entire document on the video screen.

Although a full-text data base would require a much larger computer memory and a more sophisticated program, it would seem to have all the advantages offered by the public commercial legal data bases. The major disadvantage, at the moment, is that the cost of entering all documents full-text into the computer is outrageously high. Until and if optical character recognition scanners (OCRS) are perfected to read other than a few typefaces, a human being must labor over the keyboard, typing in every single word. Because of this, very large full-text projects often are sent overseas, to countries where labor is significantly cheaper.

Deposition and trial transcripts present a significant exception to the labor-intensive costs of full-text entry. Increasingly, court reporters use computer-assisted transcription (CAT) in converting their notes or tapes into transcript form. Briefly, the computer is fed a dictionary of the reporter's own shorthand vocabulary (each reporter has a somewhat unique vocabulary). Then it can transcribe the trial notes, with the editorial assistance of the reporter, into completed transcript form, which it produces into hard copy. However, the computer tape that produced the hard copy can usually be read directly into the data base of the computer assisting in litigation. For instance, Rich, Big, and Old can get the computer tape of the day's trial testimony two hours after the court adjourns (with a special rush order); load it into their computer; and search and retrieve specific aspects of the testimony of that day's witnesses in order to prepare for tomorrow's cross-examination. This would be impossible with manual methods, which require from 10 to 20 hours to prepare a hard-copy transcript from a normal day's testimony. The mountains of pretrial depositions can be similarly searched, at a more leisurely rate.

As law offices and business offices in general become more automated, more and more documents will be available in "machine-readable" form. In other words, they will be created on some medium—tape or disk—that can be read into the computer without being retyped. Unfortunately, since computers have many different operating systems and storage media, it may not be possible to load the information directly into a different computer. However, there are vendors who will perform this conversion function. In most businesses, payroll accounts and invoices of all kinds are already in this form, so is any document that has been produced by a word processor. Although it should not be a problem to obtain evidence in this form from your own client, it is also possible to subpoena the opposing party for evidence in "machine-readable" form. There are some special requirements in drafting this sort of subpoena, and there is a growing body of law (beyond the scope of this book) that deals with the discovery and admissibility of evidence in "machine-readable" form.

The work products of the litigating attorneys—memoranda, pleadings, briefs, and so on—should also be in machine-readable form if they are produced on a word processor or a word-processing program of a computer. These could be entered full text into the data base of documents, but there is some concern regarding security from discovery by the other side. Although this is theoretically privileged information that is unavailable to the other party, if a subpoena specifies the whole of the data base, privileged materials will be difficult to separate out. For this reason attorney work-products generally are kept in a separate data base.

Documents that are entered full text will not need extensive analysis and coding, but it is common to "enhance" them in some fashion. This may mean that all the proper names, dates, and places are put in standardized form, according to an authority list, to ensure that the computer will not miss them because they are spelled differently from the search query. It may also mean that a short descriptive summary will accompany a longer document, or that some general subject codes will also be used to facilitate easier retrieval. Enhancing a document has strategic value as well, since this can turn a document that may be subject to discovery by the other side into an attorney's "work product," immune from discovery.

### *b. Extracts, Abstracts, Bibliographic Indexes*

Most documents in large cases are still not entered full text, and on microcomputers this is not a real option right now. Sometimes it may not even be desirable to enter a document full text, since only part of it may actually be useful. For instance, lengthy business correspondence may contain only small portions that deal with the issues in litigation. Relevant extracts may be the solution in this case, although it takes considerable analysis to decide what is relevant. Extracts would then be treated as full text in terms of search and retrieval.

The most common form of data entry is in bibliographic format, possibly with an abstract. For these entries a document coding form, or DCF, is most commonly used. The DCF, which may be specially designed for one case or may be a standardized version, presents appropriate spaces for bibliographic information (where the document originated, where it was sent to, dates, and so on) and for subject codes. It may or may not provide a space for an abstract.

**SAMPLE DOCUMENT CODING FORM**

**ACCESSION:** 00A10284 **DOCUMENT DATE:** 76/04/02

**MICROFORM:** AP0010634/0635

**DOCUMENT TYPE:** Letter

**DOCUMENT SOURCE:** Army

**TITLE:** Designation of Contracting Officers Representative.

**AUTHOR:** Jakovich D; Procurement Div

**ADDRESSEE:** DFAE; Kelly GP

**COPIED TO:** Capous Contracting; Contracts Branch; Finance

**X REFERENCE:** TAB026

**PRODUCED:** Y

**DISCOVERY/PRODUCTION:** GVT 78/11/15 Interrog 01

**RELEVANCE:** Relevant

**ABSTRACT:** Outlines authority of technical representative. Acknowledgement signed.

**INDEX TERM:**

CT04000 Contract Amendment

CT06100 Description of Work

CT06200 Material & Equip Approval

CT06500 Technical Specifications

QC03000 Government Inspection

**DUP CHARACTER CHECK:** TERMINATION

**CREATE DATE:** 82096 **UPDATE DATE:** 82096

On large cases, the coders usually fill out the cards for each document, either directly at the location of their origin, or after screening, back in the office. They can either type them on a typewriter with fonts (typefaces) that are readable by an OCRS, or they can use special handwriting-recognition systems, such as Datapad or Micropad, where the forms are attached to a pressure-sensitive pad that converts the data into machine-readable form. It is also common to take ordinary handwritten document-coding forms and send them in huge batches overseas (probably to Asia), for keying onto magnetic disks or tapes. These are then mailed back and fed right into the computer.

On smaller cases with no remote field sites, it would be possible (and perhaps labor saving) to type this information directly into the computer, bypassing document-coding forms entirely. Sydney Solo or his paralegal could have performed this task, skipping one step in the creation of the data base. In any large case, it also is possible to mix and match several different methods. All depositions and transcripts acquired in machine-readable form can be entered full text into a large time-shared mainframe computer outside the office, since their volume would severely strain or overwhelm the in-house mini. All other documents can be coded and stored for retrieval in the mini. This means searching more than one data base, but it may prove to be much less expensive.

## SEARCHING AND RETRIEVING

The accomplishment of creating a data base of thousands of documents may seem like an end itself, but such a creation is useless unless it organizes the information to the best strategic advantage. The labor-consuming tasks of collection, coding, and entering into the computer have probably been performed by trained professional and nonprofessional support personnel, but at this point it is necessary for the attorney or inside members of the litigation team to take over. They can do this in two ways: (1) by sending requests for indexes or reports to far-away computers, where the data base is stored for batched processing, or (2) by communicating in an interactive fashion with the data base, using an in-house terminal (this is better but more costly). If the data base is stored on an in-house micro or mini, the interactive mode is, of course, the preferred mode.

The advantage of a computer over manual methods is that not only can it act as a super-indexer, calling up sets of documents at breathtaking speed by many more indexing categories than can be created manually, but also it can combine sets called for by using its powers of Boolean logic.

Boolean logic allows the researcher to restrict his request by using the qualifiers "and," "or," and "not." This means he can request all the memos "and" letters in which the proper names Brown "and" Blue appear, and "not" Green, Yellow, or Red. This could be useful to establish a private pattern of correspondence between two parties suspected of collaboration in a price-fixing suit. It would also be extremely useful to Sidney Solo in trying to sort out personal injuries. He might request all medical reports in which neck "and" head, and "not" foot "or" arm appear.

Sophisticated software, like that used by the full-service bureaus (but not the microcomputer) can also make: proximity search requests—for example, Jones must appear in the same sentence or the same paragraph as Brown; root expansions—for example, all words with the root of "pric," which would include "pricing," "prices," "price," "pricers," and so on; and time-frame requests—for example, all memos between May 1974 and July 1974.

**BOOLEAN OPERATORS**

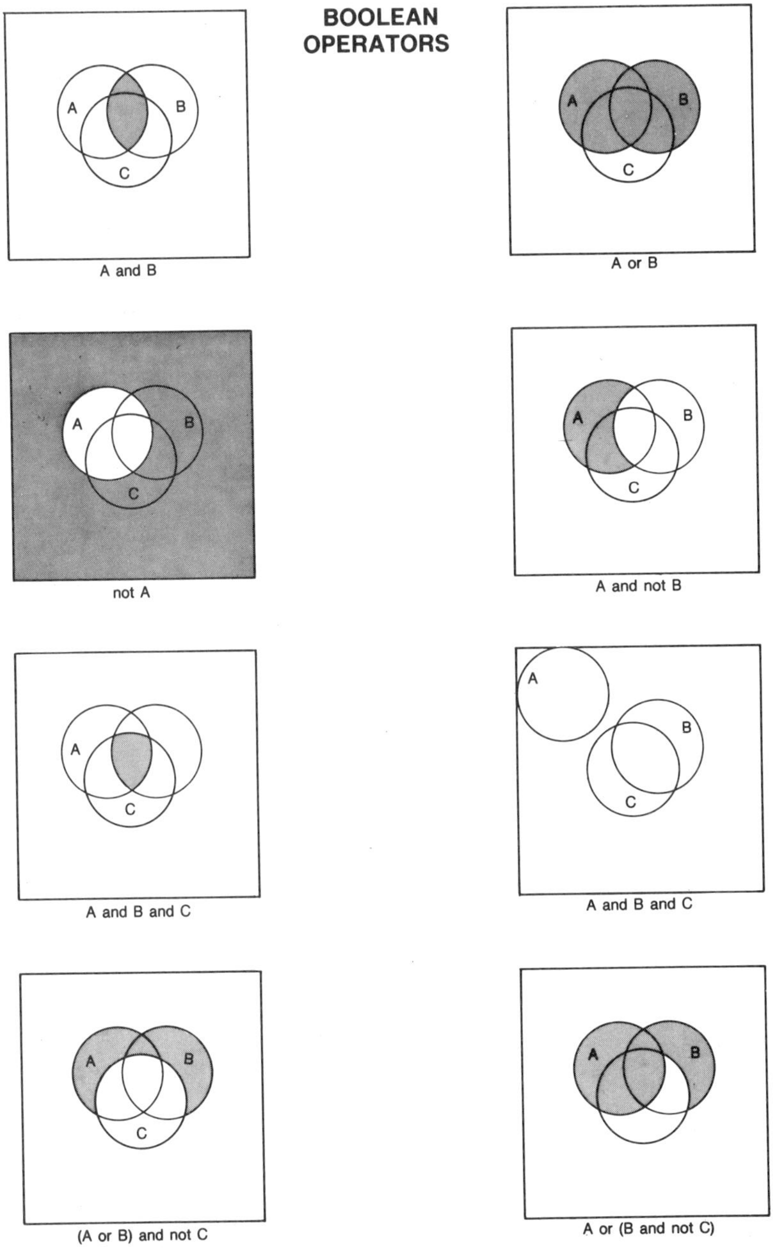


The final report or index can usually be presented in a variety of formats: alphabetical by author; chronological; and so on. It is also possible to specify how much information is desired regarding each document that has been requested: for instance, with or without the abstract; or, in retrieving full-text documents, the key-word request in the context of several sentences.

# USING THE INFORMATION

Sidney Solo and Big, Rich, and Old, could use their computerized data bases at many steps on the road to litigation.

## A. Discovery

It is a simple matter to code documents that are produced for and received from the other side. Then it is possible to match your requests for information against what is actually received, and to keep a record of documents given them. When, during the course of a trial, the opponent objects to introducing a document on the grounds that it was not produced for him, it is possible to quickly check the computer and prove that he is mistaken.

## B. Witness Preparation

One of the major uses of the data base is to sort out the story before reviewing the witnesses in deposition. By organizing the document by date, subject, and so on, the attorney can better interrogate a deponent, and prepare his own witnesses for their testimony at trial.

## C. Trial

Information from the data base can be used to prepare trial briefs, organize exhibits, develop the strategy for direct and cross-examination of witnesses, and, it is hoped, find the smoking gun. The latter may be accomplished by impeaching the testimony of an opposing witness through a quick retrieval of contradictory testimony from the full-text depositions in the data base.

# THE FUTURE OF COMPUTER ASSISTED LITIGATION SUPPORT

Computers have only begun to enter this field, and so far have been severely restricted to the very largest cases. With the decreasing cost of hardware and a computer in every office, there will be increasing demand for affordable and efficient software that will allow at least modified computer-support for cases of all sizes.

# CHAPTER 6

# Managing Words: Word Processing

Anyone who has ever labored over a yellow legal pad, sweating out a memorandum or brief, can appreciate the wonders of word processing. All the deletions, insertions, and cutting and pasting that go to produce even a rough draft are handled in seconds, and the first printed draft can be the final draft, since all the corrections have been completed by reviewing the draft on the video screen. The word processor will even correct spelling mistakes. This very paragraph has been removed, replaced, and revised without a hard-copy printout. All these changes took less than two minutes.

The product of a law practice may be information, but the medium by which this product is conveyed is paper. Therefore, law offices are small publishing houses. The volume of paper produced has increased with the rising curve of litigation, and the trend shows no sign of reversing itself. Most lawyers have recognized that the word processor is a useful weapon in this paper war; thus, the word-processing function of computers is the one that is most generally used, and probably the one that is most generally useful.

Because there is an enormous market for word processing in almost all business settings, not just law, there are literally scores of competing companies that come out almost monthly with a new or improved model with special features. The basic word-processing program, whether it operates on a microcomputer, a minicomputer, or a dedicated word processor, can provide similar basic services.

## A CHECKLIST FOR WORD PROCESSOR FEATURES

| FEATURES: | **VENDORS:** | | | |
|---|---|---|---|---|
| "stand alone" workstations? | | | | |
| can workstations share a printer? | | | | |
| central unit for workstations? | | | | |
| maximum # of workstations: | | | | |
| # of diskette drives | | | | |
| diskette storage capacity: | | | | |
| hard disk? capacity, if any: | | | | |
| software-based (upgradeable)? | | | | |
| print speed: | | | | |
| proportional spacing? | | | | |

---

| | | | | |
|---|---|---|---|---|
| stored phrases and formats: | | | | |
| automatic page-end adjustments? | | | | |
| page and paragraph numbering? | | | | |
| automatic footnotes? | | | | |
| automatic headers and footers? | | | | |
| spelling dictionary? size, if any: | | | | |
| document merge (e.g., mailing lists)? | | | | |
| sorting? # of criteria: | | | | |
| selecting? # of criteria: | | | | |
| special function keys (easy to use) | | | | |
| multiple tasks? | | | | |
| full page screen? | | | | |
| horizontal scrolling? | | | | |

---

| | | | | |
|---|---|---|---|---|
| telecommunications? | | | | |
| electronic mail/messaging? | | | | |
| scheduling/calendar control? | | | | |
| DP programing? | | | | |
| special application packages: | | | | |
| | | | | |
| | | | | |
| | | | | |
| | | | | |

# FUNCTIONS

## A. Text Editing

This lets you push around words, phrases, and whole blocks of text any number of times at rapid speed, and without a hard-copy printout. Letters, words or phrases can be deleted or moved with a single keystroke, and whole blocks of text can be kept in memory to be inserted at a later time.

## B. Merging

The text of one file can be merged into the text of another. This is very valuable with a repetitive document, where most of the document remains the same but a few words or phrases may change. This is obviously suited to legal forms, and is also commonly used for mass mailings, where each letter is personalized with the addressee's name and address.

## C. Storage

The product produced by the word processor can be stored permanently or temporarily on the medium on which it is produced: usually, a floppy or hard disk, or possibly a mag card. This storage allows the user to retrieve it at any time and re-edit it, or print it again just as it is.

The more sophisticated the word processor is, the more special functions are available. These may include spelling checks, records management, global search and replace, repagination, math functions, docket/calendar control, communications, and photocomposition interfaces.

## D. Spelling Checks

Spelling programs can check the user's accuracy and be customized for the vocabulary of the individual user.

## E. Records Management

Some word processors will sort files according to specific requests, such as by zip code, or alphabetically. The most sophisticated word processors permit searching and retrieving of specific documents by many different field designations.

### F. Global Search and Replace

A repetitive word or phrase in a document will automatically be replaced by another word or phrase. This is a useful feature for many standard legal forms.

### G. Repagination

Each time a revision is made, the page numbers are automatically corrected.

### H. Math Functions

Special programs can be added to certain word processors that will allow basic mathematical computations.

### I. Docket/Calendar Control

This permits the status of each case and the calendar of every attorney to be maintained.

### J. Communications

Many dedicated word processors are equipped to talk to other word processors, a central computer, or the outside world through telecommunications. It is also possible for several brands of word processors to tie into WESTLAW for legal data base research. Many microcomputers that function as word processors have the same ability.

### K. Photocomposition Interfaces

Some of the most sophisticated word processors are capable of photocomposition interface for the typesetting of printed materials. This eliminates the labor-consuming step of retyping documents, such as trial exhibits or appellate briefs, which might normally be typeset and published.

## APPLICATIONS

Word processing works wonderfully for any document that needs revision, or any document that is repetitive. This covers almost everything that is produced in a law practice, with the exception perhaps of a perfunctory business letter. Some specific applications include the following.

## A. Memoranda, Briefs, and Pleadings

Any major writing product that includes research and legal analysis undoubtedly needs revision, perhaps several revisions. Once the product is produced, it must be stored for easy retrieval and re-use, since there is no sense in redoing research that has already been done. Hard-disk storage is growing more popular for this purpose since it allows a firm to keep its entire library of memoranda or briefs on a single disk for easy access. Floppy disks have a much more limited storage capacity.

## B. Litigation

In addition to pleadings, civil litigation requires discovery-related documents, such as interrogatories or subpoenas, which may well be similar or almost identical from case to case. Production, storage, and re-use of these documents can be a great time-saver.

With personal-injury litigation taken on a contingency basis, the time saved can be directly translated into money saved, since the hours of labor cannot be billed to a client. This kind of litigation also creates its own specialized documents, such as settlement letters, medical releases, and so on.

## C. Corporate Practice

Articles of incorporation, partnership agreements, filings, shareholders agreements, and so forth often require only a few changes in text from one client to another.

## D. Family Law, Probate, Bankruptcy, and Immigration

These areas of the law generate real paper blizzards. They all require numerous repetitious filings of documents with the court; therefore, they are wonderful candidates for word processors.

## E. Real Estate and Estate Planning

Although these substantive areas do not require as many court filings, they generate long, complicated documents of a repetitious nature, such as living trusts, sale or lease agreements with extensive property descriptions, and so on.

## F. Tax

Most word processing programs are not capable of the mathematical computations necessary to figure out tax returns or projections. For that purpose, another computer program must be used.

However, the opinion letters, briefs, or memoranda relating to tax issues are suitable candidates for a word processor.

## SAVINGS

The amount of time saved by using a word processor is a heated subject for debate among management people. A promotional brochure for a Wangwriter (one of the most popular dedicated word processors) claims a 50 percent savings in time over the time savings provided by an electric typewriter. And a survey by Altman and Weil,[1] a noted law-office management consultant firm, reports that with the most sophisticated distributed logic system, the daily page-production can increase by a factor of ten over a conventional electric typewriter (that is, 120 finished pages can be produced, rather than 12).

No one disputes that word processors are faster than typewriters. But where any individual case falls in this great range between 50 and 1000 percent is determined by the kind of word processor, the configuration in which the word process fits. whether or not an OCR (optical character device) is used, how well trained the typist is, and the organizational level of the office.

The next most controversial question is the degree of savings in personnel—i.e., how many secretaries can you take off the payroll? Those whose jobs may be in jeopardy will be soothed to know that a 1981 survey conducted by Baer, Berkow Associates of 150 law firms in New York, Philadelphia, and Washington, D.C., found that there was little correlation between the increase in the investment in word-processing equipment and the decrease in the number of secretaries. In general, the ratio of secretaries to legal staff has decreased, but word processing did not seem to be a critical factor in this overall trend.

This study also found that law offices were using only the most routine capacities of word processors—text editing, filling in forms, and docket control—and that they rarely made use of more sophisticated math or communications facilities, even when they were available.

The results of this study, and the great range of increased productivity experienced in different law offices, indicate that although the legal profession has embraced the concept of word processing, it has not yet learned how to take maximum advantage of its benefits.

At the same time, the word-processing market is exploding with new products and new technology. Whole new configurations of

**1.** Altman and Weil Study, reported in Arentowicz and Bower, *Law Office Management and Technology,* New York: Matthew Bender & Co., 1980, Sec. 7.05[3].

law-office automation equipment are being introduced, rendering much of the existing word-processing equipment obsolete.

# HARDWARE FOR WORD PROCESSING

In the 1970s, word processing was more or less synonymous with the IBM "mag card" typewriter. But in the 1980s there is a bewildering choice of word-processing hardware to choose from, ranging from a $1,000 Radio Shack microcomputer with a word-processing application program, to a $75,000 word-processing application program for a 120 MB hard-disk minicomputer. All have in common: an input device (usually a keyboard, or possibly—with more sophisticated equipment—an OCR device); some form of main memory (although this can be minimal in dedicated word processors); and an output device (almost always a printer). The range of speed and quality among printers is enormous. (See Chapter 1, "Output Devices.")

## A. Microcomputers as Word Processors

For a sole practitioner or very small law firm, it is difficult to decide whether to buy a small dedicated word processor or a microcomputer that has a word processing program in addition to others. The main advantage of going the microcomputer route is that you can combine basic data processing (i.e., number-crunching) functions, including billing, accounting, time keeping, and so on, with traditional word-processing capacities, such as text editing and merging of documents. Although some dedicated word processors have mathematical abilities, they are usually only the most primitive.

The popular APPLE IIe and IBM PC have their own operating systems and their own software programs, which include word-processing programs. Other popular brands, such as WordStar and EasyWriter, are written for them as well as for the CP/M market. (See Chapter 3, "What Size Is Your Computer?").

As an example of this genre, the popular WordStar, which retails for about $500, can be purchased with a spelling correction program, SpellStar, and a Merge package. It performs all the basic text-editing functions, using a control key and regular keyboard letters for commands rather than special-function keys. It allows for automatic return, right-hand justification, pagination, footnoting, underlining, on-screen formatting, and special print commands such as "boldface type." It also has the capability of global search and command, and when used with the Merge package it can perform all merge functions.

It does not sort files, create indexes, or alphabetize them, but these functions can be very well performed by a data base management software program, many of which are available for the popular brands of microcomputers.

Most microcomputers that use a CP/M or MS–DOS operating system have a dual disk-drive that uses minifloppies, with a capacity of up to 250 pages. It is both possible and increasingly popular for many of these microcomputers to add on Winchester hard disks, which could provide up to several thousand pages of storage. It is also possible for microcomputers to communicate with each other, and perhaps share the data stored in a hard disk.

There is a very wide choice of printers that can be used with a microcomputer. A letter-quality daily wheel printer, which prints at a rate of 55 characters per second, can be purchased for under $1,500; a dot-matrix printer can be purchased for around $500. More money can buy more features, such as automatic single-sheet feed. A buffer, or additional memory, can also be purchased so that printing can be done at the same time as editing new material without tying up the main CPU with one function.

For a range between $5,000 and $10,000, then, it is possible to purchase a microcomputer with a word-processing package and a letter-quality printer. Perhaps the major drawback in choosing a versatile microcomputer, rather than a limited dedicated word processor for approximately the same price, is that at this stage of the microcomputer's infancy it takes some time and ingenuity on the part of the purchaser to put together a good, workable system. Different manufacturers are producing the computer, the software, and the printer, and someone must put it all together. The word-processing programs also are rather difficult to learn. They may be quite sophisticated, as is WordStar; but without special-function keys it takes some practice to learn the commands. In this low price range there are no vendors who will supply complete installation, training, and trouble-shooting. In this fast-evolving field, however, this kind of service will undoubtedly appear to meet the market demand.

## B. Stand-Alone Dedicated Word Processors

A stand-alone word processor is one in which all the components are sold together and operated by one person. The technology in this area is so fast-changing that the machine that dominated the '70s, the "mag card" typewriter, is now completely technologically obsolete (although it is still used in many law offices). This consists of a keyboard, a magnetic card that can hold one page of text, and a printer. Today's stand-alone products resemble a microcomputer in that they have a keyboard, often a video screen, and a separate printer (usually high speed). They may have dual disk-drives and some main memory as well. If they do feature a video display screen, they can print one page while editing a second. This process is known as split keyboarding, and is a great advance over earlier models.

The resemblance between today's modern stand-alone word processor and the microcomputer goes beyond just appearance. Many of the new models have a microcomputer base, and some, such as the IBM Displaywriter, do not have the word-processing program written into ROM memory at the factory, but do offer software packages that can be upgraded or changed.

Stand-alone word processors, however, are dedicated only to word processing. Their keyboards, with their special-function keys, make word processing easier than with microcomputers. They also come as a complete unit and are usually supported by installation, training, and trouble-shooting services from the vendor.

You pay for ease and vendor support, however, and most stand-alone video screen word processors are in the $10,000 to $20,000 range, depending on the speed of the printer and special features offered. This is often more than twice as much as the microcomputer system, and does not provide the data-processing applications. In an effort to be competitive, some word-processing companies have offered lower-priced models with less dealer support. The IBM Displaywriter (which starts at $7,000), has been upgraded every year since its introduction in 1980. It offers good editing capabilities but no installation or training by IBM.

## C. Combinations and Permutations

The larger the firm, the larger the volume of paper that must be both produced and stored. Competitive manufacturers have presented several different solutions to this problem.

### *1. Shared-Logic Word-Processing Systems*

A shared-logic system uses a central CPU—usually a minicomputer with up to 256K main memory and hard-disk storage, and as many "dumb" (without computing ability), terminals as needed, up to the limits of the system. It may also use both letter-quality, and nonletter-quality printers. It is a dedicated word-processing system in the sense that it performs no other functions.

Because it has a more powerful CPU, this system can usually perform more sophisticated functions than a stand-alone word processor. For instance, it can manage a large central data base consisting of all firm work-products, pleadings, memoranda, and so on, and retrieve them quickly from hard-disk storage. Initially it is quite a major investment—a minimum of $30,000 for the CPU, two terminals, and a letter-quality printer—but the cost goes down per terminal in comparison with stand-alone processors.

A major drawback to this type of system is that it is totally dependent on a single CPU. If the CPU has trouble, the whole firm is in trouble, and 20 to 30 terminals can be stilled.

*2. Distributed-Logic Word-Processing Systems*

In this arrangement, the terminals each have a small memory that allows them to perform about 90 percent of the required editing functions, independently of the central CPU and central hard disks drives. This puts less pressure on the central system, but is somewhat more expensive.

*3. Shared-Resources Word-Processing Systems*

This is another level of independence and expense, in which the terminals are essentially stand-alone word processors wired to central disk drives for access to storage, and to a main CPU for additional power. If the central CPU fails, the office can still go on relatively smoothly.

*4. Networks*

A system can provide any combination of dedicated word processors, dumb and intelligent terminals, and a central CPU, provided that the appropriate communications software is available. If the hardware is all from the same manufacturer, this is more likely. Many manufacturers, such as Wang and IBM, are promoting these mixed networks. This same network could also include facsimile devices, micrographic machines, and reproduction machines.

## OPTICAL CHARACTER RECOGNITION UNITS

With any of the combinations described above, an OCR device (see Chapter 1) can greatly increase the productivity. An OCR will read the text of any document typed with the appropriate typeface into a computer or stand-alone word processor. It has the feature of ignoring red felt-tip ink; therefore, any document produced on any ordinary typewriter (with the proper typeface) can be edited in red and entered into the computer for final production.

Conceivably, it could have the capacity of entering any document received from the outside—from opposing counsel or the courts, for instance—into the computer for storage or editing. Unfortunately, the state-of-the-art of these devices is still developmental, and the devices will work only with carefully prepared documents. At present time, they are also quite expensive, ranging from $10,000 to $40,000.

## THE COMPUTER MARRIAGE OF WORD PROCESSORS AND DATA PROCESSORS

The most significant new trend in the development of word-processing systems has been the combination of word-processing and data-processing functions in one large computer system. With this marriage, the same computer that edits a document will also figure out the billing and accounting, keep the docket, and perhaps also provide computerized litigation support. This, of course, is what microcomputers do on the smaller, less expensive end of the spectrum. The advantages of this marriage of convenience are rather compelling.

### A. Data Base Management

A data base is a collection of interrelated data, stored together to serve one or more application. An attorney, before taking on a new matter with an old client, may be very interested in the previous billing arrangement and the status of the account. In the back office, the accountant may need updated biographical information for that same client. Rather than keeping several information files for the same client, a well-organized central data base can ensure easy access and updated information. A large computer can also retrieve this information more quickly and accurately than a word processor.

There are obvious issues of security, since the front office may not want the back office to have access to all the information. However, all data-base systems have some system of control, often a password.

### B. Sophistication

The larger the computer, the more sophisticated the programs can be. Data-base management programs that are also used for litigation support are a primary example. Smaller computers or word processors cannot handle sophisticated search and retrieval of large amounts of information.

### C. Cost

Combining two smallish computers into one larger one is usually less expensive. When the savings of maintaining one central data base rather than two or more are added, the advantage can be substantial.

## D. Disadvantages

### *1. Inadequate Software*

There has been a rush to the market by large numbers of computer manufacturers and software houses that are offering combination word and data processors. Unfortunately, many of these products are old data processors with a word-processing program, or vice-versa, offering a deteriorated version of the old single-purppose computer. The chaos that can occur when a new system that is controlling all vital law office functions fails, is frightening and is experienced as a threatening vision by the rest of the profession. Optimistically, these problems will be resolved with time and testing.

### *2. Cost*

A large new computer represents a significant investment, particularly if the office is already automated in some fashion (e.g., several stand-alone word processors and a small data processor). It will take some time to recapture the investment.

### *3. Reorganization of Personnel*

Everyone needs to be retrained, and the division between the data processors and the word processors becomes blurred. This can have the benefit of creating new skills, greater challenges, and higher morale. It can also initially be very confusing.

## E. Offspring of the Marriage of Word Processing and Data Processing

The same combinations that are available for word-processing configurations are possible with the combined system: shared logic with dumb terminals: distributed logic with slightly more intelligent terminals; and shared resources (which would probably mean using microcomputers as terminals in order to provide maximum power and flexibility). Networks combining different combinations and other equipment, such as reproduction machines, are also possible.

# RESTRUCTURING THE LAW OFFICE

Whether a single microcomputer or a dedicated word processor is introduced into a very small law office, or a hard-disk-drive large minicomputer is introduced into a large law office, the first results will probably be the same: confusion and anxiety. Not only is it difficult to get used to doing something a new way, but it also means that most workers will be doing somewhat different tasks.

## A. The Secretary

The legal secretary is affected first and most directly. Large typing jobs will be done by the word-processor specialist, and once the data base of pleadings, forms, brief, memoranda, and so on is developed, there will be fewer large jobs, even for the word-processor specialist. The traditional one-to-one ratio of attorney to secretary will fall; indeed it has already succumbed.

There are several possibilities for the displaced secretary: he may work for several members of the legal staff, possibly in a team concept (i.e., the real estate team, the labor law team, etc.); he may upgrade his skills (preferably with the aid of some formal training) and take on some paralegal tasks (e.g., basic legal and factual research, or organization of documents for litigation;) or he may try his hand at word processing and become one of the firm's word-processing specialists. What he cannot continue to do is maintain his exclusive relationship with one attorney.

## B. The Paralegal

Most firms of any size have already hired paralegals although these people often are not used as effectively as they might be. Word-processing equipment opens up many possibilities. The drafting of many legal documents requires some legal knowledge; however, with a prototype already on a disk, the drafting may amount to only a few revised words or phrases. A paralegal with his own terminal could retrieve the model, key in the few changes, and send off the draft on in-house electronic mail for the attorney's approval. The attorney could then review it and send it off for first and final printing. Little secretarial help would be required. Documents of this nature could include: pleadings of all types; marital-settlement agreements; complete probate, bankruptcy, and workers compensation proceedings; all forms of discovery; and so on. There is no real limit to the tasks that a trained paralegal could perform, with appropriate attorney supervision.

The team concept is particularly appropriate for paralegals who have specialized skills. The concept of a litigation team is fairly popular, but it could be applied to almost any other substantive area of the law.

## C. The Attorney

Many attorneys have become accustomed to using computer terminals for legal research, but in order to make full use of the wonders of word processing, the attorney should actively participate. As with the paralegal, an attorney may need to add only a few words or phrases to a document that is already on a magnetic medium. While this does mean putting hands on a keyboard, it also saves a great deal of personnel and turn-around time. Then there is the question of the yellow pad. It is very hard to change old habits, but any attorney who is willing to make the effort will find drafting and revising on the keyboard of a word processor a great deal faster than drafting and revising on a yellow pad. For short letters or memos that normally are dictated, the attorney's time will probably still be used more efficiently if he dictates them for input and revision on a word processor; but for the kind of writing that takes a great deal of thought and is not normally dictated, direct keying with the word processor is more efficient.

Unfortunately, voice recognition by computers is still a long way down the road for all but the most limited vocabulary. The keyboard will be the major form of input, at least for this decade.

## D. Law-Office Managers

It is a rare managing partner who understands computers well enough to make maximum use of their powers, or who can supervise the reorganization of the front- and back-office personnel to meet the new technical demands of the computer system. For this purpose, consultants often are brought in on a temporary basis and, increasingly, professional managers are hired on a permanent basis. These managers may have experience in financial planning, systems management, and computer-systems analysis. Hiring a manager indicates that the law firm recognizes itself as a sophisticated modern business, not as a cottage industry. It may take some of the charm out of practicing law, but it increases profits.

For smaller firms or sole practitioners, where the luxury of a manager is not a possibility, an attorney or a legal staff member must take the responsibility of supervising the computer machinery and reorganizing the office for maximum efficiency.

Ultimately, every member of a law firm must be retrained and re-educated. If not, then the computer may become an expensive enemy that drains profits and energy.

# CHAPTER 7

## Case Management: Docket/Calendar and Conflict-of-Interest Systems

One morning, Attorney Brown receives a phone call from Client Blue. Blue complains that he hasn't heard from Attorney Brown for many months, and he wonders what is happening to his personal-injury suit. Attorney Brown assures him that he will check the file and get back to him immediately. He calls up the file from the file room and notes, with a sinking heart, that the statute of limitation on filing Blue's claim has passed two months before.

This is every attorney's nightmare; and unfortunately, it is too often a reality. The largest single cause of malpractice claims—about 30 percent—are missed statutes of limitations; the next-largest source is a related phenomenon—missed appearances.[1] This is probably the result of two factors: (1) clients are clearly more willing to sue for what they consider negligent behavior (the number of attorney malpractice suits has doubled in the past decade), and (2) the rate of litigation is increasing, creating more appearances and deadlines that are possible to miss.

The soaring rates of malpractice insurance reflect the huge increase in attorney malpractice filings. In response, all insurance companies now require attorneys to describe in detail their calendaring procedure, and to maintain at least one back-up system. It is also possible that the insurance company will not pay out a mal-

**1.** Altman and Weil 1977 Survey, reported in Arentowicz and Bower, *Law Office Management and Technology,* New York: Matthew Bender & Co., 1980, Sec. 12.01.

practice claim if the calendaring system was not established as described on the application.

## DOCKET CONTROL/CALENDAR SYSTEMS

Unfortunately, computers will not solve the main problem of missed deadlines, which is human failure to enter appropriate information into a system. The computer does not (yet) answer the phone or open the mail. Nor does it check whether the responsible attorney who is scheduled for a court appearance is actually home in bed with the flu. But what the computer can do is provide a more secure, more organized system: slips of paper do not fall out on the floor and get lost, and the docket information can be retrieved in more formats than is manually possible.

### A. Manual Systems

The key to all successful docket-control systems, calendar systems or tickler systems (as they are sometimes called) is a single responsible person—usually *not* a lawyer—who makes all changes and entries. A single person should be responsible for this task, whether there are one or one hundred attorneys. This person should be familiar with local court rules and with pleadings of all sorts; therefore, a paralegal is a good choice. All new information is received by this person from the secretary or attorney who takes the phone message or opens the mails. This person must also be responsible for making sure that an appearance or deadline is covered by someone else if the responsible attorney is, in fact, in bed with the flu.

There are many commercially available manual calendar systems, and they all provide at least one (usually two) back-up systems. The main concern is to provide plenty of advance warning for any deadline, and usually more than one reminder, before the due date. A common procedure is to issue a firm- or department-wide notice of the entire week's calendar at the end of the previous week and then to issue daily calendars during that week.

### B. Computer-Based Docket-Control Management

A docket-control system is a relatively easy records or data base management function for any computer. There is plenty of software available at all levels, micro or mini, to perform this task. In fact, it is possible to use any standard data base management software package. Usually, the information that needs to be entered in a docket-control system includes: case name and number; date entered; type of activity (deposition, appearance, etc.); responsible attorney; court; judge; or any other relevant informa-

**SAMPLE DOCKET FORM.** The Docket can be printed for any month, forward or backward, and serves, therefore, not only as a traditional docket, but also as a complete calendar and diary. The Docket will print by attorney, client, matter number or by date.

* * * SAMPLE DOCKET PRINT-OUT * * *

To print the entries by ATTORNEY, designate the provider's # in the appropriate line. Only those docket entries for that attorney (provider) will be printed.

*** DOCKET ***

7/25/83

START: 7/1/83 STOP 7/30/83 PROVIDER: 2 CLIENT #.MATTER

| DATE | DOCUMENT #/DESCRIPTION | PROV | CLIENT #.MATTER # | NAME |
|---|---|---|---|---|
| 07/10/83 | CONSULTATION W/ CLIENT | 2 | 81001.01 | NEWMAN |
| 07/12/83 | COUNCIL ZONING HEARING | 2 | 81001.01 | PATRICIA NEWMAN |
| 07/19/83 | MEETING W/ MITCHELL | 2 | 81002.01 | PATRICIA NEWMAN |
| 07/21/83 | COURT APPEARANCE 10:30 | 2 | 81001.01 | PATRICIA NEWMAN |

*** DOCKET ***

7/25/83

To print all the entries pertaining to a CLIENT.MATTER #, the designated the client.matter # in the appropriate line.

START: 7/1/83 STOP: LAST PROVIDER: ALL CLIENT #.MATTER #:81002.01

| DATE | DOCUMENT #/DESCRIPTION | PROV | CLIENT #.MATTER # | NAME |
|---|---|---|---|---|
| 07/02/83 | CALL INSURANCE AGENT | 2 | 81002.01 | BRETHERTON |
| 07/19/83 | COURT APPEARANCE 10:30 | 2 | 81002.01 | BRETHERTON |
| 07/30/83 | FILE PROCEEDINGS W/COURT | 1 | 81002.01 | BRETHERTON |

*** DOCKET ***

7/25/83

To print the entries by DATE, enter the date using the month, day, and year for which you would like to begin printing your docket entries.

START: 7/1/83 STOP: LAST PROVIDER: 2 CLIENT #.MATTER #: ALL

| DATE | DOCUMENT #/DESCRIPTION | PROV | CLIENT #.MATTER # | NAME |
|---|---|---|---|---|
| 07/02/83 | CALL INSURANCE AGENT | 2 | 81002.01 | BRETHERTON |
| 07/03/83 | COMMISSION MTG - 9:30 | 2 | | HOUSE BUILDING |
| 07/10/83 | ZONING HEARING | 2 | 81001.01 | PATRICIA NEWMAN |
| 07/11/83 | COUNTY COUNCIL - 8:30 | 2 | | AT CITY HALL |
| 07/11/83 | LEASE AGREEMENT DUE | 2 | 81004.02 | SMITH |
| 07/19/83 | COURT APPEARANCE 10:30 | 2 | 81002.01 | BRETHERTON |

DOCKET 1

[D750]

tion. The advantage in using a computer is that the information can be retrieved not only by date or case name, but also by judge, court, type of activity, back-up attorney, or any other field topic that is created. For instance, if the back-up attorney is sick or leaves the firm, the computer can report almost instantly which activities require a new back-up person.

The computer is fairly infallible in the security of information it stores, but it is subject to human error in entry and retrieval. Therefore it must be backed up with some kind of manual system.

### C. Word-Processor-Based Docket-Control System

Because the function is relatively simple, many dedicated word processors also advertise a docket-control system as part of their sort-and-select records-management function. Although many word processors can do this, they usually are limited in their storage capacities to a single floppy disk, which makes it improbable for anything but the smallest firms.

## CONFLICT-OF-INTEREST SYSTEMS

Big, Rich, and Old was involved in a multimillion-dollar breach-of-contract suit in which they represented the plaintiff, Radio World (an electronics retailer) against Audiotech (a manufacturer of receivers). In spite of the firm's best professional efforts, their client, Radio World, lost the suit. Six months later Radio World brought a malpractice suit against Big, Rich, and Old, claiming that the firm had simultaneously represented in another law suit, Genetex, the parent company of which Audiotech was a subsidiary. The malpractice claim alleged that this constituted a conflict of interest and prevented Big, Rich, and Old, from giving their best efforts to Radio World.

Conflict of interest, which can be the basis of a malpractice suit or of an appeal or dismissal, is a very slippery concept. The ABA Code of Professional Responsibility requires that the attorney "resolve doubts concerning potentially differing interests against undertaking the representation." Furthermore, "it is the duty of a lawyer at the time of retainer to disclose to the client all the circumstances of his relations to the parties, and any interest in, or connection with the controversy, which might influence the client in the selection of counsel." [2]

The potential conflict can take many forms, including:

1. When the interest of any former or present client might affect the quality of representation.

2. When a new or prospective client has been involved in prior litigation with a current or existing client. There may even be a problem with personal relationships if, for instance, the attorney is the son-in-law of the opposing party.

The combinations and permutations possible for potential conflict are almost endless, but a potential conflict-of-interest situation does not always mean that a law firm cannot accept a new client. If there is full disclosure and discussion and acceptance by the client, a potential conflict is not always a bar to the relationship.

2. "Canons of Professional Ethics Annotated", in *Opinions on Professional Ethics,* Chicago, Ill.: American Bar Foundation, 1967, 22.

It is the affirmative duty of the attorney, however, to discover and reveal potential conflicts. This can be very difficult in a large firm with many clients and many attorneys. The fact that the opposing party is the father-in-law of an attorney in the firm would certainly come to light, but the fact that Audiotech was a subsidiary of Genetex would not be obvious.

Almost all large firms have some sort of procedure to investigate possible conflicts, but they may be very rudimentary and subject to error.

## A. Manual Systems

### 1. *Word of Mouth*

Everyone in the office is asked if they have ever had any dealings with the new client or the opposing party in the suit. This has the obvious limitation of ordinary forgetfulness, and does nothing to uncover subsidiary or tangential relationships.

### 2. *New-Matter Memo*

This can include as much information regarding the client and case as one wishes to include. In searching for conflicts of interest, however, each card would have to be investigated one by one.

### 3. *Multiple-Index System*

Sophisticated manual retrieval systems, such as those used in manual litigation-support systems, may use techniques such as punched holes, notched codes, or color codes, and may provide easy cross-indexing of several different fields. Key information can be sought by client name, opposing counsel, opposing party, or other criteria. There is a limit (usually well under ten) of the numbers of indexing fields that a manual system can contain. If hundreds of clients are involved, the system can become impossible.

## B. Computer-Assisted Conflict Systems

At some point, the use of electronics to store, retrieve, and update potential conflict information becomes necessary. Manual systems simply cannot safely handle the volume of information.

### 1. *Word Processors*

Word processors are possible for limited conflict systems, but they have two innate drawbacks: (1) they have a limited number of terms for which they can search (usually between one and ten), and

(2) they have limited storage capacities and cannot keep information regarding hundreds of clients on floppy disks. Nevertheless, they are very fast, and may be useful for very small offices that have no other computer equipment.

*2. Computers*

A computer with hard-disk storage can store hundreds of client records and retrieve them by almost unlimited search terms. Any data base management software package should permit the creation of a sophisticated conflict system. On a microcomputer, off-the-shelf data base management packages like dBASE II allow 32 search fields and over 65,000 records. Only the type of storage (floppy or hard disk) would limit the number of records stored. On larger computer systems where storage is not a problem, the conflict information may be part of a larger data base containing a great deal more information about the matter and the client, such as calendar and billing information.

## C. The Human Factor

No matter how sophisticated the computer, a conflict system will only be as good as the human being who enters the data and keeps it up to date. As with the calendar, one person should be in charge of all entries and changes, and uniform procedures must be followed. Some sort of controlled data entry, such as the forms used in litigation support with a controlled vocabulary, are useful to keep track of the many ways in which information can be stated.

# CHAPTER 8

# Financial Management

## TIME IS MONEY

Information is the product that lawyers and law offices produce. But that product is evaluated by the hour, not by the pound or by the quality or quantity of information. This evaluation varies only in contingency arrangements, or in a flat-fee situation for a specific job, like the drafting of articles of incorporation. Whatever the ethical or practical arguments regarding using time as the measure of value for attorneys' services, the tradition is established and not likely to be changed. Keeping track of time, therefore, becomes one of the most vital aspects of a law practice. Time is literally money for an attorney.

Attorneys record from 1 to 35 time entries each day, with considerable individual variation. In a typical week, Sidney Solo may collect 60 different time entries to be charged against 12 different client accounts; while Big, Rich, and Old, with its 75 attorneys, may collect as many as 5,000 time entries in serving 1,000 clients. Paralegals now regularly bill out their time as well, adding to the volume and complexity of the time-keeping arrangements.

Attorney billing is complicated by many factors: each attorney may bill at a different rate; each client or matter may receive special billing consideration; paralegals will bill at their own rate; and then there are contingency, flat-fee, and paid-in-advance arrangements. Even within a single case, attorneys may bill differently for certain kinds of activities (e.g., trials vs. depositions).

Client disbursements are also a unique billing headache. If travel is involved, these can add up to more than the actual hourly billings. The use of computers brings up some tricky questions regarding disbursements. Although it is common practice to charge for xeroxing, telephone calls, telegrams, and such, should computer time or word-processing time be charged for the creation of documents? It has become quite well established to charge clients for research time on WESTLAW and LEXIS, but the tradition of charging computer time for other applications is not established, except perhaps in the area of computerized litigation support, when full-service or time-sharing services are used.

*Example A: Small Time*

Sidney Solo registered 120 time entries for the work of April 5th through 12th. These time entries included 32 phone calls, 2 client conferences, 2 depositions, assorted draftings of pleadings, and 1 trial brief. Disbursements covered 6 long-distance phone calls, 2 messenger charges, 360 pages of xeroxing, 45 minutes on WESTLAW, and travel fare for a one-day trip from San Francisco to Los Angeles.

During that week Solo worked on 15 different client accounts, 6 of which were on a contingency basis. Of the remaining 9 clients, 5 were billed at an hourly rate of $125.00, 2 were billed at a rate of $100.00, and 2 were billed at a rate of $75.00. Three of these clients had already paid money in advance toward their account.

Sidney Solo had just begun to use a paralegal on a part-time basis. For that same week the paralegal billed out 6 hours of time, which included 23 time entries ranging from phone calls to legal research to collection of hospital records for litigation. The paralegal served 5 clients, only 2 of whom were not on a contingency basis. He also generated 200 pages of xerox costs and 3 long-distance phone calls, plus ½ hour of WESTLAW time. His hourly billing rate was $35 an hour.

*Example B: Big Time*

Big, Rich, and Old, during that same week in April, generated 4,722 time entries. These included 1,691 phone calls, 132 depositions, 232 clients in office conferences, 20 court appearances (including 2 trials that lasted the complete week), and assorted draftings of pleadings, briefs, and memoranda, not to mention the creation of 7 articles of incorporation, 15 wills, 42 contracts, 3 marital-settlement agreements, and various other business and legal documents. The 45 paralegals also collectively generated 500 time entries, which included almost the complete spectrum of possible paralegal activities.

Big, Rich, and Old maintained a scale of attorneys' billing rates, which ranged from $75.00 for an associate to $250.00 for the senior partner. There were 5 steps on this scale. In addition, some clients were given a reduced rate on some matters, and that week the attorneys served 153 clients who were on a contingency basis. The firm reported 5,029 disbursement items, covering the gamut from long-distance calls to long-distance airplane travel. These also included 88 hours of LEXIS time.

Although the volume of time entries is obviously greater for large firms, a small practitioner such as Sydney Solo may have to face just as many complex variables. Clients increasingly demand detailed billing statements and will not accept a blank-fee charge without a narrative accounting. Both Solo and Big, Rich, and Old have to report to their clients the names of the people or companies they talked to on the phone, and how long they talked. Each bill becomes a personalized document and cannot be mass produced.

## COMPUTERS AS TIMEKEEPERS

The advantage that computers offer over manual time-keeping and billing systems is that they retrieve time entries at electronic speeds, by an almost unlimited number of criteria, and also perform complicated mathematical computations relating to each individualized bill. In addition, a good computer program can generate financial reports regarding the productivity of each attorney, the entire firm, or any other measuring stick that is requested. All sophisticated computerized time-keeping software, whether developed for micros, minis, main-frames, or service bureaus, should be able to accommodate the following needs:

A. An extensive amount of narrative should be possible with each bill. The attorney must be able to explain the 4 hours that were spent on a deposition, and who the deponent was. He must also be able to explain that the trip to Los Angeles was to study the title company's records.

B. The billing system must be able to accommodate a number of different rates for each attorney.

C. It must be possible to make changes or deletions easily in both time entries and disbursements up to the point of sending out the bill.

D. The software should be connected with a general ledger accounting program in order to keep the firm's accounting records on the same data base, and to not duplicate efforts.

E. A full range of management reports should be possible. They should include: an accounts/receivable aging report; attorney productivity records; a client-collections report; and individual histories of client accounts.

The same software may also include calendar/docket-control functions, a conflict-of-interest system, and a trust-accounting application. It is not always necessary for all these functions to be available in the same software package. However, it should be possible for different software application programs to use the same data base, without complicated adjustments.

# MORE MONEY MANAGERS

## A. Accounting—Keeping Track

Time keeping and billing present complexities that may be unique to law practice. Accounting, however, is handled in a law office much as in any other business. If the office is a large one, accounting is handled like a large business. If the office is a small one, accounting is handled like a small business. Therefore, although many of the billing and time-keeping packages do also provide accounting functions, this is not necessary; many of the general accounting software packages could be used as well. The major advantage of an integrated package (i.e., both accounting and time keeping) is that one can more easily make use of same data base. However, this may be overcome with other software programs that integrate software applications on the same computer. Any accounting package should be able to perform the following functions:

- A monthly financial statement
- The general ledger
- The payroll
- Aging of accounts receivable
- Accounts receivable and check writing

Many organizations with large main-frame computers, such as banks, offer payroll services that are relatively inexpensive. Since payroll is the kind of activity that is usually fairly continuous, without demanding constant editing, a batched payroll sent to a bank is often more economical. Therefore, although this function may be available in the accounting package, it may be desirable to separate the tasks and send the payroll out of the office.

Like any business, a law practice must keep track of its productivity. As with accounting, this application is common to all businesses, except that attorneys measure the value of their product in time. Good time-keeping software should allow the generation of productivity reports in many different forms. The software should have the capacities of a good search-and-retrieval system, and should be able to create reports based on any number or variety of criteria requested. Management reports commonly requested include:

- Time-use analysis for each attorney
- Profitability analysis for each attorney, department, and field of law, or type of activity
- Case list by attorney and department
- Analysis of aged unbilled time and disbursements

## SAMPLE BILLING STATEMENT

YOUR FIRM
ATTORNEY AT LAW
YOUR ADDRESS
YOUR CITY ST ZIP
YOUR PHONE #

2/28/82

PATRICK GEORGE NEWMAN III
AD DEVELOPMENT CO.
1234 NORTHEAST DEVONSHIRE DR.
NORTH HAMPTON MD 21201

MATTER 81001.001 REAL ESTATE DEVELOPMENTAL PLAN

| ITEM | *** ACTIVITY THIS PERIOD *** | | | | TOTAL |
|---|---|---|---|---|---|
| 1 | 1/9/81 | CONSULT WITH CLIENT CONCERNING ZONING | 1.50 HRS AT | $60.00 | 90.00 |
| 3 | 1/10/81 | RETAINER FOR SERVICE | | | 300.00 |
| 4 | 1/19/81 | DRAFT DOCUMENT | 3.50 HRS AT | $60.00 | 210.00 |
| 5 | 1/15/81 | SCHEDULE ZONING | 0.50 HRS AT | $60.00 | 30.00 |
| 6 | 1/25/81 | FILING FEE ADVANCED | | | 52.50 |
| 7 | 2/6/81 | PREPARE TESTIMONY | 3.70 HRS AT | $50.00 | 185.00 |
| 8 | 2/10/81 | TRANSCRIPT OF ZONING HEARING FOR CLIENT | | | 78.00 |
| 11 | 3/4/81 | LONG DISTANCE CALL | | | 5.45 |

| ITEM | *** AMOUNTS OUTSTANDING *** | | TOTAL |
|---|---|---|---|
| 12 | 2/28/82 | SERVICE THIS PERIOD | 515.00 |
| 13 | 2/28/82 | EXPENSE THIS PERIOD | 135.95 |

HELD IN RETAINER 300.00

| | | SERVICE | EXPENSE |
|---|---|---|---|
| RA 1 | PREVIOUS BALANCES | 0.00 | 0.00 |
| | PAYMENTS RECEIVED THIS PERIOD | 0.00 | 0.00 |
| | | ========= | ========== |
| | BALANCES FORWARD | 0.00 | 0.00 |
| | BILLED THIS PERIOD | 515.00 | 135.95 |
| | | ======== | ========== |
| | CURRENT BALANCES | 515.00 | 135.95 |

TOTAL NOW DUE 650.95

*** TIMEKEEPING & BILLING PAGE 14 *** (D901)

Sophisticated software could produce a comparison either month by month, or year by year, and possibly generate some graphical models to represent this analysis. With a sophisticated system, one should also be able to project future profits or trends by computing the addition of new factors, such as new attorneys or new paralegals employed, or rising office expenses.

# COMPUTER OPTIONS

Since the application of computers to financial management is the most popular use of computers in law offices (next to word processing), there is a great competition for performing these services. The financial applications of a computer often are called data processing, since numbers and computations are involved, as opposed to word processing, which involves text editing and revision. As discussed earlier, it is common to separate these two functions in a law office and to have a computer system dedicated to each. However, it is increasingly popular to combine both of these functions in one computer, or to link the word processor and data processor together in some kind of networking system. Among the many possibilities for using computers in financial management are service bureaus, minis, and micros.

## A. Service Bureaus

It is very common for large, medium and even very small (sole practitioner) law firms to send out some or all of their financial-management tasks. Service bureaus have become very competitive and can be less expensive than buying the equipment and training personnel for in-house use. Time keeping/billing and payroll are the functions most frequently delegated to service bureaus. Service bureaus normally have mini or even mainframe computers, and most often they will provide batch-processing arrangements. With batch processing, the firm sends all its billing and all its payroll to the service once a month. The service then produces the report or check. The other possibility is on-line service. A law firm will have a terminal directly on-line to the main computers and it can enter new information at any time. This is considerably more expensive, and therefore it is not as popular. The main disadvantage of service bureaus, especially for time keeping, is that they have their own format and do not usually customize billing reports. Since billing is so complicated and so individual to each office, this can be very frustrating. With the batch-processing system, it also is not possible to change or to enter information more than once a month. This means that it usually is impossible to find any kind of account of work in progress.

These problems are less common to payrolls, since the information does not vary as much and does not need to be individualized. Therefore, it is an increasing trend to send a payroll to a large service bureau, which will provide all the proper withholding, deductions, and other payroll concerns.

## B. Minicomputers

The trend is to beef up and consolidate in-house minicomputers, providing communication among the terminals and sharing a common data base. Financial management is certainly one of the major activities of these fast-growing consolidated in-house systems often referred to as networks. The various hardware and software configurations possible (see Chapter 1 for a discussion of these) include: dealing with separate vendors for hardware and software; purchasing turnkey systems, which provide both hardware, software, training, and continuing assistance; and adapting existing word-processing and computer equipment to new software, and/or to new communication systems linking the hardware together.

## C. Microcomputers

Although many microcomputers (for example, the IBM PC and Apple IIe) provide their own software, there is a large market for independent software that can run on many machines, particularly those that support a CP/M operating system or MS–DOS. It is common for software manufacturers in this area to provide several different versions for machines that have different operating systems—for example, a CP/M version and an IBM PC version. Therefore, there is no lack of financial management software covering the gamut from billing and time keeping to docket control, accounting, and management-report functions; and more are coming on the market each day. Some of the currently popular off-the-shelf financial application packages include: Advanced Legal Software, VERDICT, and DATALAW/PC (for the IBM PC XT).

*

# PART THREE

# Computers and Research

## AN INTRODUCTION TO COMPUTER-ASSISTED LEGAL RESEARCH

Computer-assisted legal research (CALR) is just coming into its own after more than two decades of research, development, and investment. It represents the critical nexus of the transformation of the practice of law by computers.

### A. Public and Private Data Bases

Technically, computer-assisted legal research refers both to the public, commercially available legal data bases and to the private collection of documents gathered by each law firm to prepare for litigation or to maintain for reference. Commercial legal data bases such as WESTLAW and LEXIS provide: full text of all recent state and federal court decisions; the U.S. Code; and specialized libraries of tax, securities, labor, energy, patent law, and other major areas of substantive law. The private data bases of a law firm might include depositions, legal memoranda and briefs, pleadings, and summaries or indexes of a wide variety of documents and information.

Recently, commercial services such as Public Affairs Information and Commerce Clearing House's ELSS offer on-line legislative tracking of all bills before Congress and the legislatures of all 50 states.

Other commercial services such as ORBIT, DIALOG, NEXIS, and BRS provide massive data bases of nonlegal information, which include the complete texts of some journals and newspapers and bibliographic indexes to almost all existing technical and scientific resources. Strictly speaking, these are not legal data bases, but the factual or technical information they contain can be just as critical in preparing a case for trial as the leading case law.

Part III of this book deals primarily with public data bases, both legal and nonlegal. Private data bases are covered in Part II, in the chapters on litigation support and in-house information processing. However, the same characteristics of storage and retrieval are common to both public and private data bases, and together they form an integrated research process.

## B. Information Storage: The World on Your Desk

Most attorneys and some legal workers spend a significant portion of their professional lives engaged in legal research. The average legal researcher maintains or shares a library that probably carries: the state reporter and codes; a state digest; several secondary sources, including some kind of legal encyclopedia; two or three form books; Shepard's Citations; and one or two looseleaf services, most likely in the area of tax or business law. If the researcher is lucky, he will be located within half an hour (including parking) of a major law library. The researcher may not have the space nor the money for a larger office library.

Computerized data bases literally bring the world to the legal researcher's desk. With a subscription to WESTLAW and DIALOG, he can instantly retrieve on his desktop terminal the full text of cases from all state and federal jurisdictions, and more tax and business information than are probably available at his local major law library. He can also immediately determine the status of any bill that is before any legislature in the country, using one of the available legislative tracking services. Through telecommunications, he can obtain nonlegal information from technical journals, newspapers, and many other published sources that he may not be able to locate anywhere in his city. In his private data base he can store unlimited numbers of documents, either full text or in summary, that would be physically unmanageable in files, boxes, or crates. This private information may be stored on a single hard disk (which is smaller than a breadbox) or, if the volume is great, in a far distant large computer, to which the researcher has immediate access by telephone line.

## C. Information Retrieval: Lightning Access

Information is retrieved from both public and private data bases in a similar manner. Any word, phrase, or number that appears within the text of a case, newspaper article, bibliography, deposition, or other document can be used as the key to finding the document. Each commercial service may require a somewhat different format for phrasing the search inquiry, and some may insist on a coded vocabulary, but the principle is the same.

Let's say that one of the researcher's clients is the daughter of a woman who took the drug DES while pregnant. The daughter now has strange physical symptoms. In order to discover the current law, the researcher could retrieve all relevant cases in any jurisdiction simply using the term "DES" with WESTLAW. The researcher could then transfer to a nonlegal information data base such as DIALOG, and search the chemical and medical abstracts for articles relating to DES. In this instance it might be necessary to further limit the search by adding the phrase "birth defects," since there may be articles that deal with DES in a more theoretical way with no concern for its medical consequences.

The attorney may also be aware of a bill pending in Congress that would, in part, determine liability for the class of victims of DES. A subscription to Public Affairs Information would allow him to call up information regarding the status of this bill on his desktop terminal.

As the case progresses the researcher may choose to put the full text of all the witnesses' depositions into his private data base, as well as abstracts of other documents such as medical reports, technical literature, and interrogatories. In preparing his case for trial the researcher can almost instantaneously retrieve specific information by using key words or phrases. If it were necessary, for instance, to establish a life-long pattern of fainting spells, the researcher could search all the depositions of family members and the medical records for the terms "faint" or "fainting."

Manual indexes, of course, such as case digests, technical bibliographic indexes, and notched card indexes for private files, could have provided some of the same information as the computer search. But a computer search has several inherent advantages: not only is it astonishingly fast (when given the correct terms, of course), but also it is not limited by the focus of the professional indexer; the researcher becomes the indexer. The indexer of digests, for instance, would not have created a special section for DES cases, and the researcher might have a difficult time locating them manually in the topics of medical malpractice or negligence. The computer also facilitates the location of cases or facts by using arbitrary combinations of words or phrases. For instance, the researcher could search all cases to find only those where both "DES" and "birth defects" appear, or where a certain attorney and DES appear (often critical information for trial strategy).

To perform sophisticated searches, however, the researcher must have a good grasp of the issues in order to use words or phrases that will retrieve the appropriate material. Not all searches are as straightforward as the example used with DES. It can be easier to miss important information than with a manual index, since the manual indexer is in the profession of thinking up as many terms as possible in any given area of substantive law. The researcher must come to his search well prepared in both legal and factual issues.

It is also not uncommon for a new researcher, particularly in dealing with a legal data base, to use terms that are too broad and to end up retrieving several hundred documents. This occurs because the computer is searching the full text of all the documents in the data base requested. The words or phrases requested may appear in a document that is otherwise completely inappropriate to the search. For instance, it is possible that the term DES might retrieve many cases dealing with trademark or patent litigation that included the drug DES.

WESTLAW offers the advantage of restricting the search first to specific digest topics and/or key numbers and then further qualifying it with factual terms. Many of the nonlegal data bases also provide subject descriptors, which restrict the focus of the search. Details of the search strategy will be offered in Chapter 10, "A User's Guide to WESTLAW and LEXIS."

# CHAPTER 9

# Public Legal Data Bases

Legal data bases are truly in the forefront of the information revolution because they offer full text rather than bibliographic information. This not only allows much wider searching but also eliminates several steps from the research procedure. Conceivably, a researcher can complete the entire research process while seated at the terminal, and not have to locate the printed text, which may be in a distant library or available only through mail order.

## THE PROS AND CONS OF USING A LEGAL DATA BASE

Most researchers have already formed some opinions about the commercially available legal data bases, WESTLAW and LEXIS—not necessarily based on a great deal of experience. These opinions, often hotly debated, generally fall into the following categories:

*Advantages:*

- Speed of information retrieval
- Availability of a large law library in your office
- Access to specialized material in areas such as tax, securities, and so on
- Ability to reach very recent cases not yet indexed
- Accessing documents by judge, court, attorneys, and so on that are not possible with manual research
- Shepardizing in a fraction of the normal time

*Disadvantages:*

- Cost
- Difficulty in using for inexperienced researchers

- Limits of data base (e.g., no very old cases, few statutes, few secondary sources)

All these points will be addressed in this chapter and in the chapter on using the systems, to help the researcher make a more informed evaluation.

## THE DATA BASES

Several legal data bases are available in America, and there are several in Europe as well. The two most prominent in America, WESTLAW and LEXIS, serve the public; however, there are others available only to federal and state entities—most notably, FLITE (a service provided by the Department of Defense), JURIS (the system developed by the Department of Justice), and RIRA (serving only the I.R.S.).

Spectacular new data-base services have very recently become available in the area of legislative-bill tracking. Two national services, Public Affairs Information and Commerce Clearing House, now offer complete national coverage, and several commercial services are devoted to individual states. The federal government and most states have developed some sort of computerized legislative system that usually is available only to insiders, and which may contain confidential information regarding fiscal impact, etc.

## WESTLAW AND LEXIS

### A. Operation

The two competing commercial legal data bases, WESTLAW and LEXIS, have many more similarities than differences. Both are on-line interactive systems, which means that the user can carry on a dialogue with the central computer that stores the data base. WESTLAW, a service of West Publishing Company, has its central computer in St. Paul, Minnesota; LEXIS, a service of Mead Data Central, maintains its computer in Dayton, Ohio. Seated at a terminal (a device consisting of a keyboard and display screen), the researcher makes contact with the central computer using a telephone link via a modem. The terminal itself stores no knowledge and has no program (software) to search the data base; it simply provides the equipment (hardware) to put in a request (1) for specific information to the central computer by means of the keyboard (input), and (2) to view the information the computer has retrieved on the video screen (output) via the telephone line. The telecommunications used may be a private communications network—such as TYMNET or TELENET, which provide fast service with minimum distortion—or a private leased line, dedicated exclusively or almost exclusively to this task. Once the information has been retrieved, the researcher has the choice of browsing or quickly skimming the information on the video screen, and of printing relevant sections on the high-speed printer that most often accompanies the terminal.

The terminal may be anywhere in the country where there is a telephone line. Theoretically, it could take any shape, including a briefcase terminal. WESTLAW can be accessed by increasing numbers of popular-brand microcomputers and word processors, which may include briefcase models in the near future. It may soon be common to see attorneys sitting in airports, in courthouse corridors, or on the back deck, retrieving relevant cases on their briefcase terminals. At the moment, however, CALR is normally performed on a terminal in the law library or at a law office.

The search request that the researcher enters through the keyboard of the terminal consists of words, phrases, numbers, or combinations thereof that describe a legal problem. The researcher can address thousands of cases, statutes, and other legal documents in any state or federal jurisdiction, and receive the documents that contain those terms at a fantastically fast rate. Any search term can be modified by the user to include or exclude additional terms. This interactive dialogue between the user and computer gives the user greater freedom in framing and modifying search requests than is possible with standard published digests and indexes.

Both systems provide full-text retrieval of court decisions. WESTLAW offers the full text of opinions augmented by headnotes, digest topics, key numbers, and synopses. This allows WESTLAW researchers to limit their research queries to topic areas or to focus more closely on specific facts. Both WESTLAW and LEXIS are continually adding to their libraries. They both enter all new decisions into their data bases very quickly (some jurisdictions more quickly than others) and are extending their coverage backward in time as well.

The original emphasis for both WESTLAW and LEXIS was case law. Now they both maintain data bases of state and federal court opinions within the past 15 to 30 years and are expanding in many different directions, including tax, energy, securities, and many other specialized areas of business and administrative law. The specialty data bases contain statutory authority, judicial decisions, administrative regulations, and, sometimes, advisory opinions. A very current catalog or viewing the menu on the terminal itself is always necessary to assess the contents of the data bases.

Although the operation of the two systems is very similar, there are some differences between them that may be of importance to the researcher. Also, it is likely that the researcher will have access to one rather than both, of the systems. Therefore, a detailed examination of each system follows.

## WESTLAW

West Publishing Company introduced the WESTLAW service in 1975. Originally it offered only the West headnotes, which are the headnotes found in its National Reporter system; but beginning in 1978, it switched completely to full text, since researchers found that full-text retrieval was far more useful. WESTLAW now offers both full text plus headnotes and case synopses, exactly as they appear in the National Reporter system. In fact, the same computer tape that is entered into the WESTLAW data base is also used to print the National Reporter volumes. Because preparation of the headnotes and synopses takes some editorial time, WESTLAW cases (with the exception of the U.S. Supreme Court and the U.S. Circuit Courts of Appeals, which are printed first without headnotes) take somewhat longer to enter the data base than those of LEXIS, which offers only the opinion. Its offerings are expanding rapidly, and the user must refer to the most current bulletin, published monthly. WESTLAW is competing vigorously with LEXIS in the expansion of its data base. It is also assertive in its marketing; and in spite of its late start WESTLAW is now seriously competitive with LEXIS.

### A. Equipment

WESTLAW is in the process of expanding its compatibility to suit virtually any existing microcomputer or word-processing terminal that has communications capabilities. Currently, it is compatible with more than 60 of the most popular models, including the IBM PC and Radio Shack TRS–Models 2, 12, and 16.

WESTLAW also offers a custom terminal called WALT (West's Automatic Law Terminal), with a video screen and printer that is specifically designed for access to the WESTLAW data base. This system can offer some features that are not available in converting a regular word processor or microcomputer to a WESTLAW system. Although it is a larger capital investment, it also means that the terminal is always free for legal research. It often happens that a word processor or microcomputer is too heavily used to make it available to the researcher when it is most needed. Access to the central computer is either direct on leased or dedicated lines, or indirect by way of TYMNET or TELENET switching systems.

## B. Operation

WESTLAW is a full text database. When the text of a document is put into the computer, a concordance, or index, is developed for almost all the words and numbers. This means that the concordance contains a word such as "pension," and can immediately indicate all the cases where that word can be found in the particular database or library that the user is searching. It also responds to requests based on Boolean logic; e.g., universities "and" colleges, "but not" high schools.

The concordance will not include some very common words, such as "and," "the," and "or." The method of retrieval will be discussed in Chapter 10, "A User's Guide to WESTLAW and LEXIS." One major difference between WESTLAW and LEXIS in this respect is that the searcher can also make search queries based on West's Topic and Key Number system. If use of a West Digest has taught the researcher which topic and key number are appropriate to the problem, the researcher can use the system as a master digest. For example, he can call up Divorce, keynumber 18, to find cases on pension rights and divorce in any of the data bases. Or he can use this as only one of the qualifiers in the search, including factual terms. For researchers accustomed to using the West Key Number system, this can be a great advantage; for those not accustomed to using the Key Number system, it can help focus the search. An impossible number of terms might be retrieved using only the factual terms without the restriction of a topic. With WESTLAW the searcher has the option of viewing cases retrieved in one of several forms: full text, synopsis only, digest paragraphs only, or a list of citations. This is because when WESTLAW publishes its volumes of the National Reporter System the information is put immediately on machine-readable tape. Therefore, the same text, including headnotes and synopses, which is found in the published version of the National Reporter System is also available in the WESTLAW data base.

## C. WESTLAW Data Bases

### *1. Legal Data Bases*

WESTLAW has divided its case law into libraries. Coverage is, of course, continually expanding in all these libraries. The term "full text plus" indicates that the opinion is accompanied by headnotes and synopses, exactly as reported in West's National Reporter System. (A complete listing of the libraries is contained in Appendix A.)

*a. Federal Libraries*

A. U.S. Supreme Court Reporter, 1925 to date.

B. Federal Reporter 2d, U.S. Courts of Appeal decisions from 1945 to date.

C. Federal Supplement, which includes:

1. U.S. District Courts, 1950 to date.

2. U.S. Court of Claims, 1954 to 1960.

3. Other specialized federal courts include Court of International Trade cases, Regional Rail Reorganization Act Special Court, and so forth. (For a complete listing see Appendix A.)

D. Federal Rules Decisions, 1978 to present, headnotes 1961–1977.

E. U.S. Code, official text.

F. Code of Federal Regulations, all 50 titles.

G. Federal Register.

*b. State Libraries*

All 50 states and District of Columbia are included in state law libraries, organized according to the regional reporters. State libraries include full text of state cases plus synopses and headnotes from at least 1965 to date. Headnote coverage is available in most states from 1957–1964.

*c. Specialty Law Libraries*

In this area WESTLAW has rapidly closed the gap with LEXIS, which held a large lead in early years. WESTLAW has developed extensive specialty libraries in the areas of: federal tax; federal securities; antitrust and business regulations; federal government contracts; patent; trademark and copyright; federal communications; federal labor; Delaware corporation law; admiralty and federal bankruptcy. By the end of 1983 these libraries will offer roughly equivalent coverage to those presented by LEXIS. The only significant subject-matter difference between the two at this point is that LEXIS offers a specialized library in the area of energy, and WESTLAW offers an admiralty law library. Each system is developing the unique library offered by the other. WESTLAW offers the Military Justice Reporter with Courts of Military Appeals and Courts of Military Review cases from 1978. WESTLAW has also developed specialized libraries for California and New York in the areas of family law, insurance law, and education law. Other states and federal cases will be added.

As with LEXIS, these specialty libraries contain a combination of federal court opinions, administrative tribunal decisions, regulations, private letter rulings, and so on, which focus on that topic. For instance, the Securities data base includes SEC Decisions, SEC Releases, and SEC No-Action Letters as well as relevant federal cases and relevant sections of the U.S. Code and U.S. Code of Federal Regulations.

*d. European Libraries*

It is now possible, through an arrangement with EUROLEX, to access an extensive library of Common Market, English, and Scottish legal materials.

*e. Shepard's Citations*

WESTLAW provides full coverage of Shepard's Citations, allowing the researcher instant verification of the status of the case he is relying upon, and providing additional research information. Shepard's is much more interactive in WESTLAW than in LEXIS and consequently much easier to use. The user can go directly from a case to the list of Shepard's Citations which pertain to it, and from there directly to the citing cases.

*f. Insta–Cite*

This service is an integral part of WESTLAW and can serve to discover case history and validate information about decisions, as well as obtain parallel citations.

*2. Nonlegal Data Bases*

Although WESTLAW does not provide its own nonlegal data base as LEXIS does with NEXIS, the WESTLAW video display terminal can be linked up through TYMNET or TELENET to a variety of data base services, including DIALOG, Dow Jones News Retrieval Service, and ORBIT. (The utility and variety of the nonlegal data bases will be closely examined in Chapter 11, "Public Nonlegal Data Bases.")

## D. WESTLAW as a Litigation Support System

WESTLAW offers the use of its computer for private libraries, but does not aggressively market litigation support services at the present time. Because of the variety of compatible equipment such as the IBM Displaywriter or CPT terminals, however, one system can work for various purposes.

### E. Costs for WESTLAW

Although WESTLAW, like LEXIS, is increasingly prominent in law libraries, particularly those connected with law schools, the vast majority of users still gain access through private subscription. WESTLAW is very competitive with LEXIS in its pricing. A detailed analysis of pricing is beyond the scope of this text, but equipment, including a printer can be purchased or leased for approximately $240 per month. The first three hours of research are charged at a rate of $115 an hour, and the amount reduces to $65 for every hour more than 100. Unlike LEXIS, there are no surcharges or search units.

Special rates are offered for law schools and government users and a discount is given for members of the American Bar Association.

## LEXIS

LEXIS is the older of the two systems. In the late 1960s the Ohio Bar undertook a study to see how computers could aid lawyers in their research. A small company named OBAR began putting Ohio case law into its data base, and was soon taken over by the Mead Corporation. In 1973 LEXIS was offered to lawyers as a service of Mead Data Central. LEXIS has grown remarkably, both in the breadth of its data base and in the volume of its users, which now number in the thousands.

### A. Equipment

At the moment, LEXIS is available only through hardware supplied by Mead Data Central and a small number of microcomputers. This equipment consists of the terminal (keyboard and display screen) for access to the data base, and a printer (usually high speed) to deliver a hard copy of the information requested. It is also possible to purchase a printed copy of any information retrieved from Mead Data Central; it will arrive by mail in a few days. There are various terminal models, with different price tags, including a desktop model. The special equipment is an advantage in that the equipment is specifically designed for use of this system; however, it also means a substantial leasing fee. Terminal access to the computer in Dayton, Ohio, is through Mead's network of private leased data lines.

### B. Operation

When the text of a document is put into LEXIS, the computer notes the location of each word used in the document. The computer then produces a "concordance" for each file. A concordance is a listing of the location of all the words in the file, with the exception of about 100 of the most commonly used words, such as "a" and "the." A file is a separately searchable collection of documents. Files are usually organized by either type of document (e.g., California State courts) or by type of document and date (e.g., U.S. Circuit Courts of Appeal, 1945 to 1959). When a search request is made, the computer will search the concordance of that file, not the actual texts within the file. Mead Data Central claims that LEXIS can complete 90 percent of all searches within a single file in fewer than 15 seconds.

For example, if the researcher asks LEXIS to search for the word "university" in the California state court file, the computer will search the concordance for that file and retrieve all the documents in which that word appears. The software program that instructs the computer uses Boolean logic, which means that it can request the computer to search the concordance for strings of terms connected by "and," "or," or "not," rather than single terms. Therefore, the researcher can request all documents that contain the terms: university "or" college, "and not" high school.

Specific instructions on how to narrow or broaden search terms and when to retrieve the full text or segments of a document will be given in the Chapter 10, "A User's Guide to WESTLAW and LEXIS." At this point, it should be noted that the search may not stop with one file: the researcher may wish to investigate U.S. Supreme Court cases in addition to California courts. To do this he would call up the file on U.S. Reports and search the concordance of that file for the same terms.

## C. LEXIS Data Bases

### *1. Legal Data Bases*

The legal information available through LEXIS is grouped first into what LEXIS refers to as "libraries." These libraries are organized around a particular jurisdiction. The following is a general description of what these libraries contain (a specific listing is found in Appendix B). Coverage in these libraries is continually expanding, and current listings from Mead Data Central must be checked.

#### *a. Federal Law Libraries*

This data base includes full text of cases decided by the U.S. Supreme Court, Court of Appeals, District Courts, and Court of Claims. The U.S. Code is also included. The Federal Register has recently been added, beginning in 1980, and the Code of Federal Regulations is now on-line.

### *b. State Law Libraries*

These libraries include full text of cases from all 50 states and the District of Columbia. Coverage begins at varying times, most often starting in 1965. State statutes are included for a few states. State statutes are expensive to put on-line and to maintain, but they must certainly be added in the future if computer-assisted legal research systems hope to take the place of traditional law libraries.

### *c. United Kingdom Law Libraries*

Includes cases and statutes from the United Kingdom. Coverage begins in the 1940s. Special files on tax, industrial relations, patents, intellectual property, European communities, and local governments are also included.

### *d. French Law Libraries*

Public law, private law, and statutes and regulations beginning in the 1960s are available.

### *e. Auto-Cite*

This system, a service of Lawyer's Cooperative Publishing Company, but made available through LEXIS, is mainly useful for checking the accuracy of a case citation that the researcher is relying upon, and for obtaining parallel cites. It will also list any appellate cases that directly affect his case's validity as precedent. Recently, Auto-Cite has expanded its services to provide a citation to any American Law Reports annotation that cites the case at hand. This can provide a useful research tool, since the ALR annotation may cite many other on-point cases in the same area of law.

### *f. Shepard's Citations*

Shepard's provides parallel citations, and a statement of the subsequent history of the case at hand, including the treatment given the case by judges deciding other cases. Shepard's Citations for all federal, state and regional reporters is offered. This is an indispensable tool for any researcher in order to ensure that the case he is using is still good law.

*g. Specialty Law Libraries*

Here CALR can make significant and unique contributions. It is possible to pull together various strands of law, including cases, statutes, reports, regulations, and rules, around a topic area. In this way the computer performs a similar function to commercial looseleaf reporters, but can provide coverage of many more areas. Currently, LEXIS provides topical coverage in the areas of tax, securities, trade regulation, patent, trademark, copyright, communications, bankruptcy, labor, energy, and public contracts. These libraries include relevant cases that will also appear in the state and federal libraries, statutes, regulations, legislative history, administrative decisions, rulings, and releases.

*h. Matthew Bender Publications*

Full text of some Matthew Bender publications are being placed in the LEXIS data base. Currently, 20 legal treatises are on-line.

*2. Nonlegal Data Bases*

Nonlegal data bases offer enormous research support for attorneys in almost every area of law practice. (See Chapter 7.) LEXIS offers the following nonlegal data bases.

*a. NEXIS*

This is a full-text document-retrieval system that is also available from Mead Data Central. As with LEXIS, access to the documents is through the words actually used in the text. The offerings include a wide range of business and general news periodicals. The NEXIS service is available to LEXIS subscribers and is also marketed heavily in the nonlegal business community. Coverage includes: *The New York Times* Information Service (a recent acquisition); *The Washington Post; U.S. News and World Report; Newsweek; Business Week; The Economist; The Federal Register* (also available in the LEXIS Federal library); the *Congressional Quarterly Weekly;* the Associated Press and United Press International wire services; and many other news sources.

These sources can be valuable for tracking down evidence in trial preparation.

*b. LEXPAT*

This is a new data base that will offer full text of all utility, plant, and design patents issued by the U.S. PTO from 1975 to date.

This data base can be searched full text or by a class, subclass, or patent number.

*c. DIALOG*

As with WESTLAW, LEXIS users can access the DIALOG service.

*d. Accounting Information Library*

This data base includes annual reports of corporations listed on the New York Stock Exchange, the American Stock Exchange, and corporations quoted over the counter.

*e. Britannica 3*

The 10-volume *Micropaedia* and the 19-volume *Macropaedia* are made available through LEXIS.

## D. LEXIS as a Litigation-Support System

LEXIS offers an option of private library services; i.e., LEXIS will store the user's own documents in its central computer. All the materials stored in this private library can be searched in the same manner as the cases and statutes stored in the LEXIS data base. This service has been used most often by law offices to store documents in the course of litigation and to store work products. Documents need not be full text. They can be stored in the form of abstracts, extracts, or bibliographic information.

The litigation-support package includes the ability to sort documents by date, author, type of document, or any other appropriate index.

## E. Costs for LEXIS

Although LEXIS is available at a few law libraries, particularly those connected with a law school, the vast majority of users are private subscribers. The cost of using LEXIS is significant, and must be a serious consideration for any potential user. As with the contents of the data bases, there is continuous change and a current catalog must be consulted.

As of June 1983, charges are broken down into several categories: initial installation; training; the monthly subscription and library access fees; monthly charges for terminals and printers; the use charge based on LEXIS computer time; and the search surcharges based on the number of occurrences of the words being searched and the number of sub-searches. There are also printing charges for printing requested from the LEXIS central facility. There is a downward sliding scale for the installation of multiple terminals, and also for increasing numbers of computer hours used.

The price reduction for multiple terminals provides incentive for wider distribution within law firms and for sharing among attorneys not belonging to the same firm. It makes it possible for a number of law offices in the same building, for instance, to share the expense.

Law firms using LEXIS most often bill research time at the rate of $2.50 to $3.00 per minute. At least one federal court, in *Pitchford Scientific Instruments Corp.* v. *PEPI Inc. et al.,* 440 F.Supp. 1175 (W.D.Pa.1977), ruled that LEXIS costs could be included in attorney's fees as well. Total charges now average about $150 per hour, although there is great variation depending upon usage and equipment. Most or all of this charge can be recouped by billing the client.

The other factors that must be considered in a cost evaluation are the savings in research time, and the quality of research that can be produced.

## LEGISLATIVE TRACKING SYSTEMS

Computerized legislative tracking systems offer an enormous breakthrough in the very difficult process of following the progress of a specific bill through a state legislature or Congress. Attorneys very often have clients, such as corporations, labor unions, schools or universities, who have a critical interest in the outcome of pending legislation. The input of the client at a crucial juncture could make the difference between passage and defeat. By taking advantage of the up-to-date information provided by a computerized tracking system, the attorney can literally have the answer at his fingertips, on his desk terminal.

Currently, there are two national systems that cover all state legislatures and Congress: ELSS, or Electronic Legislative Search System (offered by Commerce Clearing House), and Public Affairs Information. Public Affairs Information, which began as California Research and merged with Martin Haley Companies, Inc. in 1982 to provide national coverage, claims the largest number of subscribers—500, with 100 in California alone. At the moment these subscribers are almost exclusively corporate clients with specific legislative interests, such as the American Petroleum Institute and IBM. PAI advertises that it will design client-owned or leased computer systems that will provide other applications, such as word processing, and will be connected on a time-sharing basis with PAI's main computer. PAI also provides a range of other legislative services, including: lobbying programs; political profiles; political education training and seminars; and federal and state legislative assessment and analysis. The client can sign up for any or all of these services and can receive hard-copy and/or on-line reports on a daily or weekly basis. Usually the client will subscribe to one or two special-interest areas, and the searches will be restricted to these. The number of jurisdictions that will be searched is determined by the client.

No figures are available for the numbers of subscribers to the newly offered ELSS, but they are advertising for an attorney market and they charge on a "use-only" basis after the initial registration fee (determined by the numbers of subjects and jurisdictions). ELSS advertises that its service, available by telecommunications, is compatible with most word processors and microcomputers. The subscriber either chooses specific subject areas and specific jurisdictions, or chooses to have access to all subjects and jurisdictions. ELSS provides: descriptions of bills and resolutions, including short titles, sponsors, dates, or introductions and committee referrals; all committee and floor assignments; vote counts affecting the passage of federal legislation; and disposition of bills (whether enacted, defeated, tabled, or pending).

There are also several data-base services, and many more in the works, that offer strictly state coverage. One such service in California, LEGITECH, provides both legislative tracking services and information on political contributions. With this system it is possible to discover precisely who contributed how much to any candidate. This service has become available to the public through at least one public library.

The federal government, as well as several states, also maintains its own legislative data base for legislators, their staffs, and other authorized governmental employees. These systems can provide a wide variety of information, including legislative tracking and statutory searches. LEGIS, the federal government's legislative data base system, provides a wide range of information, including special research reports on pending bills.

## GOVERNMENTAL DATA BASES

### A. JURIS

JURIS is a computerized legal research system developed and operated by the Department of Justice to assist federal attorneys in finding the law. This service is not restricted for the use of Department of Justice attorneys, but is also used by Legal Services Corporation Migrant Legal Action Program. JURIS is an interactive system, similar to LEXIS and WESTLAW. Searches can be made in one of two ways:

a. *Index searching*

This restricts search to West's headnotes and it is done with the cooperation of West Publishing Company.

b. *Full-text searching*

This gives the user access to the entire JURIS data base.

The JURIS data base is developed by means of a concordance, similar to that of WESTLAW and LEXIS. Each word in the data base is indexed in a concordance so that it can be immediately located for retrieval. The method of forming the search query is similar to that of WESTLAW and LEXIS also. The user must choose a specific file and enter a search request, which may be words, numbers, or phrases, grouped together with connectors. As with the other systems, choosing the correct words or phrases as a search query is the most important first step. It is also possible to research by logical segments such as opinion, circuit, or citation. This limits the search to a smaller number of potential cases.

Since JURIS is for the exclusive use of federal attorneys, its data bank naturally reflects the interests of this group. In addition to all recent lower federal court cases and U.S. Supreme Court cases from 1900, JURIS offers the U.S. Codes and the current uncodified public law. It also contains all of West's Federal Digest, the holdings of the Courts of Military Review, published Controller General sessions, selected U.S. Attorney General opinions, and Nuclear Regulatory Commission Decisions.

## B. FLITE

FLITE is a batched rather than interactive system. This means that the researcher mails his request to the data base computer, where attorney advisors perform the search and then mail the results back by mail. This system has obvious assets and drawbacks. The attorney advisors are very skilled in retrieval, but the client cannot change his research query in response to the information he receives, as he could in an interactive system. And of course the retrieval time is determined by the post office.

The clients of FLITE are departments and agencies throughout the federal government. Research services are provided without fee to clients from the Office of the Secretary of Defense, to all DOD components, the U.S. Coast Guard, the president of the United States, Congress, and the U.S. Supreme Court. Clients from other federal departments and agencies are charged $50 per database search.

FLITE has access to the JURIS data base, and to Lockheed's DIALOG data bases. In addition to all federal cases and codes, which can be obtained through JURIS, FLITE also maintains Court Martial Reports and the Military Justice Reporter. As for specialty libraries, it maintains a labor law data base, which includes decisions and interpretations of the Federal Labor Relations Counsel, and a tax library that includes Tax Court Reports and Board of Tax Appeals Reports. It offers specialized material regarding internal management, procurement, and federal administration. Through DIALOG, it has access to Federal Register Abstracts and Congressional Administrative News as well as scores of other general and technical data bases.

## C. RIRA

This database serves the IRS exclusively, and its contents reflect that agency's needs. It includes: federal and tax court cases; regulations; rulings; private letters; and other relevant agency information.

## D. LAWNET

This newly developing data base is projected to serve all law libraries. It will allow researchers to discover instantly which library contains a specific reference. It then may be possible to obtain a copy of that reference through interlibrary loan. It also allows each participating library to automate its own indexes. At present, over 50 law libraries are contributing to the effort, and more will join.

# CHAPTER 10

# A User's Guide to WESTLAW and LEXIS

Computer-assisted legal research is different from traditional methods because of the comprehensiveness of the indexing. With the full-text systems, retrieval is achieved by searching for terms actually used in the text of the document. This provides the researcher with many more possible access points than traditional techniques would afford. He is freed from the constraints of manual indexing. In addition to text searching, the researcher can retrieve documents by judge's name, counsel's name, name of court, author of the majority opinion or dissenting opinion, and so forth.

Like most other new skills it takes some practice to become proficient at retrieval, but it by no means requires specialized technical knowledge of computers. Both WESTLAW and LEXIS provide self-programmed training packages, which take no more than two hours. They also offer personal training sessions with company representatives. After a few hours of practice in retrieval, the researcher should begin to feel at home.

LEXIS and WESTLAW, the two systems that most researchers will have access to, have many more commonalities than differences in the method of retrieval. There are, however, some differences in their language of retrieval. Therefore they will be treated separately in this chapter. This treatment is by no means a complete exposition of these two very sophisticated systems, but it may serve as a primer. Each of the systems offers detailed instruction manuals for the user.

# USING WESTLAW

## A. Step 1. Formulating the Search Query

A good deal of preparatory work is done before the researcher turns on the computer. Cases and other legal documents are retrieved from WESTLAW by typing a search query on the keyboard. A query will include search terms, but these will be combined with connectors and modifiers that instruct the computer to search for these terms in a specified relationship: for example, in the same sentence or paragraph. Since computer time is expensive, this query should be carefully worked out before coming to the keyboard.

### *1. Stating the Issue(s)*

Just as with traditional research, the research process begins by extracting the issue or issues from a fact situation.

Fact Situation 1

A client comes to you in the winter of 1983, hoping to buy a home. The seller had taken a mortgage from a California state chartered savings and loan institution in 1979 at a 9 percent interest rate. The institution claims that under federal law this loan, which contains a "due on sale" clause, is not assumable.

Issue 1

In this fact situation, there is really only one important legal issue: Is a home mortgage loan from a state-chartered savings and loan bank assumable under federal law?

### *2. Determining the Key Words*

As with traditional research, the key search words must be pulled out. This is the point at which computer-assisted legal research pulls far ahead of traditional research, since the researcher is not limited by an index; rather, the text of all judicial opinions becomes the index. Terms consisting of more than one word can be searched as a phrase by enclosing them in quotations.

home mortgage state chartered "savings and loan" assumable "due on sale"

This determination of key words differs somewhat from traditional research in the sense that you can search for very specific terms; therefore, broader concepts such as real estate, which would be useful for digest research, are not necessary. With WESTLAW, it is possible to use the West digest topics and key numbers in addition to, or instead of, these carefully chosen key words. This strategy is often very useful.

### 3. *Synonyms*

Since judges might use words phrased differently than the researcher, it is important to consider synonyms as well. These can be added to the search terms. For example: residential for home.

### 4. *Roots*

Some of the search terms may appear in an opinion as plural forms, or different forms of verbs or adverbs. WESTLAW solves this problem very easily. Find the smallest useful root of your search term and place an exclamation point after it. For example:

residen! mortgag! (this will retrieve mortgagor, mortgagee, mortgages) assum! (this will retrieve both assumable and assumption)

An asterisk is used to replace a single letter in a word, e.g. wom*n will retrieve both woman and women.

### 5. *Restrictive Connectors*

The order in which these search terms appear, and their proximity in the body of the opinion, are important for retrieval. These connectors reflect the Boolean logic used by the computer for searching strings of words. (See discussion of Boolean Logic in Chapter 9.) The most commonly used restrictive connectors are the following:

- _ A single space between words indicates "or". This is most commonly used between synonyms. The computer will then retrieve either of the terms.
- & The ampersand symbol means "and". It requires that one of the terms on both sides of the & be in the same case.
- /p One of the terms on both sides of the /p must be in the same paragraph.
- /s One of the terms on both sides of the /s must be in the same sentence.
- +s One of the terms in front of the +s must precede one of the terms following the +s in the same sentence.
- % The computer will not retrieve cases that contain any of the terms following the percent sign.

These symbols soon become almost automatic to the researcher. In our query, the appropriate connectors would be:

"savings and loan" /p "state chartered" /p home residen! /p mortgag! & assum! & "due on sale"

At this point it should be mentioned that several different search words and combinations of search words would probably retrieve the same law. There is no single "correct" search query.

## B. Step 2. Entering the Computer

With search query in hand, the researcher is now ready to sit down at the WESTLAW terminal, enter his password, and press db (data base) to see the menu of all the libraries contained in the WESTLAW data base.

The researcher knows that the question is federal law. Therefore he has the choice of the Supreme Court Reporter, the Federal Reporter, the Federal Supplement, or the U.S. Code. The researcher has probably also heard that there is a recent Supreme Court decision in this area—and, under any circumstances, this is a wise place to begin.

The message on the screen asks for a query and the researcher types in:

"savings and loan" /p state chartered /p home residen! /p mortgag! & assum! & "due on sale"

A few seconds pass while the message on the screen says that his search is proceeding. Then the screen flashes:

There are no documents which correspond to your search query

## C. Step 3. Changing the Search Query

The researcher new to CALR needs some practice in formulating a search query that is neither so narrow that no cases will contain exactly that wording, nor so broad that too many opinions will be retrieved. Rather than abandoning the search in the Supreme Court data base, the researcher should try simplifying the query, keeping only the most critical terms. He might simply try:

home residen! /p mortgag!

The screen now flashes that there are 26 documents that fill this search request, and it immediately displays the title page of:

U.S. 1982

Fidelity Savings and Loan Association v. de la Cuesta

102 S.Ct. 3014

Quickly scanning the synopsis, the researcher finds this case relevant, since it pertains to the assumability of loans. He then has the choice of striking P and reading through the case page by page, or T and only retrieving those pages that satisfy the search term query. With WESTLAW he can also peruse the headnotes and synopsis before entering the text of the opinion. This can be a great timesaver. By either method, the researcher would soon discover that the decision forbids the assumption of home mortgages, but clearly limits this decision to federally chartered savings and loans, leaving state-chartered savings and loans to state discretion. The researcher can now make use of the printer to print out relevant pages for documentation.

This is the most recent case on point so it may not be necessary to investigate any of the other 26. By pressing L, for list however, the researcher can retrieve citations to all these cases and print them for further use if he wishes, or call up some of the other more recent cases for perusal.

## D. Step 4. Changing the Data Base

The researcher has discovered the most recent holding of the highest federal court, which says that it will only enforce "due on sale" clauses where the lender is a federally chartered savings and loan association. But judicial opinions are only one source of federal law. In order to thoroughly search federal law, the researcher must also investigate statutory law, i.e., the U.S. Code. In order to change the data base and maintain the same query, the researcher simply types s db and the data-base menu appears. The researcher chooses the USC data base and waits for the full text of the U.S. Code to be searched.

The search query yields two sections of the U.S. Code, one dealing with investment banking, the other with the F.H.A. It is at this point that experience and training with WESTLAW pay off. Since the language of statutes is much more narrowly written that that of judicial opinions, it is easier to miss relevant sections. In order to avoid this, the researcher should try all possible search terms. The researcher would then type q for last query and try several different combinations of the original search terms. Upon entering:

assum! & "due on sale"

WESTLAW retrieves:

12 USCA s 1701j–3. Preemption of due on sale prohibitions.

This complicated statute, passed on October 15, 1982 (popularly known as the Garn-St. Germain bill), directly relates to his client's problem. Basically, it allows all state and federal lenders to enforce "due on sale" clauses after October 1, 1982. It does, however, contain exceptions. One of the exceptions is that contracts made under any prevailing state law governing this matter after 1978 will be enforced until October 1, 1985. The researcher has now learned that the situation is complicated and he must go to prevailing state law to determine whether his client falls under the exception. He types in q db to preserve his query and change data bases. Since this matter arose in California, the appropriate data base to choose would be the California Reporter, which is entered as CRP.

In a few seconds the most recent case will appear:

1 of 32 documents

Cal. App. 1982

Hutton v. Glicksberg, 180 Cal.Rpt. 141.

By using either the page or term mode, the researcher can quickly peruse the case and print relevant sections on the printer. This case affirms the 1977 California Supreme Court "Wellenkamp rule," which holds that loans from state-chartered savings and loan institutions are assumable when ownership of private residences changes. The command L will give the citations to the 32 documents that meet his search request in chronological order. It may not be necessary to investigate these, since the most recent case has established the current law.

This case indicates that under California law the borrower can assume the loan from a state-chartered bank, since the loan was made after the Wellenkamp decision. The new federal law specifies that it will allow this ruling to stand for three years unless the state legislature chooses to intervene.

## E. Step 5. Shepardizing

With all proper case research, the researcher must "shepardize" the case he is relying on in order to ensure that it is still good law. Most researchers consider "shepardizing" a necessary evil, since it often requires searching through several volumes and pamphlets in order to cover the span from the time the court opinion was delivered to the present. This is both tedious and time-consuming. With both WESTLAW and LEXIS, this can now be done in seconds! This feature may win over more converts to CALR than any other single factor.

The researcher may access Shepard's Citations by entering sh and the citation. For instance:

sh 180 CRP 141

or by simply entering sh when the case is displayed on the terminal. He may limit the Shepard's citations that are called up to a particular history or treatment. For example:

limit r—which limits the display to citations reversing the original cases

or to a particular headnote,

limit 4

When Shepard's Citations are displayed on the screen, the citing cases that are retrievable by WESTLAW will have a number, and they can be called up instantly by simply entering WL and the number. Once the case is displayed, only the pages where your case is cited will be retrieved.

The case at hand yielded no citations, which means no subsequent courts have mentioned it in any way, indicating that it is still good law, and probably the most recent case. This case could be checked further for validity by using WESTLAW as a citator as well as consulting INSTA–CITE.

## F. State Statutes

In order to finally determine the answer to the client's problem, it must be determined whether the California state legislature has acted to limit the three-year period of grace offered by the federal statute. At this point we run into the limits of the current data bases of both WESTLAW and LEXIS: they do not contain state statutes. At present, therefore, the researcher must leave the terminal and go to the library shelves to find the most recent published edition of the California Codes.

## G. Evaluation

By the time the researcher has formed a search query, modified that search query, called up relevant cases in both the Supreme Court Reporter, the U.S. Code and California Reporter data bases, perused the cases, printed relevant sections, and shepardized the key cases, perhaps no more than 10 or 15 minutes have passed. Beginning researchers will obviously need more time, but it does not take very long to become proficient. How does this compare with traditional research? Research time in at least two digests, the U.S. Code, several reporter volumes, and several Shepard's volumes would be necessary to duplicate this search. Copying relevant sections with a duplicating machine would be an additional task. A rough estimate of the length of this manual search would be at least $1\frac{1}{2}$ hours.

Perhaps an even more important advantage of WESTLAW over traditional research is illustrated by researching this loan issue. The critical case—the U.S. Supreme Court Fidelity Savings case—is only a few months old, and the so-called "Garn bill" is only a few weeks old. With traditional digest research it might have been possible to miss this case and this code, since the pocket parts are not kept up to date that frequently, nor are the supplements to the U.S. Code. Usually, but not always, very recent cases will be found by shepardizing an older, important case. But this works only if the judge specifically mentions the older case. In addition, WESTLAW enters federal Supreme Court and some Circuit Court cases into its data base almost immediately upon decision by the court.

With the problem at hand, at least, it seems clear that WESTLAW can provide a much faster and more thorough research job than traditional research methods.

## H. Further Research Techniques

### 1. *Field Searches*

With the search query developed in the above example, the computer searches for the key words in all parts of the cases, including headnotes and synopses. It also searches the entire data base that has been chosen. Often the researcher wants to pinpoint his search more precisely. WESTLAW has divided all cases into seven fields, and all data bases into individual jurisdictions. Therefore the researcher can focus on one or more of these eight fields with his search query.

#### a. *Court*

The researcher may limit his search to a particular jurisdiction within the data base.

#### b. *Title*

When searching for a specific case for which half the title is already known, the researcher can use the following command:

title(Bakke) or title(Bakke & Board & Regents).

In this way he can use the computer as he does the Table of Cases or the Defendant/Plaintiff Index.

#### c. *Citation*

The researcher can also retrieve a specific case by using the volume and page number from its citation; the publication name is replaced by +s.

citation(112 +s 495).

#### d. *Judge*

For strategy reasons, the researcher may wish to retrieve all the cases decided by a certain judge:

judge(white)

This cannot be accomplished by traditional research methods.

*e. Synopsis*

The researcher may choose to search only the synopses, which are prepared by the West editors. One of the main values of this search is to retrieve all the dissenting opinions of a particular judge, since this is mentioned in the synopses:

judge(white /s dissent!)

*f. Opinion*

The computer can be instructed to search only the official opinion, without the headnotes or synopses. This is often useful in locating decisions participated in by specific attorneys:

opinion(bailey)

Again, this kind of research strategy cannot be duplicated by traditional methods.

*g. and h. Topic and Topickey*

This feature provides the the major advantage that WESTLAW has over other CALR systems: the computer is instructed to search the West headnotes to find cases with a particular digest topic or—even further—with a particular digest topic and keynumber (topickey). WESTLAW gives all digest topics a number, which is found in the reference manual. Usually these topic and topickey commands are combined with other search terms. In this way it is possible to further refine your query beyond what you could do with a traditional digest search.

Examples: The WESTLAW number for the digest topic Criminal Law is 110. The issue here is rape. An appropriate query would be topic(110) & rape. The researcher already knows that the key number for rape is 2922, but wishes to further refine the terms to statutory rape:

topickey(110k2922) & statut!

By using topic and key search strategies it is possible to narrow the number of cases retrieved to only the most relevant.

*i. Digest*

The Digest field includes headnotes, topics, keynumbers, title, court, year, and citation. If the researcher wants to search only this portion of the case the search terms:

digest(rape /s statut!)

*j. Time-Period Searches*

The search may be specifically limited in time by typing the time span to be searched at the beginning or end of the query:

date (is 1982) or date (after 1976) or date (before 1978 and after 1972).

## I. Specialized Searches

*1. Statutes and Regulations*

WESTLAW carries only the U.S. Code and the Code of Federal Regulations. At the moment, no state codes are included in the data base. As noted in the above example regarding the "due on sale" issue, accessing the U.S. Code is very similar to retrieving a case. The researcher first chooses the appropriate data base, either USC or CFR. Then the appropriate search query must be formulated. Since statutes and regulations often are worded more precisely than court opinions, it may be necessary to consider more synonyms; and, as in the "due on sale" example, it often is critical to try a number of search queries in order to catch the exact wording. The U.S. Code may also be searched by fields, similar to cases. The major fields are:

1. citation.

2. prelim, which consists of the superior subtitle, chapter, subchapter headings.

3. caption, which contains the section numbers.

As with cases, these fields are useful if you know some or all of the sections of a specific code that you wish to retrieve. Unlike case research, however, there usually is not more than one code section on point.

*2. Specialized Libraries*

Most of the specialty libraries offered by WESTLAW consist of many different kinds of legal documents, which can be found in several data bases. For example, the tax library, which is the most fully developed specialty library, is made up of the following data bases:

FTX–USC—Internal Revenue Code

FTX–CS—Federal Tax cases

FTX–SCT—U.S. Supreme Court Decisions involving tax questions

FTX-CTA—U.S. Court of Appeal and Court of Claims Decisions involving tax issues

FTX-DCT—U.S. District Court Decisions involving tax questions

FTX-TCT—U.S. Tax Court decisions

FTX-ADM—Federal Tax Cumulative Bulletin, including revenue rulings, revenue procedures, delegation orders, executive orders, and treasury department orders

FTX-WD IRS—Written determinations, including private letter rulings

FTX-PL—Public Laws

FTX-CLCT—Claims Court Cases

FTX-CFR—Tax Regulations

FTX-NR—News Release

FTX-IA—International Acts

All tax cases in these several data bases can be retrieved as in all other case law: through a strictly descriptive word search query, which searches the whole document, or through a field-search query, which limits the search to judge, synopsis, and so on.

The Internal Revenue Code, which is part of the U.S. Code, may be searched in the same manner as the U.S. Code. However, I.R.S. Written Determinations may only be searched by descriptive words or by citation.

## USING LEXIS

Since LEXIS and WESTLAW are so similar in their methods of operation, only the differences will be pointed out. The terminals may have a slightly different appearance, since LEXIS provides its own equipment (in both a standard and a deluxe model), and WESTLAW offers its own equipment or a large choice of other compatible terminals. The keys on the LEXIS terminal have some different commands than WESTLAW, since the language of retrieval command is somewhat different. LEXIS claims that its system LEXIS 80 computer is much faster than WESTLAW and that the computer is more user-friendly and helpful. This is difficult to judge, since both systems are easy to use after a few hours of practice.

### A. Step 1. Formulating the Search Query

As with WESTLAW, a large part of the research process takes place before the terminal is switched on. First the issue(s) must be stated clearly. Then the key words must be determined.

### *1. Determining the Key Words*

In order to better compare the two systems, let's use the same fact situation in which the state-chartered California savings and loan institution refuses to allow the buyer of a home to assume a mortgage from the seller, supposedly on the basis of federal law. Let's begin with the same key words as previously used:

home mortgage state-chartered savings and loan assumable due on sale

The LEXIS computer does not recognize about 100 very common words, including "and". Not developing a concordance for these very common words speeds the computer search. Phrases that include and, such as savings and loan, must be surrounded by quotations, but not other phrases.

### *2. Synonyms*

As with WESTLAW, one must consider all the possible ways in which the case may present the search terms. In this instance, residential might be used as a synonym for home.

### *3. Different Forms of Words*

As with WESTLAW, LEXIS will automatically retrieve plural and possessive forms of nouns, but to search different forms of other words, two different symbols may be used: * replaces a single letter at any point in a word (e.g., wom*n will retrieve both woman and women; woman**** would retrieve womanhood and womankind).

For indefinite expansion of a root, the exclamation point is used. This is used very frequently, and in our query we would probably use: residen! for residence, and residential; mortgag! for mortgage, mortgages, mortgagee, and mortgagor.

### *4. Restrictive Connectors*

LEXIS uses different restrictive connectors to establish the order and proximity of words in the search query, but their purpose is the same.

OR at least one of the words must be present in the case.

W/n n represents any number. Therefore assumable w/5 mortgage means that both words must be in the same segment and within five words of each other.

PRE/n assumable pre/3 mortgage means that both words must be in the same segment and that assumable must precede mortgage by no more than three words.

W/SEG means that both words must be in the same segment (segment is explained later).

AND both words must be anywhere in the same document.

NOT W/n

AND NOT

NOT W/SEG These three exclusionary connectors give the opposite directions from their above counterparts. For instance, mortgage NOT W/10 foreclosure, directs that no cases in which mortgage and foreclosure appear within ten words of one another will be retrieved. These exclusionary connectors are very useful when you know you want to avoid calling up certain kinds of cases; as in this case, foreclosure cases.

Now we are ready to make the first formulation of the search query. Using the above restrictive connectors, a likely formulation might be:

state-chartered PRE/6 "savings and loan" AND home OR residen! W/25 mortgag! AND assum! AND due on sale

To clarify the grouping of connectors, the researcher might put them in parentheses. In other situations parentheses may also be used to change the sequence in which the connectors operate.

(state-chartered PRE/6 "savings and loan") AND (home OR residen! W/25 mortgag!) AND assum! AND due on sale

## B. Step 2. Entering the Computer

The LEXIS computer is contacted through a dedicated telephone line. Once telephone contact is established, the researcher enters his LEXIS number and is ready to begin the search.

### 1. *Organization*

The LEXIS data base is organized in descending units called libraries, files, documents, and segments. A library is a major collection—for instance, the GENFED library contains all federal cases and statutes. A file is a smaller unit within that library: U.S. Reports is a file within the GENFED library. A document is a single retrievable item, such as a case, or a code section; and a segment is a separately retrievable part of a document. Segments vary from file to file, but for a case, typical segments would be the name of the case, the date of the decision, the citation, the author of the opinion, the author(s) of dissenting opinions, and the text of the opinion and the dissenting opinion.

Before entering the search query, the researcher must first choose a library and a file. The appropriate library would be GENFED, and with LEXIS the researcher has the option of choosing the file of all federal cases, just Supreme Court cases, or just more recent federal cases. Perhaps the best choice could be: Library: GENFED File: NEWER.

Next the researcher enters the search request:

(state-chartered PRE/6 "savings and loan") AND (home OR residen! w/25 mortgag!) AND assum! AND due on sale

LEXIS responds: 0 cases.

## C. Step 3. Changing the Search Query

Apparently the request is too restrictive. The researcher could edit the existing request, as one does with WESTLAW, or divide the existing request into levels as follows:

Level 1 (state-chartered PRE/6 "savings and loan)

Level 2 OR (home OR residen! w/25 mortgag!)

Level 3 AND assum!

Level 4 AND due on sale

The researcher first types Level 1 search, and LEXIS reports that it finds 0 cases on this level. Therefore this level must be too restrictive. Following the instructions on the screen, the researcher then punches M for modify, the transmit key, and types in Level 2, broadening the search by using OR rather than AND. This time LEXIS responds that there are 15 cases that fit the search request. He may either review Level 2, or decide that this number is too large and go on to Level 3. The computer retains Level 2 cases and searches them for the additional term, rather than searching through the whole data base once more. This does save some time, but can be expensive.

Level 3 search indicates that there are five cases that fit the search request. It will not be necessary to restrict the query further by going on to level 4. The researcher may now display the first case by pushing a special key or he may press CITE and receive a list of the cases retrieved, highest court and most recent date first. Either way, the first case presented will be:

Fidelity Savings and Loan Association v. de la Cuesta (1982) 322 U.S. 495

LEXIS does not provide a synopsis, but it does provide several techniques for scanning a case. The KWIC key displays the name, citation, and date of a case and each occurrence of the search terms with 25 words on each side. The CHG KWIC SIZE key includes 50 words on each side of the search term and this number may be changed to any number from 1 to 999. The key P will indicate the number of pages in the document. The researcher can then make the decision to browse page by page by pressing PAGE FORWARD or PAGE BACK keys.

Of course, at any point the researcher can print the information displayed on the screen to keep for further use. He may continue his search while it is being printed. Experienced researchers find that they rarely need to print whole cases; usually only relevant portions are best to print.

## D. Step 4. Changing the Data Base

Research in the GENFED NEWER federal case library has informed the researcher that, according to the Fidelity Savings decision, federal law in this area of the assumability of residential mortgages applies only to federal lending institutions. The researcher must then examine the other area of federal primary authority: the U.S. Code. The Code is also found in the GENFED library, so the researcher only has to push the CHG FILE key and then enter CODE. In researching the Code, the researcher will probably make use of all terms of the search query, in order to make sure that no precisely written laws are missed. In the instant example, it is only with the term, "due on sale", that the Garn-St. Germain bill, 12 USCA s 1701j–3, is retrieved.

The researcher learns from the Garn-St. Germain bill that although "due on sale" clauses in loans made from state-chartered savings and loans institutions can be enforced after October 1, 1982, there may be some exceptions made for loans contracted between 1978 and 1982, according to prevailing state law.

In order to complete the search, California law must be investigated to determine the prevailing law for California between 1978 and 1982 regarding state-chartered savings and loan associations and "due on sale" clauses. The researcher then presses the CHANGE LIBRARY key and chooses a new library and file. California will be the new library, but the researcher will have a choice between all cases, or only Supreme Court or Appellate Court decisions, or more recent cases. Recent cases would be the wisest choice, and the previous search request will automatically appear on the screen. It is possible to edit that request or formulate an entirely new request.

The search in the California library will then proceed in the same manner as in the GENFED library, with the researcher using various techniques to scan the cases, and using the printer to print appropriate sections for further reference or for incorporation into a legal document.

The researcher should find the most recent case:

Hutton v. Glicksberg, (1982) 26 Cal.App.3d 242

This is the same case that WESTLAW would find, affirming the "Wellenkamp rule," which holds that loans from state-chartered savings and loan institutions after 1977 are assumable.

As with WESTLAW, it is now necessary to leave the terminal and search the printed volumes of the California Code in order to determine whether the legislature has made any determination on this issue, since there currently are no state statutes in the data base.

## E. Step 5. Auto-Cite and Shepard's

LEXIS has added Shepard's Citations to its data base, although it is not yet completely on-line. For many years, it has made a system of Lawyer's Cooperative Publishing Company called Auto-Cite available as an option to subscribers. To check a cite in Auto-Cite, the researcher presses the Select Service key on the terminal and then enters the volume number, any commonly used reporter variation, and the paragraph or page number of the case he wishes to check. Auto-Cite verifies the accuracy of the citation transmitted, gives complete parallel citations to that case, and cites any case that directly affects its validity as precedent. This provides a more accurate citation than Shepard's, since Shepard's does not provide the name of the case. However, it does not provide all the information that Shepard's does regarding how other courts have treated the case. For example, if a judge in a different case had questioned the authority of the case it would not appear in Auto-Cite, since the case is still good precedent. Most researchers, therefore, feel more comfortable with the scope of information provided by Shepard's.

Recently, Auto-Cite has been expanded to include citations to all ALR Annotations where the case has been cited. This can be a valuable research tool.

## F. Further Research Techniques

### *1. Segment Searches*

All documents on LEXIS are made up of segments, which are natural divisions of that document. For instance, cases are made up of segments such as: name of the case; date of the case; the citation; the author of the opinion; the authors of dissenting opinion(s); names of counsel; and the text of dissenting opinions. Each file has somewhat different segments, and statutes and legal specialty documents may have completely different kinds of segments.

Segment searching is very useful in order to limit precisely the scope of the search. By searching only segments and not the entire file, total research time will be lessened as well. Segment searching compares with WESTLAW's field searches, but it is much more limited. LEXIS cannot offer the digest topic, key number, and synopsis searches that are available with WESTLAW.

For example, the researcher wishes to find all Supreme Court opinions written by Supreme Court Justice Douglas that have something to do with civil rights. As with all segment searches, he names the segment, and then places the desired word or words in parenthesis: WRITTENBY(Douglas)

Then he adds the connector AND and the other search terms: civil rights AND WRITTENBY(Douglas).

### 2. *Citations to Statutes and Regulations*

By using the citations of statutes, regulations, or constitutions as search terms, cases that mention these terms can be retrieved. This variation is most useful if the search is for a specific law—for instance, Section 1103 of the Internal Revenue Code.

### 3. *Searching Statutes and Regulations*

As illustrated above, a researcher would call up the U.S. Code by choosing: Library: GENFED, File: CODE. If the title and section are not known, he can formulate a descriptive word-search request in the same manner as case research; e.g., civil rights AND color.

If the researcher has a specific code section already in mind, he may request: SECTION(42 AND 1170). This will retrieve 42 USC 1170.

## G. Specialized Libraries

LEXIS has many specialized libraries, which gather cases, administrative rulings or regulations, and other relevant legal documents that deal with a particular subject such as tax law, security law, trade regulation, bankruptcy, patent, trademark, communications, and labor law. These specialized libraries are made up of individually researchable files.

For example, the securities library contains the following files:

Relevant sections of Title 15 of the U.S. Code Administrative Determinations

No action letters beginning in 1971

Selected Securities and Exchange Commission

Administrative decisions beginning in 1933

Regulations

Cases

Supreme Court decisions

Court of Appeals decisions

District Court decisions

Legislative History

House, Senate and Conference reports associated with 1933 and 1934 Acts

Information is retrieved from specialized libraries in the same manner that cases and statutes are accessed. A library and file are chosen, and a descriptive word search or a specific code or regulation search are entered. Each file is also composed of segments, which may be separately searched.

## H. Nonlegal Data Bases

In addition to the legal data bases, LEXIS makes available several nonlegal data bases as additional subscriptions which are useful for factual research. For instance, if the researcher were preparing a product-liability case regarding a faulty gas tank, he would want to research all the news articles regarding other accidents that involved faulty gas tanks.

NEXIS is the major nonlegal data base offered by LEXIS. It contains full text of newspapers, magazines, wire services, and newsletters; most notably the newly-acquired *New York Times* Information Service, *The Washington Post, Newsweek, Business Week,* and UP and AP wire services. These are researched in the same manner as the legal data bases, using a descriptive word-search request.

LEXIS also offers an Accounting Information Library, parts of *Britannica 3,* and DISCLO, which are abstracts of reports filed with the SEC.

## Conclusion

With only a few hours of practice, the researcher can experience much greater speed and accuracy with either WESTLAW or LEXIS than is possible with traditional research. As the data bases of these two systems expand, CALR will become an ever-increasing standard to be used when performing thorough legal research.

While we wait for the costs to decline to the point where every individual researcher can make use of his own desktop terminal, we hope that there will be more low-cost availability through law libraries, law schools, and attorney sharing-arrangements.

# CHAPTER 11

# Public Nonlegal Data Bases

There is virtually no area of law practice where an attorney does not have need for factual as well as legal information. Practitioners dealing with personal injury or medical malpractice regularly require specific medical information. Corporate attorneys negotiating contracts or mergers with industries producing any technical product must have an understanding of both the technical issues and the financial status of the corporations involved. Criminal attorneys need access to the latest social scientific studies in order to prepare their defense. The kinds of factual information required are as varied as the attorney's clients and their problems.

Attorneys, however, are not trained to perform factual research in law school, and they often find this a difficult and frustrating aspect of their work. General reference libraries are not as well indexed in many subject areas as law libraries, or may not carry the relevant journals or books. It may be necessary to search several specialty libraries in order to find a necessary piece of technical information, such as the price of hogs over the last decade.

Fortunately, the information revolution has already spawned over 1,500 computerized data bases of nonlegal information, and there is no end in sight. Typically, these data bases store references to, or summaries of, articles in periodicals and journals, books, news stories, scientific and technical reports, statistical charts, government data, and so on. They can provide the demographic material, financial statistics, and economic indicators contained in literally tens of millions of references, summaries, and statistics going back several years. These data bases are created and maintained by a variety of private and public organizations, including the National Library of Medicine, the *New York Times,* and many government, scientific, and social scientific professional associations.

## LEGAL VS. NONLEGAL DATA BASES

Although the concept of storage and retrieval is similar with legal and nonlegal data bases, a significant difference is that nonlegal data bases (with some exceptions), do not provide the full text of the document referred to. Most commonly the reference will contain the author, title or publication, some key descriptor terms, and perhaps a summary or abstract.

The following is a typical reference produced from the CHEMCON data base in response to a query regarding ozone generation in the atmosphere of American cities:

CA08422L54908R

Test of the theory of ozone generation in Los Angeles atmosphere

Author: Calvert, Jack G.

Location: Dep. Chem. Ohio State Univ., Columbus, Ohio

Section: CA059002 Publ Class: J

Journal: Environ. Sci. Technol. Coden: ESTHAG Publ: 76

Series: 10 Issue: 3 Pages: 248–56

Descriptors: ozone generation Los Angeles, smog Los Angeles, ozone, simulation model ozone generation

In many ways this data base is like a legal digest, which allows the researcher to select appropriate cases. Like a digest, the data base will often be accompanied by a printed descriptive-word index (often called a thesaurus), which will help identify the exact descriptors used for that data base. Having discovered the appropriate reference in the data base, in most instances, the researcher must still obtain the full text of the document. Although, as will be later explained, it is often possible to directly order the document from the computer service, the document must be sent through the mail; thus, it is rarely possible to have the answer almost instantly, as it is with full-text legal data bases.

Nevertheless, nonlegal data bases can often lead to information that was previously totally inaccessible to the attorney, such as ongoing government-contract research, or current medical studies. It means that the researcher does not have to leave his office, and can avoid long, frustrating hours in libraries.

## PROS AND CONS OF NONLEGAL DATA BASES

Most legal researchers will be less familiar with the commercially available nonlegal data bases than with the legal data bases, WESTLAW or LEXIS. Therefore they may not have clear opinions about the value of the nonlegal data bases in legal research. To help them determine whether subscribing to one or more nonlegal data bases is worth the effort, this and the following chapter will examine the relevant factors.

Possible Advantages

- Access to a vast amount of information that is often unavailable or difficult to locate
- Speed of information retrieval
- Ability to go beyond conventional indexes and search many different data bases

Possible Disadvantages

- Cost
- Difficulty in use
- Relevancy in law practice

# SPECIALIZED DATA BASES

There are hundreds of available data bases, and obviously attorneys will use some more than others. It is rare that an attorney needs to find out what hog prices have been over the past ten years; but it is an everyday occurrence for an attorney to want to discover a company's standing in the Dow Jones average over that same ten years. Following are selected data bases in information areas that are more likely to be requested by attorneys. At least one commercial service that offers each data base is noted; many data bases are offered by more than one such service.

## A. Legally Related Information

A major breakthrough in the indexing of legal periodicals and journals has occurred with the development of the Legal Resource Index and the Criminal Justice Periodical Index.

### *a. Legal Resource Index*

Covering a period from 1980 to the present, this data base provides cover-to-cover indexing of over 660 key law journals and five law newspapers, plus legal monographs and government publications from the Library of Congress MARC database. The LEGAL RESOURCE INDEX comprehensively indexes articles, book reviews, case notes, president's pages, columns, letters to the editor, obituaries, transcripts, biographical pieces, and editorials, providing access to valuable secondary information for the legal profession. (Available through DIALOG.)

*b. Criminal Justice Periodical Index*

This provides comprehensive cover-to-cover indexing of 120 administration-of-justice-and-law-enforcement periodicals and journals, from 1975 to the present. (Available through DIALOG.)

## B. Congressional and Legislative Information

On-line legislative tracking systems, such as Public Affairs Information and Commerce Clearing House's ELSS, were examined in Chapter 9, "Legal Data Bases." The following services provide access to the publications put out by Congress, and fall more accurately into the category of legislative history rather than legislative tracking.

*a. CIS/Index (Congressional Information Service)*

The CIS data base is the machine-readable form of the Congressional Information Service's Index to Publications of the United States Congress. CIS provides current comprehensive access to the contents of the entire spectrum of Congressional working papers published by the nearly 300 house, senate, and joint committees and subcommittees each year. Coverage is available from 1970 to the present. (Available through DIALOG.)

*b. Congressional Record Abstracts*

This data base provides comprehensive abstracts covering each issue of the Congressional Record. Coverage includes Congressional activities regarding bills and resolutions, committee and subcommittee reports, public laws, executive communications, and speeches. Data on bills, roll-call votes, reference to floor debates, and specific issues are included. Coverage is from 1976 to the present, and is updated weekly. (Available through DIALOG.)

*c. CRECORD*

CRECORD provides comprehensive, highly current coverage of the Congressional Record. References are indexed and cross-referenced in 275 legislative areas. (Available through ORBIT.)

## C. Business and Finance

There are scores of data bases that are designed for use by business or financial managers. The following may be particularly useful for attorneys in corporate practice.

*a. CLAIMS/U.S. Patent Abstracts*

This data base contains citations and abstracts for all patents classified by the U.S. Patent office in the areas of: aerospace and aeronautical engineering; chemical engineering; chemistry; civil engineering; electrical and electronics engineering; electromagnetic technology; mechanical engineering; nuclear science; and general science and technology, from 1978 to the present. (Available through DIALOG.)

*b. NEWS/RETRIEVAL*

This data base has a range of 90 days. It provides instant access to news of interest to the business community. It makes available complete text of articles from the *Wall Street Journal,* financial analysis of companies and industries from Barrons, and up-to-the-minute news from around the world. Data becomes available within seconds of its appearance on the Dow Jones newswire.

*c. PTS F & S/Funk and Scott Index*

This data base accesses domestic and international company, product, and industry information. The data base includes information on such topics as: corporate acquisitions and mergers; new products; forecasts of company sales and profits; technological developments; new capacity additions by companies; and factors affecting future product demand and productions. Coverage is from 1972 to the present, updated weekly. (Available through DIALOG.)

*d. DISCLOSURE II*

This data base provides current extracts of reports filed with the U.S. Securities and Exchange Commission by publicly owned companies. These reports, filed by 8,500 companies, provide the most reliable and detailed source of public financial and management information on these companies. Useful for: marketing intelligence; corporate planning and development; portfolio analysis; accounting research; and corporate finance. (Available through DIALOG, Dow Jones).

## D. Medical and Technical

It is perhaps in these areas that computerized information data bases make their most dramatic contribution. These data bases make it possible to keep current not only with completed research results, but also with work in progress. The researcher can enjoy the benefits of information networking (drawing together research from many different fields) to focus on a specific problem.

There are more data bases in this area than any other—reflecting, no doubt, the continuing explosion of information in these fields. For the attorney who deals with medical or technical issues (and there are few who do not), the following data bases represent only the tip of the iceberg of those available.

*a. MEDLINE (MEDLARS on-line)*

Produced by the U.S. National Library of Medicine, this is one of the major sources for biomedical literature. MEDLINE indexes articles from over 3,000 international journals published in the United States and 70 countries. Over 40 percent of records added since 1975 contain author abstracts. Over 250,000 records are added each year. Coverage is from 1966 to present. (Available through BRS, DIALOG and others.)

*b. TOXLINE*

This database identifies human and animal toxicity studies, effects of environmental chemicals and pollutants, and adverse drug reactions.

*c. International Pharmaceutical Abstracts*

This data base provides information on all phases of the development and use of drugs, and on professional pharmaceutical practice. The IPA data base is growing at a rate of 7,000 citations per year, indexed and abstracted from more than 500 pharmaceutical, medical, and related journals. Its scope ranges from the clinical, practical, and theoretical to the economic and scientific aspects of the literature. Coverage is from 1970 to the present. (Available through DIALOG, BRS and others.)

*d. NTIS*

Produced by the National Technical Information Service, the NTIS data base consists of government-sponsored research, development, and engineering, plus analyses prepared by federal agencies, their contractors, or their grantees. It is the means through which unclassified, publicly available, unlimited distribution reports are made available for sale from such agencies as NASA DDC, DOE, HEW, HUD, DOT, Department of Commerce, and some 240 other units. State and local governments are now beginning to contribute their reports to the file. The NTIS database includes material from both the hard and soft sciences, including substantial material on technological applications, business procedures, and regulatory matters. Coverage is from 1964 with biweekly updates. (Available through DIALOG and others.)

*e. SCISEARCH*

This database is a multidisciplinary index to the literature of science and technology prepared by the Institute for Scientific Information. SCISEARCH covers every area of the pure and applied sciences, and includes 90 percent of the world's significant scientific and technical literature. Citation indexing is provided, which allows retrieval of newly published articles through the subject relationships established by an author's reference to prior articles. The index contains all significant items (articles, reports of meetings, letters, editorials, correction notices, and so on) from about 2,600 major scientific and technical journals. From 1965 to the present. (Available through DIALOG.)

*f. SOCIAL SCISEARCH*

A multidisciplinary data base indexing every significant item from the 1,000 most important social sciences journals throughout the world, and social sciences articles selected from 2,200 additional journals in the natural, physical, and biomedical sciences. From 1972 to the present. (Available through DIALOG and BRS.)

## E. General News and Information

Very often, newsworthy events affect the decisions that lawyers must make. If a client owns a football team and the attorney hears of a football merger that might affect his client's plans to sell, he would want to learn the exact details of the story. Fortunately, there are several data bases that provide current coverage of general news.

*a. NEWSEARCH*

This is a daily index of more than 2,000 news stories, information articles, and book reviews from over 1,400 of the most important newspapers, magazines, and periodicals. Every working day the previous day's news stories are indexed and added to NEWSEARCH. (Available through DIALOG.)

*b. The New York Times*

All articles, features, columns, editorials, letters and news stories from the final late edition of the weekday *New York Times,* and the

Saturday and Sunday editions. Full text from 1980. (Available through NEXIS.)

c. *National Newspaper Index*

This data base has monthly updates, providing front-page-to-back-page indexing of *The Christian Science Monitor, The New York Times,* and *The Wall Street Journal.* It is particularly useful for answering general reference questions. From 1979 to the present. (Available through DIALOG.)

## ACCESS TO NONLEGAL DATA BASES

There are several ways by which a researcher can gain access to these computerized data bases. As with WESTLAW and LEXIS, the large mainframe computer that contains the information may be anywhere in the country. The information is transmitted via telecommunications, through a modem, and into the user's terminal. Many of these data bases allow you to use your own microcomputer or word processor, so that you don't have to rent a terminal. In some cases it is also possible to obtain the information from a third party, called a retailer, who has access to many data bases and will do your research for you.

With some variations, access is usually obtained through single or multiple data bases, as described below.

### A. Single Data-Base

Some major single data-bases, such as MEDLINE allow direct access without requiring you to go through a broker. You deal directly with that data base, dialing up their number and receiving the information on your terminal through the telephone line, much as you would with WESTLAW or LEXIS. This would be most useful and economical for a specialist, such as a physician. It would be less useful for an attorney, who normally has a wide range of information needs.

### B. Multiple Data-Bases

In the past few years, many information brokers have begun to offer their services. Typically, a broker maintains a large mainframe computer anywhere in the country, and stores many different data bases from different sources in that computer. The broker may specialize in certain types of data bases, such as energy, or banking and general news (as NEXIS does), or it may offer a wide range of data bases. Some of the largest brokers—such as Lockheed's DIALOG, ORBIT, and BRS—may offer over 100 data bases ranging across the complete spectrum of available information. Others—such as *Reader's Digest's* SOURCE, which is aimed at the home-computer market—offer a wide variety of services: for example, electronic games, travel and dining information, checkbook balancing, and electronic mail, in addition to wire-service news and financial information.

Usually, these services are accessed via a telecommunications service, such as TYMNET or TELENET. The user dials the local TYMNET or TELENET number. Once he receives the signal, he places the phone into the modem attached to his terminal. Most microcomputers are equipped to access these services, via an added telephone-modem. The user can also rent a nonintelligent terminal (without computer capabilities) to connect to the telecommunications line.

This method of accessing the information broker's computer is the same as that used to access both WESTLAW and LEXIS. In fact, users of WESTLAW and LEXIS have the option of subscribing to the largest of the information brokers, DIALOG, on the same terminal they use to retrieve the legal data bases.

## USING DIALOG

### A. Data Bases

Since Lockheed's DIALOG is the largest of the information brokers and is compatible with both WESTLAW and LEXIS equipment, it will be used to illustrate the genre of multipurpose, multibase information brokers.

DIALOG contains over 170 data bases, representing more than 50,000,000 records. Records—or units of information—can range from a directory-type listing of specific manufacturing plants, to a citation with bibliographic information and an abstract referencing a journal, conference paper, or other original source. The data bases offer subject coverage in science, technology, engineering, social sciences, business, and economics. It is difficult to conceive of any question a researcher might have for which DIALOG would not offer at least one appropriate data base, perhaps several.

Each of these data bases is individually owned and maintained, and each charges a different fee for the time used. This fee may vary from $35.00 per hour for the GPO monthly catalog to $165.00 for SCISEARCH. The size of the data base is the main factor in cost. Each data base also has a separate rate for off-line printing. There is no start-up or monthly subscriber fee, however, so the user pays only for actual search time. This is a significant advantage for the subscriber over systems such as WESTLAW and

LEXIS, where the monthly-subscriber and equipment-rental fees are substantial.

## B. Operation

A subscriber almost anywhere in the U.S. using his own terminal and a modem, can make contact with the DIALOG computer in Menlo Park, California.

A typical user may not be certain which data base will answer his information request. He can select topic words and enter DIALINDEX, a program that will indicate which of the data bases are appropriate for his request. The user can then search each of these data bases separately, but maintain the same search query.

Let's say that the researcher wants to find the latest research on computerized legal reasoning. He would first have to phrase the search query. This phrasing is similar to that used with WESTLAW or LEXIS, since it uses a form of Boolean logic. However, since the computer is not searching full text, many of the restrictive commands are not used. The search is expressed in levels rather than on the same line.

The search command could be phrased as follows:

1 computer?

2 legal (W) analysis

3 legal (W) reason

4 (2 1 and (2 or 3)

DIALINDEX indicates that the appropriate data bases are LEGAL RESOURCE INDEX and SOCIAL SCISEARCH.

Most data bases have their own thesaurus, or controlled vocabulary. These printed documents are sold separately (and are usually expensive), but they are very useful for researchers who work regularly with the same data base. Without the thesaurus it is possible to "free search," simply trying the most likely terms.

In this example, the researcher chose the LEGAL RESOURCES INDEX and entered the "free search" query developed above. After 15 seconds, the video screen displayed a list of six references, beginning with:

1916064 DATABASE: LRI File 150

Computers and legal reasoning.

Grossman, Gary S; Solomon, Lewis D.

A.B.A.J. 69 66–70 Jan 1983

This is a small number of references, but this data base begins coverage only in 1980. A search of the SOCIAL SCISEARCH data base yields 15 references, three of them duplicates of those found in the LEGAL RESOURCES INDEX. Each data base provides somewhat different information; some offer an abstract, as well.

### C. Following Through

Since DIALOG data bases contain bibliographic information or an abstract, but not the full text, the user will most likely need to examine the full text of the information discovered. With DIALORDER, the user enters the accession number of the document and its vendor. DIALOG then places the order with the vendor, who sends the document by mail and bills the user directly. The user also has the option of locating the reference in a traditional library.

For an additional monthly charge, the user may receive by mail a regular update of his search request, as new information is added to that data base.

DIALOG and other information brokers provide training seminars for new users. They also provide catalogs and appropriate thesauri for each of the data bases.

## NEXIS

This system is produced by Mead Data Central, which also produces LEXIS. It is available to all LEXIS users, but it is being marketed to a wider business community, as well. What distinguishes NEXIS from other information brokers is that, like LEXIS and WESTLAW, it offers full-text data bases rather than abstracts or indices. Therefore it can be searched in the same manner as the legal data bases and is not limited to descriptor words. Also, the researcher does not usually need to order a printed copy of the document. Instead, he can either peruse the document on the video screen or order it to be printed on his own high-speed printer.

The NEXIS data base currently contains full text of several newspapers and wire-service accounts from 1977, and of magazines from 1975. It has recently added the *New York Times* Information Service. Currently, its data base emphasizes banking, mining, oil, and foreign-affairs journals and newsletters.

## RETAILERS

Enterprising entrepreneurs have responded to the information revolution by offering full-service information services. Trained researchers who work for these services simply take your information request—for example, "Has there been any controversy, legal or technical, relating to the drug ARNVON?" The researchers will then produce a full report and bibliography, or just a bibliography, depending upon your request.

These services usually do not specialize in legal information (although there are a few that do). Instead they focus on a wide business and professional market. Usually they have access to all the major data bases, often subscribing to several of the commercial brokerage services. They can provide market surveys, complete reports, and extensive bibliographies in any field. They will also deliver the full text of documents requested from any source. The advantage of these retail services is that they have expert researchers who may find information more easily than the novice researcher. The disadvantage is that they are relatively expensive and not as convenient as a desktop terminal.

# CHAPTER 12

# The Future of Public Data Bases

Most attorneys have developed sentiments for the printed word, ranging from affection to passion. The printed word has provided most of their knowledge of the world and the skills with which they make a living. Although attorneys may accept the computer as a useful device, like the dishwasher, the thought of the video screen of a terminal completely replacing print-on-paper is very upsetting.

There is, in fact, a great deal of controversy regarding the future of print-on-paper publications versus data-based electronic publications. An overview of the increasing involvement of computers in the publishing field may help clarify this controversy.

## COMPUTER TYPESETTING

The computer first entered the publishing field because of the significant economic advantage of computerized typesetting. This use of computer technology, however, did not really provide a new tool; rather, it made an already existing tool more efficient, and therefore less expensive.

The distinctly new advantage—a spin-off of this computer application—was that the typesetting tape was now in machine-readable form and could be stored in a computer's memory and retrieved electronically. Most major newspapers, periodicals, and new books are typeset by computer. Most legal publications, including all of West Publishing Company's National Reporter System, are typeset by computer.

## DATA-BASE PUBLISHING

This term is confusing, since it often is used to describe different operations. Most commonly, however, data-base publishing means that information can be stored in shared or unified data bases. This permits the publication (either by print on paper or electronically) of information that previously was inaccessible or very difficult to obtain. For example, a geologist may be able, through the use of a wide variety of full-text journals offered by NEXIS, to write an article or book on recent shale oil technology, using information from several sources that would be almost impossible to obtain through traditional methods.

One of the difficulties with organizing a unified data base is that even with printed material that has been typeset by a computer, there are many different typesetting systems and no standardized language. This makes it difficult and expensive to enter material that has been typeset with different systems into a common data base. A successful example of a shared data base is the use of the magnetic tapes from Shepard's Citations in the WESTLAW data base.

Another aspect of this problem occurs with the legislatures' and, increasingly, the courts' use of computerized typesetting systems to produce slip opinions or bills. Theoretically, a publisher could use these machine-readable tapes and not have to completely retype them. But with varying typesetting standards, this often becomes impractical.

There is also the very serious and expensive problem of entering old printed material that has not been computer typeset. This includes all of case law before 1970, and most of the remaining contents of a law library. The same problem exists for nonlegal printed material. It is an enormously labor-consuming project to keystroke all this information into a computer. However, in the future new technological advances in the area of optical character recognition may allow any printed material to be entered with an electronic scanner.

Yet despite these technical difficulties, the continuing incredible growth of information data bases seems assured. WESTLAW, LEXIS, and the hundreds of nonlegal data bases are only the beginning of the complete entry of print-on-paper publications into unified computer data bases.

## ELECTRONIC PUBLISHING

The next logical step in this technological cycle would be to eliminate print-on-paper publication and to receive information only from the electronic print on the video terminal. If the receiver had a high-speed printer, any or all of the information could be transformed into print on paper, on demand.

This is the step at which most bibliophiles balk. In a sense this is what both WESTLAW and LEXIS have done with recent case law, by providing full text of the opinions, and making it possible to entirely bypass the use of the print-on-paper publication for these references (although the cases are still published in that form). Most of the nonlegal data bases do not yet provide this option, since their contents are not available in full text form.

The advocates of this brave new world of electronic publication make the following points about cost and desktop terminals.

## A. Cost

At some time in the not-too-distant future, the unit cost of delivering the information electronically will be less than the unit cost of delivering it through a print-on-paper publication. Without question, currently it is very expensive to read thoroughly a 20-page case on a WESTLAW or LEXIS terminal—possibly $40.00 or $50.00. However, with the option of a high-speed printer as an accessory to the terminal, the case can be printed for perhaps $5.00 worth of time and read off-line. And, of course, it is not always necessary to read the complete case. Another factor is that an attorney needs to research only a slight fraction of the cases he purchases in bound volumes, creating a problem of cost-efficiency and storage.

While the costs of print-on-paper publication will inevitably soar, as the electronic advocates claim, the cost of data-base use will go down as more subscribers are added and the initial costs of data base creation are returned.

## B. Desktop Terminals

With the amazing drop in price and ascent in quality of microcomputers, it is both possible and desirable for every professional to have a personal computer, both in the office and at home. With increasing miniaturization, it is also possible to carry one when traveling. This makes what is now a limited market of users a potentially unlimited market.

Critics of electronic publishing claim that the costs will never be competitive with print-on-paper publication for full-text reading: the cost of computer hardware may go down, but the cost of telecommunications will not drop, and it has already experienced inflation over the past few years. In fact, with the expansion of satellite telecommunications, these costs could drop dramatically.[1]

The critics also claim that you cannot curl up with a computer when you go to bed or plug into a telephone line while riding the bus.

## DISK PUBLICATION

An exciting new frontier in computer technology is laser-disk technology. (See Chapter 1.) It is unclear when and if this technology will be perfected, but the potential applications are overwhelming. For instance, it may be possible to put the entire contents of a law library on a single disk. Unlike microfilm, which simply miniaturizes the sources, all the incredible powers of storage, search, and retrieval of enormous computers would be available on the desktop computer. At the moment, search and retrieval of such massive amounts of information is well beyond the capacities of small computers; however, with the rapidly increasing size of main memories, nothing seems impossible.

This system, if perfected, would completely eliminate the cost of telecommunications, and it could conceivably make insignificant the costs of personally owning a major law library or general-reference library.

Immediate and important objections come to mind. The creators and maintainers of data bases could lose control of the distribution. The data-base business might become like the record industry, where pirated discs are a continuing problem. It would then be economically infeasible to maintain and update the data bases. The user also would have the problem of updating, certainly a crucial factor in legal research. Telecommunications might be used for only the most current information, as a supplement to the disk.

Some of these speculations are futuristic, and some are based on current technology. Perhaps the only sure prediction is that computerized data bases will continue to gain an ever-larger role in the production and distribution of information.

**1.** Shapiro, "Data Base Publishing", in Bigelow, ed., *Computers and the Law,* 3d ed., A.B.A. Section of Science and Technology, 1981, 273.

# PART FOUR

# Computers as Reasoners, Predictors, and Teachers

## INTRODUCTION

Thus far, this book has viewed the computer as a super-efficient mechanical helper that lets the user perform the necessary but mundane tasks involved in practicing law faster and more accurately, just as a jet plane is more efficient than a car for traveling from New York to San Francisco. Even in the area of researching legal and nonlegal data bases, the computer provides no more than speedy retrieval; it offers no real advice or direction. If the researcher decides that his key word is negligence, with no qualifying term, the computer will obligingly retrieve several thousand cases.

A computer does have greater abilities, however, and the most exciting new development in applying computers to law is their use in the process of legal reasoning. This concept covers a lot of ground, beginning with computerized document preparation and stretching into the use of computers as consultation machines. The ultimate apocalyptic scenario in this evolution is that of an ordinary citizen relating the facts of his complicated legal problem to a computer, which then immediately dispenses the proper advice and/or legal document, totally avoiding the use of a lawyer. Rest assured that lawyers do not have to fear being obsoleted by computers in the near future; but computers will significantly affect the way in which law is practiced in the next decades.

A different but significant application of the computer's ability is in the area of mathematical modeling and prediction. A number of studies have been published that deal with the prediction of judicial decisions and with the use of computers for jury selections.

Knowing in advance, with a high degree of probability, what the judge's or jury's decision will be in a given case would certainly change the practice of law dramatically.

Yet another application of the logical powers of computers is beginning to be put to use in legal education and in legislative drafting. Computers prove to be superb teachers of logical reasoning, helping law students and lawyers think and write in a more precise fashion.

# CHAPTER 13

# From Document Preparation to Legal Consultation

## AUTOMATED DOCUMENTATION–PREPARATION SYSTEMS

The most immediate, and perhaps ultimately the most useful, application of computers as reasoners is the development of automated documentation-preparation systems. In the next ten years or so, it is almost a certainty that these systems will revolutionize the practice of law. At this writing, the first entries in what is sure to become a flood of software have already been developed, and marketed to a limited degree. The existing systems have a wide range: from a package of simple and specific forms that can be used with a word processor to complete a legal transaction (such as drafting a will by substituting names and clauses), to sophisticated computer programs that can be applied to almost any legal transaction and will create an automated system that completely drafts the finished document.

### A. Automated Word Processing Substantive Systems

Most well-organized law practices already have a number of manual substantive systems that they have developed out of the experience of their practice. The system may include: a customized interview sheet, which allows the interviewer to gather relevant facts from a client; a checklist to determine whether there are other facts to be discovered, in addition to the interview; and a form file that contains previously drafted documents, which can be modified to suit the individual case. A very useful book has been written by Roberta C. Ramo for the American Bar Association, entitled *How to Create Your Own Legal System.*[1] This book carefully guides practitioners through the creation of such a system.

Whatever can be done manually can be done much more efficiently with a word processor. The major advantage that a word processor can provide is the ability to produce perfect documents without the labor-consuming effort of retyping them. Only the customized changes regarding names or clauses need to be re-entered.

Several publishers of legal forms are now beginning to present automated versions for use on word processors, or on computers with word-processing capacities. These packages, usually in the form of floppy disks, include a variety of appropriate forms for a legal transaction (such as a divorce or will), with spaces to fill in individual names and a choice of appropriate alternative clauses.

Among the more ambitious of these offerings are the systems being developed by Matthew Bender for California and Illinois. The California systems will include: domestic relations; wills and trusts; corporations; partnerships; personal injury; and probate. Most of these are not yet completed. As an example of this genre, the California domestic relations system, which is completed, provides a nine-volume attorney's manual. This includes: a hard copy of all the forms; commentary about their use; intake sheets and questionnaires; and practice aids, such as testimony checklists, financial-rule checklists, and special guides and charts. Another three-volume operator's manual includes: hard copies of the forms; directions for production of documents on various word-processing equipment; and general information on proper format. This system provides 21 forms on floppy disks. Currently, they are produced only for dedicated word processors, but they soon will be available for micros as well.

These disks are not software application programs, since they give no instructions to the word processor or computer; rather they are data disks upon which the word-processing software performs its editing functions. The number of these packages for use with word processors is certain to expand rapidly in the next few years.

## B. Automated Computer Document-Preparation Systems

A giant step away from the most efficient manual systems and word-processing systems can be taken with computers. The computer has the ability to make choices regarding the appropriate wording of a document, and to produce a completed draft with no

1. Ramo, ed., *How to Create A System for the Law Office,* Section of Economics of Law Practice, American Bar Association, 1979.

human involvement beyond the entry of factual information. A well-programmed computer can even direct the interview, soliciting different subsequent information depending on the answers to the initial questions.

The prototype for computer document-preparation systems is that developed by James A. Sprowl of the American Bar Foundation. The ABF Processor, as it is called, is a two-step procedure. In the first step, documents and statutelike procedures are drafted in ABF language. ABF language is a computer language that more closely resembles English than other programming languages, such as Fortran or Cobol. When the attorney drafts a document in ABF language, he uses deductive reasoning to make decisions between alternative clauses in a document. For instance, if conditions A or B exist, then clause C must be included. An example of a document drafted in ABF language would be:

> I leave all my personal effects and household goods to my [the testator's spouse, a husband or a wife], [the spouse's name], if [he or she, the spouse's subjective pronoun] survives me, and otherwise to my children who survive me in equal shares.

Optional passages are preceded and followed by bracketed commands to the computer, indicating the condition(s) that are to control their inclusion or exclusion:

> [IF the death taxes ARE to be paid out of the rest of the estate INSERT] I instruct my executor to pay all death taxes out of the rest of my estate so that the legatees and devisees do not have to pay any such taxes out of their individual gifts. [END IF].[2]

Bracketed commands also are used to indicate different data insertions, such as names or places. Putting all documents into ABF language does not require sophisticated computer-programming training, but the attorney drafter does need some instruction in order to break a document into its deductive parts.

In addition to the documents, the ABF language can also be applied to statutelike procedures that define how the documents are to be assembled. Here the procedures are broken down into their deductive parts, and bracketed commands are used to instruct the computer which procedural choices to make.

Once the document and procedures are drafted in ABF language, they are entered into a computer that is equipped with an ABF processor, which then can completely automate the document assembly. When an attorney, paralegal, or secretary needs to have a document prepared for a specific client he calls on

**2.** Sprowl and Staudt, "Computerizing Client Services at the Law School Teaching Clinic. An Experiment in Law Office Automation," 1981 *American Bar Foundation Journal,* no. 1, 706.

the computer to "process the form document into a client-customized version."

Sophisticated ABF-processor programs also can include the computational ability of the computer. In a real estate closing contract, the computer can compute the prorated tax by figuring the closing date as a percentage of the annual rate, and include this in the contract. Any contract, tax document, or legal document that requires computation can include the computational instructions in the document-preparation program. This capability opens endless possibilities for the practice of law.[3]

The original concept of the ABF processor was that it could be applied to document preparation in any substantive area, and that it would be possible for attorneys and assistants to develop the programs without the aid of professional programmers, since the ABF language was so much simpler than most programming languages.

The first real applications of the program have produced mixed results. In an experiment with a legal-services teaching clinic, attorneys and secretaries were trained to design automated practice systems. Despite the simplicity of the ABA processor language, the development of automated systems proved to be initially time consuming and often frustrating. Following improvements made in the system, the experimental team produced five automated systems, including a divorce system, a guardianship system, a will system, a trust system, and a real estate system. The will system ultimately was used to produce 450 wills.

The divorce system, the most complicated, begins with an interactive client interview in which the computer poses a number of questions, most of which can be answered either by a yes, no, or selection of the most likely possibility from A to E. The computer stores 8 major documents, along with 18 passages that are incorporated by reference into 1 or more of the major documents, 63 computational procedures, 1 data file, and 1 document that controls the selection of which major documents are to be prepared for a client. The ABF processor produces the final documents immediately upon the conclusion of the initial interview. If the client requires the maximum number of documents, the completed printed copy will be 42 pages long.[4]

This prototype system suggests so many possibilities that already there are many spin-off efforts aiming ultimately toward commercial distribution. A second generation of the ABF processor has been developed at Lewis and Clark in Oregon, using the computer language PASCAL, with the goal of developing

3. *Ibid.,* 705.

4. *Ibid.,* 701.

systems for microcomputers. Legal Management Systems in Michigan has already adapted the model of the ABF processor to produce software, the LMS system, which can be operated on a microcomputer. A different approach has been tested by a group at Brigham Young University, where the appropriate automated system at a central computer can be reached with an in-house terminal by means of telecommunications.[5]

Since so much "up-front" attorney time is needed to develop a system from scratch (i.e., to put the documents and procedures into computer language), the most widespread use of substantive systems will probably come with the marketing of fully developed software packages that can be used on a wide variety of micros and minis, or with a central computer on a time-sharing basis. For specialized needs, attorneys will be able to use software packages like the ABF processor to design their own systems.

The substantive areas of the law where automated systems are likeliest to be the most useful are those with a number of set forms and some required computations. This definitely includes all areas of tax practice, trusts and estate planning, probate, divorce, real estate sales, and bankruptcy. Of course, the systems would have to be developed to account for differences among individual states.

The legal and ethical implications of fully automated systems already are being addressed. A brand-new secretary, with no legal training, can type in the answers to the interview questions posed by the computer and press the print button at the conclusion of the interview. This brings up the possibility of computer malpractice and attorney dispensability.

However, fully automated document-preparation systems do not really provide sophisticated legal analysis or give advice. They simply provide the most efficient method of dealing with routine legal transactions. Paralegals and legal secretaries using manual systems and word processors have long offered the first step toward automation.

## COMPUTERS AS CONSULTATION MACHINES

The ability to give correct legal advice in response to a novel or complicated fact situation is a serious challenge to the ability of the computer and the programmer. There is a great deal of experimentation in this area, but the results are still far from practical. This differs from computerized document-preparation systems, where the basic technology has been worked out and mass marketing will soon begin.

**5.** *Ibid.*, 732.

The best-known experiment is TAXMAN, developed by L. Thorne McCarty, specifically to identify B and C reorganizations under the Internal Revenue Code. While the ABF processor reasons by deductive logic, TAXMAN utilizes a programming language developed for artificial intelligence to reason by analogy. Relevant portions of tax cases and the tax code are represented according to their relationships in what is termed "semantic networks," and are stored in the computer. The user enters into the computer a set of statements in a formal, non-English language that defines relationships in a specific fact pattern. The computer then searches for similar relationships in the law. From the facts of a corporate reorganization, it can recognize which of the various statutory patterns best fit those facts.[6]

TAXMAN tackles a very narrow area of law, but one that has a balanced mixture of statutory and case law. Therefore it can serve as a model in many substantive areas. Another analogical system has been developed by Jeffrey Meldman, focusing on assault and battery. His model requires as input a series of word groups describing the facts. The computer then responds by identifying cases with similar fact patterns, or stating that it needs additional data.

All analogic legal-reasoning systems face similar problems. The first and most serious is that developing a legal data base represented by semantic networks is an overwhelmingly complex and time-consuming task. The existing systems attempt it in only a tiny patch of law, which in itself is a formidable chore.[7] It is difficult to imagine the whole of the WESTLAW data base, for instance, ever being represented by semantic networks.

The second obstacle is that the user also must put the facts into a special relational format in order to establish an analogy to the law. This requires a technical expertise that is likely to seriously limit the use of the system.

On the positive side, technical difficulties have a way of getting worked out in the computer field. If the whole of substantive law could be accessed simply by presenting a fact situation, research would become incredibly fast and accurate. By combining both analogic and deductive capacities, the researcher could both find the relevant law and could deduce whether his fact situation fit the formal requirements of a rule or statute. The human lawyer would still be necessary to resolve conflicts of law and to decide on actual strategy.

**6.** Grossman, "Computers and Legal Reasoning," 69 *American Bar Association Journal,* January, 1983, 67.

**7.** *Ibid.,* 68.

# CHAPTER 14

# Computers as Predictors and Educators

## COMPUTER AS PREDICTORS

Any attorney who specializes in litigation spends part of his professional life trying to predict what a judge or jury will decide. The litigator believes that the judge and jury will be objectively convinced by the weight of the law and the facts in a particular case; however, as a child of this social-science-minded twentieth century, he knows that there are other nonobjective factors that will influence the decision. These factors might include the social and economic background of the judge or jury, their age and sex, previous experience in this particular area of the law, or the prevailing political climate.

### A. Judicial Decisions

Social scientists, particularly political scientists, have long urged the use of statistical methodology in legal analysis. For more than 20 years, the computer has been used by social scientists to apply mathematical models to judicial decision-making. Although there is a great deal of literature in this area, there have been very few practical results.

In order to use the computer to aid in analysis and prediction of judicial decisions, a mathematical model must be developed that truly represents how judges respond to the various factors involved in any particular decision. In dealing with an appellate court where there are several judges, these factors might include: personal interactions among the members of the group; the influence of interest groups; threats to the court authority; and, of course, the individual socio-economic background of each of the judges.

Predicting judicial decisions is more difficult than predicting political behavior in other contexts, such as the president's response to a Soviet arms-control proposal, since legal theory must also be taken into account in the analysis. A judge may act as a political person, but he is also acting as a lawyer who is trained to respond to legal arguments. Therefore, the task of analyzing the weight of legal precedents and theories in a judge's decision is a very complex one. It requires a thorough analysis of both precedent and new law in any area, and this analysis must be plugged in as only one factor in the process.

Some of the most interesting work in this area has been done by Reed C. Lawlor, who has developed a mathematical model of personal *stare decisis.* Lawlor observes that although there are disagreements among judges, each judge is consistent with his own decisions. It is a time-consuming and tedious task to develop a data base concerning a particular issue decided in a substantial number of cases by a particular court or judge, but Lawlor reports a predictability rate exceeding 90 percent.[1]

Recently, Charles M. Haar, John P. Sawyer, and Steven J. Cummings completed a successful model to predict appellate court decisions in Connecticut zoning-amendment cases. In this study, two lawyers and a statistician worked together to provide both legal and statistical analyses. They developed a legal data base of zoning amendment cases, which they coded according to the 19 variables that they determined most important in the legal reasoning process. Using the statistical tool of regression analysis, they entered legal reasoning as one factor in a predictive model. This model included more traditional factors, such as socio-economic background, small group dynamics, and so on.[2]

The field of judicial prediction is a very complex task in which the basic concepts are just beginning to be understood. At least in the near future, an attorney will not be able to buy a software package in which he plugs in a variety of requested data and receives an accurate prediction.

## B. Jury Selection

The most successful work in judicial prediction has been accomplished at the appellate level, where the facts are frozen and

**1.** Lawlor, "Computer Analysis of Judicial Decisions," *Computer Science and Law,* New York, N.Y.: Cambridge University Press, 1980, ch. 15.

**2.** Haar, Sawyer, and Cummings, "Computer Power and Legal Reasoning—A Case Study of Judicial Decision Prediction in Zoning Cases," 1977 *American Bar Foundation Research Journal,* no. 3.

the judges normally have a long personal history of judicial decisions that the researcher can analyze. Although one hears a great deal about choosing juries by computer, the realiability of these predictions is far less accurate, since one can know relatively little about each individual juror, and since there is no history of decision as a group. Nevertheless, using a computer to predict the decision of any individual jury is a dramatic and attractive idea.

As in the area of judicial prediction, the necessary mathematical technology has been available for more than 40 years. By 1950, there were already well-developed standardized attitude and personality scales, as well as studies of the relationship between various demographic characteristics (such as sex, age, race, religion, and so on) to attitudes. The availability of computer-data storage and statistical analysis in the '60s simplified the complex process of statistically correlating demographic survey data to jurors' attitudes. The computer can also easily perform multiple regression analysis, where a number of variables can be taken into account simultaneously rather than one at a time, and each of these variables can be given a predictive weight. For instance, in a given case, religion may be deemed a more important predictive variable than sex, and this can be accommodated in a predictive equation. However, the predictive equation only reveals probabilities for the population surveyed, not for the individual prospective juror.

The use of computers for jury selection dramatically attracted public attention in several celebrated political trials in the 1970s. The first occurred in 1971, when the Harrisburg Seven Defense Committee assembled a team of specialists to aid in jury selection. The team first conducted a telephone survey of 840 randomly selected registered voters, and then sent 45 trained volunteers to personally interview 262 of the original 840. The interviewees were questioned about media contacts, knowledge of the Harrisburg case, individual values, attitudes toward the government, children's ages and activities, organizational membership, attitudes toward potential trial issues, and tolerance toward antiwar activities.

The results of the interviews were analyzed to determine the key factors, that related to attitude preference. With this demographic predictive model in hand, jurors were chosen who most closely matched this demographic model. The jury in the Harrisburg case voted 10–2 for acquittal on the conspiracy charge.[3]

Obviously, this kind of demographic survey is very costly, and not possible for every case. However, it is possible to conduct surveys that can be used in more than one case. For instance,

**3.** Wanamaker, "Computers and Scientific Jury Selection: A Calculated Risk," in Young, Kris, and Trainor, *Use of Computers in Litigation,* Chicago, Ill.: American Bar Association, 1979, 235.

periodic surveys of the population in a certain jurisdiction regarding attitudes toward liability of manufacturers in product-liability cases, or attitudes toward damage amounts in personal-injury suits, may be applied toward many cases.[4] Obviously, the more general the survey, the less accurate the predictive model.

With the rapidly increasing availability of computers to individual lawyers at relatively low cost, the use of computers for analysis in jury trials will undoubtedly grow. Packaged software to meet general situations, such as attitudes toward embezzlement or draft registration, will probably flourish as well, although the accuracy of these generalized models is not well proven.

## COMPUTERS AS EDUCATORS

### A. Law School Education

In some undergraduate colleges, students are issued a microcomputer on the first day they arrive as freshman. This has certainly not yet occurred in any law school, but there is a growing interest in making use of computers in legal education. The focal point of this burgeoning interest is the newly established Center for Computer-Assisted Legal Instruction, a joint effort between the Law School of the University of Minnesota and Harvard Law School. These two law schools cooperatively pioneered in the development of computer-aided instruction in the law during the '70s, and are now ready to widen their activities.

At this writing, about 70 computer exercises have been developed (mainly at the Minnesota and Harvard law schools) in a variety of fields, including: evidence; civil procedure; torts; trial advocacy; contracts; legal research; interviewing; client counselling; and professional responsibility. These exercises take a variety of forms. Some are simulations, as in the following video example of witness interrogation.

Q. Do you know David Defendant?

A. Yes.

Q. Is he a trustworthy person?

Student: Objection.

The Court: Sustained.

Q. How long have you known him?

A. Ten Years.

In this exercise, the computer will sustain or overrule the objection, and at the end of the exercise give the student the rationale

4. Lafitte, "The Use of Social Science Techniques in the Jury Selection Process," 2 *Review of Litigation,* no. 2, Spring, 1982, 219.

behind the ruling. In some of the simulated exercises the student can play one of several roles: he can answer the questions first as judge, then as plaintiff counsel, and finally as defense counsel. In other exercises the student may choose the best of a series of multiple-choice answers, or approve or disapprove applying a legal concept to describe a fact situation.[5]

One of the exercises asks the student to apply the concept of intent, as defined in Restatement (Second) of Torts. The student must: either approve or disapprove a proposition by applying the concept to a fact situation; identify the errors in an erroneous proposition; or indicate how the erroneous proposition can be corrected.

The computer can: display questions, drills, information, data, and problems on the screen; ask the student for a response; interpret the response; and then proceed through a program differentially, depending upon the initial response. In this respect, a computer has a great advantage over workbooks, since it is capable of complex branching, allowing a student to skip questions or exercises depending on the student's response. In some exercises it will also allow "free language" responses to questions rather than multiple-choice answers. This means that if the computer asks what the objection is to a question asked in a trial simulation, the student can reply freely without having to make a choice among a limited number of possibilities.

In some form or another, the computer always provides feedback to the student. It may explain why the student's answer was incorrect, or it will reinforce the student's correct answer. This interactive process with the student makes the exercise engaging, and most closely simulates a one-on-one tutorial session. Since law school classes often have more than 100 students, these individualized exercises can nicely supplement the regular classroom experience. Some instructors require that students complete the exercise before coming to class, thus guaranteeing a prepared audience.

Over 50 law schools have experimented with at least one of the computer exercises, and more than 20 law schools will become members of the Center for Computer-Assisted Legal Instruction during 1982–1983. The big breakthrough in distribution is now occurring with the transfer of the programs to microcomputer software. Originally the programs were stored on the University of Minnesota computer and accessed by EDUNET, a network developed by a consortium of higher-education institutions (EDUCOM) to share computer resources for the support of education and research. Time on EDUNET was billed at a rate of nearly $20.00 per hour, and of course a terminal was required. The Center for

5. *National Law Journal,* Special Edition, January, 1982.

Computer-Assisted Education has now transferred all the teaching exercises to software, which will work on all microcomputers using UCSD Pascal. These include Apple II, Terak, IBM-PC, and Xerox 820. Soon all the exercises will be compatible with the CP/M operating system, which will expand the microcomputer choices to include the TRS–80, Northstar, and many more. Soon, microcomputers may be required equipment for all first-year students.

Other microcomputer applications include an instructional exercise for normalized legal drafting for use on Apple II, produced by Professor Layman Allen at the University of Michigan Law School. This ground-breaking project is a method of rewriting legal language with the use of symbolic logic. These exercises help students to develop a better sense of syntax in legal drafting, and therefore to communicate more clearly.[6]

The Center for Computer-Assisted Legal Instruction has wide-ranging plans for developing computer uses in law-school education. According to its executive director, Russell Burris, the Center will "establish standards for hardware, software and courseware; coordinate the distribution and use of computerized instructional exercises in law; support authors in the development of new instructional programs; and sponsor research for advancing the quality and effectiveness of the exercises."[7] Recently the Center and the Law School have been awarded grants to develop and field-test network configurations of microcomputers for multipurpose uses. The network will be connected to different mainframes on the University of Minnesota campus, and to national and international computer-based resources through networks such as TELENET.

In addition to academic exercises, students will be able to use the microcomputers for legal writing and research. Software routines to check spelling, punctuation, and split infinitives, and to provide stylistic analyses will be adapted and developed. WESTLAW, DIALOG, and the *New York Times* Index will be available for research. If the experiment at Minnesota proves fruitful, it may significantly change the style of legal education, and of continuing attorney education.

**6.** Burris and Stein, "Law School's Leadership Role: Computer Uses/Applications in Law/Legal Education," unpublished draft of article, 2.

**7.** *Ibid.,* 6.

# APPENDIX A

## Glossary

ABF PROCESSOR A prototype for computer document preparation systems produced by the American Bar Foundation.

ALU (Arithmetic Logic Unit) The part of the Central Processing Unit that performs arithmetic and logical operations.

AUTOMATIC SPEECH RECOGNITION The ability of the computer to understand and respond to an ordinary human voice.

AUTOMATED SUBSTANTIVE SYSTEMS Using the computer to help prepare all the necessary documents in a legal transaction such as a divorce. Systems range from simple forms on disks, to computer programs that make choices and perform computations.

AUXILIARY MASS STORAGE or MEMORY All data and software programs not kept in main memory are stored in an auxiliary storage medium which includes floppy and hard disks, magnetic tape, and laser disks. When these storage media are "on line" they can be directly accessed by the CPU.

BOOLEAN LOGIC An algebraic process that permits the user to search the computer data base for sets of information using the qualifiers, "and", "or", and "not".

BINARY DIGIT (BIT) In the binary number system, either the character 0 or 1.

BINARY NUMBERS The basis for calculation in all computer systems is a two digit number system, 0 and 1, in contrast to a 10 digit decimal system.

BRS (Bibliographic Reference Service) One of the major non-legal data base brokers. Contains over 70 data bases covering a wide range of technical, non-technical, and news services.

BYTE In most computers data is stored and transmitted in multiples of eight bits, called a byte.

CALR (Computer Assisted Legal Research) Making use of a computerized data base of legal sources, such as WESTLAW or LEXIS to perform legal research.

CAT (Computer Assisted Transcription) Making use of a computer to transcribe the court reporter's notes into finished text. These transcripts can then be entered full-text into a data base for storage and retrieval.

CLS (Computerized Litigation Support) Using the computer to assist in the storage and retrieval of documents in preparation for trial. Can also include using computers for graphical representations and statistical analyses for trial exhibits.

COAXIAL CABLE Used for telecommunications. Most telephone lines utilize this, and transmit in analog, not digital signals.

COMMUNICATIONS PROGRAM The software program that allows one computer to exchange data with another.

COMPILER A software program designed to convert a computer program written in another programming language (like BASIC) into a language readable by the computer.

CONTROL UNIT The part of the CPU that monitors and supervises the operation of the entire system. Directs and schedules movement of data within the CPU and between the CPU and peripheral devices.

CP/M A popular operating system used by many 8 bit microcomputers.

CPU (Central Processing Unit) The essential core of the computer system, contains the Arithmetic/Logic Unit, Main Memory, and the Control Unit.

CRT (Cathode Ray Tube) One of the names given to the video screen which most often is found as part of the computer terminal.

DATA BASE MANAGEMENT A system in which information is organized efficiently for storage and retrieval. Can be a common data base with access by many user terminals.

DATA BASE PUBLISHING The delivery of information in electronic form.

DCF (Document Coding Form) A form used to index each document in preparation for litigation. May be computerized, or noncomputerized.

DIALOG The largest non-legal information broker. Offers over 170 data bases in technical, non-technical, and general news.

DISK Used for auxiliary mass storage. Magnetic disks can be flexible (floppy), or hard (Winchester). Laser disks are a new possibility.

DISTRIBUTED LOGIC A network focusing on a large central CPU with intelligent terminals that have some processing abilities.

ELECTRONIC MAIL The use of telecommunications to forward electronic information from one computer to another.

IMPACT PRINTER A printer which creates a printed character by striking the paper with some device.

INTERPRETER A software program that is used to translate a higher level language, like BASIC, into machine language. Each instruction is translated as the program is run.

KILOBYTE One thousand bytes. A byte is usually composed of 8 bits.

LASER PRINTER A laser printer creates a character by burning a hole in the paper. These printers are very fast and very expensive.

LEXIS One of the two major legal data bases, produced by Mead Data Central. Contains all recent judicial opinions and a great deal of law in specialty areas such as tax, corporate and labor law.

LSI (Large Scale Integration) The process of integrating a large number of circuits into a single chip of semiconductor material.

MACHINE–READABLE Data in a form that can be understood and used by a computer.

MAINFRAME The largest type of computer, it can have a main memory of several megabytes, and because of its great speed, support hundreds or thousands of users.

MAIN MEMORY or STORAGE The part of the Central Processing Unit where data is stored for instant retrieval and processing by the ALU.

MEGABYTE One million bytes.

MICROCOMPUTER A small, multi-purpose computer which contains at least 64 kilobytes of memory and can be purchased for under $5000, (without printer or software).

MINICOMPUTER Between a microcomputer and a mainframe. Costs more than $10,000 and can support multiple users.

MODEM The piece of hardware required to change computer digital signals into analog signals for transmission along telecommunications wires.

MOS Memory (Metal Oxide Semi-Conductors) The main memory of most modern computers is stored on MOS chips. This information is volatile, which means that data is lost when the power to the computer fails.

MS–DOS One brand of operating system. Most popular for 16 bit microcomputers, including IBM PC.

NETWORKING A term generally used to describe a communications network in-house which might include computers, word processors, printers, OCRs, and other electronic devices.

OCR (Optical Character Recognition Unit) An input device which converts printed characters to computer machine language for storage on magnetic medium, or for entry into the CPU for processing.

OEM (Original Equipment Manufacturer) A misnomer since the term refers to a dealer who puts together a complete hardware and software package, (referred to as a "turnkey system"), often from different manufacturers.

OFF–LINE The user does not have direct access to a CPU, but prepares data to be later processed by the computer—very common with monthly billing services.

ON–LINE The condition when the CPU has direct access to information. This can refer to accessing a far-away central computer by an in-house computer, or to the CPU and floppy disk of an in-house terminal.

RAM (Random Access Memory) Bits of information stored in main memory which can be accessed in any random order. Extinguished when the computer is turned off.

ROM (Read Only Memory) Bits of information stored in main memory which are permanent. Cannot be altered or extinguished.

SERVICE BUREAU A dealer with a large computer that may provide a wide variety of services from time-sharing, to complete project management. Service bureaus are used frequently in the areas of timekeeping/billing and litigation support.

SHARED LOGIC A computer system with one central CPU and several "dumb" terminals.

SHARED RESOURCES A Computer system based on several independent microcomputers which can communicate with each other to share data bases and perhaps programs.

SOFTWARE The program instructions which tell the computer what to do. Software programs include: operating systems; language assemblers, compilers or interpreters; utility programs and application programs.

SOFTWARE HOUSES Companies that provide application software, either in off-the-shelf packaged form, or for individual clients.

SUBSTANTIVE SYSTEM A system designed to handle all aspects of a legal transaction, such as a trust, or a divorce. The system may be computerized or manual.

TAPE STORAGE A form of auxiliary storage which uses magnetic tape. Inexpensive, but slow for retrieval, since it must be accessed in a serial, rather than random order.

TELECOMMUNICATIONS The process of transmitting information electronically from one location to another.

TELENET One of the major private telecommunications networks. Less expensive and provides better transmission than telephone lines for long distances.

TERMINAL The most common input/output device used in a law office. Usually consists of a keyboard and CRT.

TIME–SHARING Renting time on a large computer outside the office. Necessary for accessing information data bases, and often used for litigation support.

TRANSPARENT The user is not aware of its existence. This is true for operating systems, telecommunications devices, etc.

TYMNET The largest of the private telecommunications network. Over 400 continental access points and more than 30 international access points.

UTILITY PROGRAMS Routine programs that are used to perform system-related functions such as supplying the initial instructions when the program is first turned on.

WESTLAW One of the two major legal data bases. Contains all recent court opinions and a great deal of law in specialty areas such as tax, labor and corporate law.

WORD PROCESSING A computer application that allows the editing and manipulation of text without re-typing the entire document. May be a separate machine, (dedicated word processor), or one of the application programs on a multi-use computer.

XENIX An operating system becoming popular on 16 bit computers.

# APPENDIX B

# Selected Bibliography


*A. General Works of Computer Technology*

*Books*

Davis and McCormack. *The Information Age.* Reading, Mass.: Addison-Wesley Publishing Co. Inc., 1979.

Martin. *Telecommunications and the Computer.* 2d ed. Englewood Cliffs, N.J.: Prentice-Hall, Inc., 1976.

*Articles*

Levinsa and Liberman. "Speech Recognition by Computers." 244 *Scientific American,* No. 4, April 1981.

Toone and Gupta. "Personal Computers." 347 *Scientific American,* No. 6, December 1982.

White. "Disk-Storage Technology." 243 *Scientific American,* No. 2, August 1980.

*Journals*

*Infoworld* (Popular Computing Inc., Palo Alto, Calif.).

*B. General Works on Computers and the Law*

*Books*

Arentowicz and Bower. *Law Office Automation and Technology.* New York: Matthew Bender & Co., 1980.

Bigelow, ed. *Computers and the Law.* 3d ed. A.B.A. Section of Science and Technology, 1981.

Heintz and Dill, eds. *LOCATE.* Section of Economics of Law Practice, American Bar Association, 1980.

Landsburg, Laventhal, Howarth. *Planning for Computers.* Section of Economics of Law Practice, American Bar Association, 1981.

*Articles*

Bigelow. "The Lawyers Computer." *Florida Bar Journal,* January, 1980.

Brill. "The Law Firm of the Future." *The American Lawyer,* November, 1980.

Eidelman. "Microcomputers in the Law Office." *Small Business Computers,* Sept./Oct. 1982.

*Journals*

*Law Office Economics and Management* (Callaghan & Co., 3201 Old Glenview Road, Wilmette, Ill. 60091)

*Legal Automation News* (Communications Exchange Inc. 1730 North Lynn St., Arlington, Va.)

*Legal Economics, Automation & Management* (575 Madison Avenue, New York City, N.Y.)

*The Lawyers Newsletter* (Law Publications, Inc., 1180 S. Beverly Drive, Los Angeles, Calif.)

*C. Litigation Support*

*Books*

Kinney. *Litigation Support Systems: An Attorney's Guide.* Wilmette, Ill.: Callaghan & Co., 1980.

Young, Kris and Trainor, eds. *Use of Computers in Litigation.* Chicago, Ill.: American Bar Association, 1979.

*Articles*

Lafitte. "The Use of Social Science Techniques in the Jury Selection Process". 2 *Review of Litigation,* No. 2, Spring 1982.

*D. Word Processing*

*Articles*

Berkow and Baer. "Law Firms and Word Processors: Current Status and Future Directions." 23 *Law Office Economics and Management,* Spring 1982.

Loftin. "What Can Word Processing Do For You?" *American Bar Association Journal* 65, November 1979.

Walshe. "Word-Processing Notebook-Comparing the Small Clustered Text-Editing Systems." 23 *Law Office Economics and Management,* Spring, 1982.

*E. Malpractice*

*Books*

"Canons of Professional Ethics Annotated." *Opinions on Professional Ethics.* Chicago, Ill.: American Bar Foundation, 1967.

Smith. *Preventing Legal Malpractice.* St. Paul, Minn.: West Publishing Co., 1981.

*F. Legal and Non-legal Data Bases*

*Books*

American Bar Association Section on Science and Technology. *Sense and Systems in Automated Law Research.* Chicago, Ill.: American Bar Association, 1975.

Sprowl. *A Manual for Computer-Assisted Legal Research.* Chicago, Ill.: American Bar Foundation, 1976.

*Articles*

Shulte. "A Survey of Computerized Legislative Information Systems." 72 *Law Library Journal* 99, Winter 1979.

*G. Legal Reasoning and Predictions*

*Books*

Niblett, ed. *Computer Science and Law.* New York, N.Y.: Cambridge University Press, 1980.

Ramo, ed. *How to Create a System for the Law Office.* Section of Economics of Law Practice, American Bar Association, 1979.

*Articles*

Fleiscam and Scaletta. "Use of Computer Technology in Legal Analysis and Prediction." 11 *American Business Law Journal* 3, 1974.

Grossman. "Computers and Legal Reasoning." 69 *American Bar Association Journal,* January, 1983.

Haar, Sawyer and Cummings. "Computer Power and Legal Reasoning—A Case Study of Judicial Decision Prediction in Zoning Cases." *American Bar Foundation Research Journal* No. 3, 1971.

Lawlor. "Computer Analysis of Judicial Decisions." *Computer Science and Law.* New York, N.Y.: Cambridge University Press, 1980.

Sprowl and Standt. "Computerizing Client Services on the Law School Teaching Clinic. An Experiment in Law Office Automation." *American Bar Foundation Research Journal,* 1981.

Sprowl. "Automating the Legal Reasoning Process." *American Bar Foundation Research Journal 1,* 1979.

*H. Computer Assisted Legal Education*

*Books*

Burris, Keeton, Landis, and Park. *Teaching Law with Computers: A Collection of Essays.* Boulder Westview Press, 1979.

*Articles*

Park and Burris. "Computer Aided Instructions in Law: Theories, Techniques and Trepidations." 1978 *American Bar Foundation Research Journal* No. 1.

# APPENDIX C

# WESTLAW Data Base

*Federal Statutory Law*

*The U.S. Code*

The complete, official text of the U.S. Code.

Special search methods make it easy to find the exact section or subsection you need, or scan related sections when necessary.

*Administrative Law*

*Code of Federal Regulations*

The 50 Titles of the Code of Federal Regulations give you access to current federal administrative regulations.

*Federal Register*

This is the original source for federal regulations before they are added to the Code of Federal Regulations. 1980 to date will be covered in the near future.

*Presidential Documents*

Includes Executive Orders 1936 to date.

*Federal Case Law*

*Supreme Court Reporter*

U.S. Supreme Court cases, Full Text Plus, from 1925 to date.

*Federal Reporter, 2D*

Full Text Plus:

U.S. Courts of Appeals Decisions, 1945 to date

Court of Customs and Patent Appeals cases, 1945 to date

Temporary Emergency Court of Appeals, 1945 to date

Court of Claims Decisions, 1961 to 1982

*Federal Supplement*

Full Text Plus:

U.S. District Court Decisions, 1950 to date

Court of International Trade cases (formerly Customs Court), 1950 to date

Special Court, Regional Rail Reorganization Act, 1970 to date

Judicial Panel on Multidistrict Litigation, 1970 to date

Court of Claims, 1954 to 1960

*Federal Rules Decisions*

Full Text Plus, 1978 to date; headnotes from 1961 to 1978.

*Note:* In the following special interest libraries, all Federal cases which includes cases from the U.S. Supreme Court, Court of Appeals, District Courts and Court of Claims can be searched inclusively or individually if desired.

Claims Court Decisions

Full Text Plus, 1982 to date

Comptroller General Decision

Full Text, 1982 to date

*Federal Special Interest Libraries*

*Federal Tax*

Internal Revenue Code

Federal Tax Regulations

Action on Decisions and Technical Memorandums now available in Tax Notes file (1981 to date) will be extended to 1967 in the near future.

| | **Start of Full Text Coverage** |
|---|---|
| Tax cases and other documents: | |
| U.S. Supreme Court | 1925 |
| U.S. Court of Appeals | 1945 |

| | Start of Full Text Coverage |
|---|---|
| Tax cases and other documents—Cont'd | |
| U.S. District Courts | 1950 |
| U.S. Court of Claims | 1954 |
| U.S. Claims Court | 1982 |
| Tax Court Reported Opinions | 1954 |
| Tax Court Memorandum Decisions | 1954 |
| Cumulative Bulletin | 1954 |
| Revenue Rulings | 1954 |
| Revenue Procedures | 1954 |
| Commissioner's Delegation Orders | 1954 |
| Executive Orders | 1954 |
| Treasury Dept. Orders | 1954 |
| Written Determinations | 1954 |
| Private Letter Rulings | 1954 |
| Technical Advice Memoranda | 1954 |
| Tax Notes | 1981 |
| IRS News Releases | 1981 |
| International Acts | 1954 |
| Public Laws | 1982 |
| General Counsel Memoranda | 1967 |

*Federal Securities*

Relevant sections of U.S. Code, relevant sections of CFR titles.

| | Start of Current Coverage |
|---|---|
| Cases and other documents: | |
| U.S. Supreme Court | 1941 |
| U.S. Court of Appeals | 1945 |
| U.S. Court of Claims | 1954 |
| U.S. District Courts | 1950 |
| SEC Admin. Decisions and Reports | 1934 |
| SEC Interpretive Releases (selected) | 1934 |
| SEC No-Action Letters | 1971 |

*Antitrust and Business Regulation*

Relevant sections of U.S. Code; relevant sections of CFR titles.

| | Start of Current Coverage |
|---|---|
| Cases and other documents: | |
| U.S. Supreme Court | 1925 |
| U.S. Court of Appeals | 1945 |
| U.S. District Courts | 1950 |

| | Start of Full Text Coverage |
|---|---|
| Cases and other documents—Cont'd | |
| U.S. Court of Claims | 1954 |
| FTC Decisions | 1959 |

*Labor*

Relevant sections of U.S. Code; also relevant sections of CFR titles to be added in future.

| | Start of Current Coverage |
|---|---|
| Cases and other documents: | |
| U.S. Supreme Court | 1925 |
| U.S. Court of Appeals | 1945 |
| U.S. Court of Claims | 1954 |
| U.S. District Courts | 1950 |
| NLRB Decisions | 1972 |
| OSHRC Reports | 1971 |

*Federal Government Contracts*

Relevant sections of U.S. Code; relevant sections of CFR titles.

| | Start of Current Coverage |
|---|---|
| Cases and other documents: | |
| U.S. Supreme Court | 1925 |
| U.S. Court of Appeals | 1945 |
| U.S. Court of Claims | 1954 |
| U.S. District Courts | 1950 |
| U.S. Claims Court | 1982 |
| Board of Contract Appeals | |
| Agriculture | 1975 |
| Armed Services | 1955 |
| Energy | 1980 |
| Corps of Engineers | 1953 |
| General Services | 1962 |
| HUD | 1975 |
| Interior | 1955 |
| Labor | 1973 |
| NASA | 1960 |
| Postal Service | 1959 |
| Dept. of Transportation | 1967 |
| Veteran Admin. | 1958 |

*Patent*

Relevant sections of U.S. Code; relevant sections of CFR titles.

| | Start of Current Coverage |
|---|---|
| Cases: | |
| U.S. Supreme Court | 1925 |
| U.S. Court of Appeals | 1945 |
| U.S. District Courts | 1950 |
| Court of Customs and Patent Appeals | 1945 |
| U.S. Court of Claims | 1954 |

*Copyright*

Relevant sections of U.S. Code; relevant sections of CFR titles.

| | Start of Current Coverage |
|---|---|
| Cases: | |
| U.S. Supreme Court | 1925 |
| U.S. Court of Appeals | 1945 |
| U.S. District Courts | 1950 |
| Court of Customs and Patent Appeals | 1945 |
| U.S. Court of Claims | 1954 |

*Federal Communications*

Relevant sections of U.S. Code; relevant sections of CFR titles.

| | Start of Current Coverage |
|---|---|
| Cases and other documents: | |
| U.S. Supreme Court | 1925 |
| U.S. Court of Appeals | 1945 |
| U.S. District Courts | 1950 |
| U.S. Court of Claims | 1954 |
| FCC Reports | 1975 |

*Admiralty*

Relevant sections of U.S. Code; relevant sections of CFR titles.

| | Start of Current Coverage |
|---|---|
| Cases: | |
| U.S. Supreme Court | 1925 |
| U.S. Court of Appeals | 1945 |

| | Start of Current Coverage |
|---|---|
| Cases—Cont'd | |
| U.S. District Courts | 1950 |
| U.S. Court of Claims | 1954 |

*National Defense*

Relevant sections of U.S. Code; relevant sections of CFR titles.

| | Start of Current Coverage |
|---|---|
| Military Justice Reporter | 1977 |

*Federal Bankruptcy*

Relevant sections of U.S. Code; relevant sections of the CFR titles.

| | Start of Current Coverage |
|---|---|
| Cases and other documents: | |
| U.S. Supreme Court | 1925 |
| U.S. Court of Appeals | 1945 |
| U.S. District Courts | 1950 |
| U.S. Bankruptcy Courts | 1979 |

*Delaware Corporation Law*

| | |
|---|---|
| Selected Federal Cases: | |
| U.S. Supreme Court | (currently available in WESTLAW's general federal libraries) |
| U.S. Court of Appeals | |
| U.S. District Courts | |
| Selected Delaware Cases: | |
| Reported Decisions | 1966 |
| Unreported Decisions | 1975 |

*Federal Energy*

Relevant sections of U.S. Code and relevant sections of CFR titles to be added in future.

| | Start of Current Coverage |
|---|---|
| U.S. Supreme Court | N/A |
| U.S. Court of Appeals | N/A |
| U.S. District Courts | N/A |
| U.S. Court of Claims | N/A |
| Commission (FERC) Decisions | N/A |

*WESTLAW State Law Libraries*

| | Start of Full Text Plus |
|---|---|
| *Alabama* | |
| Supreme Court | 1965 |
| Ct. of Civil Appeals | 1970 |
| Ct. of Criminal Appeals | 1969 |
| File: Southern Reporter | |
| *Alaska* | |
| Supreme Court | 1965 |
| Ct. of Appeals | 1980 |
| File: Pacific Reporter | |
| *Arizona* | |
| Supreme Court | 1955 |
| Ct. of Appeals | 1965 |
| File: Pacific Reporter | |
| *Arkansas* | |
| Supreme Court | 1965 |
| Ct. of Appeals | 1979 |
| File: South Western Reporter | |
| *California* | |
| Supreme Court | 1945 |
| Ct. of Appeals | 1955 |
| Appellate Dept., Superior Ct. | 1965 |
| File: California Reporter | |
| See also separate libraries on Family Law, Insurance Law and Attorney General Opinions. | |
| *Colorado* | |
| Supreme Court | 1955 |
| Ct. of Appeals | 1970 |
| File: Pacific Reporter | |
| *Connecticut* | |
| Supreme Court | 1965 |
| Superior Court | 1965 |
| File: Atlantic Reporter | |
| *Delaware* | |
| Supreme Court | 1965 |
| Ct. of Chancery | 1965 |
| Superior Court | 1965 |
| Corporation Law | 1965 |
| File: Atlantic Reporter | |

*WESTLAW State Law Libraries—Cont'd*

| | **Start of Full Text Plus** |
|---|---|
| *District of Columbia* | |
| Court of Appeals | 1965 |
| *Florida* | |
| Supreme Court | 1955 |
| District Courts of Appeal | 1957 |
| File: Southern Reporter | |
| *Georgia* | |
| Supreme Court | 1965 |
| Ct. of Appeals | 1965 |
| File: South Eastern Reporter | |
| *Hawaii* | |
| Supreme Court | 1965 |
| Intermediate Court of Appeals | 1980 |
| File: Pacific Reporter | |
| *Idaho* | |
| Supreme Court | 1965 |
| Ct. of Appeals | 1982 |
| File: Pacific Reporter | |
| *Illinois* | |
| Supreme Court | 1945 |
| Appellate Court | 1965 |
| File: North Eastern Reporter | |
| See also separate library on Attorney General Opinions | |
| *Indiana* | |
| Supreme Court | 1955 |
| Ct. of Appeals | 1965 |
| *Iowa* | |
| Supreme Court | 1965 |
| Ct. of Appeals | 1977 |
| File: North Western Reporter | |
| *Kansas* | |
| Supreme Court | 1965 |
| Ct. of Appeals | 1977 |
| File: Pacific Reporter | |
| *Kentucky* | |
| Supreme Court | 1965 |
| Ct. of Appeals | 1976 |
| File: South Western Reporter | |
| *Louisiana* | |
| Supreme Court | 1956 |
| Court of Appeal | 1956 |
| File: Southern Reporter | |
| *Maine* | |
| Supreme Judicial Court | 1965 |

*WESTLAW State Law Libraries—Cont'd*

| | Start of Full Text Plus |
|---|---|
| *Maryland* | |
| Ct. of Appeals | 1965 |
| Ct. of Special Appeals | 1967 |
| File: Atlantic Reporter | |
| *Massachusetts* | |
| Supreme Court | 1965 |
| Appeals Court | 1972 |
| File: North Eastern Reporter | |
| *Michigan* | |
| Supreme Court | 1955 |
| Ct. of Appeals | 1965 |
| File: North Western Reporter | |
| *Minnesota* | |
| Supreme Court | 1945 |
| File: North Western Reporter | |
| See also separate library on Attorney General Opinions | |
| *Mississippi* | |
| Supreme Court | 1965 |
| File: Southern Reporter | |
| *Missouri* | |
| Supreme Court | 1965 |
| Court of Appeals | 1965 |
| File: South Western Reporter | |
| *Montana* | |
| Supreme Court | 1965 |
| File: Pacific Reporter | |
| *Nebraska* | |
| Supreme Court | 1965 |
| File: North Western Reporter | |
| *Nevada* | |
| Supreme Court | 1965 |
| File: Pacific Reporter | |
| *New Hampshire* | |
| Supreme Court | 1965 |
| File: Atlantic Reporter | |
| *New Jersey* | |
| Supreme Court | 1948 |
| Superior Court | 1948 |
| Tax Court | 1980 |
| File: Atlantic Reporter | |
| *New Mexico* | |
| Supreme Court | 1965 |
| Court of Appeals | 1967 |
| File: Pacific Reporter | |

*WESTLAW State Law Libraries—Cont'd*

| | **Start of Full Text Plus** |
|---|---|
| *New York* | |
| Court of Appeals | 1940 |
| Supreme Court, App.Div. | 1965 |
| Supreme Court | 1965 |
| File: New York Supplement | |
| See also separate libraries on Family Law, Insurance Law and Attorney General Opinions. | |
| *North Carolina* | |
| Supreme Court | 1965 |
| Court of Appeals | 1968 |
| File: South Eastern Reporter | |
| *North Dakota* | |
| Supreme Court | 1965 |
| File: North Western Reporter | |
| *Ohio* | |
| Supreme Court | 1965 |
| Court of Appeals | 1965 |
| File: North Eastern Reporter | |
| See also separate library on Attorney General Opinions. | |
| *Oklahoma* | |
| Supreme Court | 1965 |
| Ct. of Criminal Appeals | 1965 |
| Ct. of Appeals | 1969 |
| File: Pacific Reporter | |
| *Oregon* | |
| Supreme Court | 1965 |
| Court of Appeals | 1969 |
| File: Pacific Reporter | |
| *Pennsylvania* | |
| Supreme Court | 1965 |
| Superior Court | 1965 |
| Commonwealth Ct. | 1970 |
| File: Atlantic Reporter | |
| See also separate library on Attorney General Opinions. | |
| *Rhode Island* | |
| Supreme Court | 1965 |
| File: Atlantic Reporter | |
| *South Carolina* | |
| Supreme Court | 1965 |
| File: South Eastern Reporter | |

*WESTLAW State Law Libraries—Cont'd*

| | **Start of Full Text Plus** |
|---|---|
| *South Dakota* | |
| Supreme Court | 1965 |
| File: North Western Reporter | |
| *Tennessee* | |
| Supreme Court | 1965 |
| Ct. of Appeals | 1965 |
| Ct. of Criminal Appeals | 1967 |
| See also separate library on Attorney General Opinions. | |
| *Texas* | |
| Supreme Court | 1920 |
| Court of Civil Appeals | 1950 |
| Court of Criminal Appeals | 1950 |
| File: South Western Reporter | |
| See also separate library on Attorney General Opinions. | |
| *Utah* | |
| Supreme Court | 1965 |
| File: Pacific Reporter | |
| *Vermont* | |
| Supreme Court | 1965 |
| File: Atlantic Reporter | |
| *Virginia* | |
| Supreme Court | 1965 |
| File: South Eastern Reporter | |
| *Washington* | |
| Supreme Court | 1965 |
| Ct. of Appeals | 1969 |
| File: Pacific Reporter | |
| *West Virginia* | |
| Supreme Court | 1965 |
| File: South Eastern Reporter | |
| *Wisconsin* | |
| Supreme Court | 1965 |
| Ct. of Appeals | 1978 |
| File: North Western Reporter | |
| *Wyoming* | |
| Supreme Court | 1965 |
| File: Pacific Reporter | |

*Insurance*

California and New York currently available. Other states will be added in the future.

*Family*

California and New York cases are currently available. Other states will be available in the near future.

*Education*

California and New York cases are currently available. Other states and federal education cases will be added in the near future.

*Attorney General Opinions*

Attorney General Opinions are currently available for the following states: Arizona, California, Illinois, Louisiana, Minnesota, New York, Ohio, Pennsylvania, Tennessee, Texas.

*Shepard's Citations*

Shepard's Citations allow the researcher to Shepardize cases that appear on the screen or cases that are entered separately. Shepard's includes subsequent history of a case, other cases which have cited the case, and notations as to how the case is treated in the citing cases. Researchers can rapidly move the original case, Shepard's listings and cases cited in the list.

*Special Interest Databases*

*Military Justice Reporter*

Covers reported decisions of the U.S. Court of Military Appeals and Courts of Military Review for the Army, Navy, Air Force and Coast Guard from 1978 to date.

*Forensic Services Directory*

The Directory, compiled by the National Forensic Center, lists 3700 expert and technical consultants plus translators, testing laboratories, investigators and other specialists who provide trial support services. A user may search by particular topic or specialties, by names of experts, or key words descriptive of an accident or event.

*Eurolex*

This optional service is now accessible through WESTLAW. EUROLEX provides extensive coverage of Common Market, European, English and Scottish legal materials.

*Black's Law Dictionary*

Complete text of Black's Law Dictionary helps researchers quickly define legal terms. This feature will be added in the near future.

*Insta-Cite*

West's INSTA–CITE is a new case history service available for WESTLAW. It provides instant cite verification, plus appellate history of a case.

*Case Highlights*

This special file includes current state and federal cases from around the country of general interest and significance to lawyers. This service is provided free of charge.

*On-Line Courses*

On-line training courses designed to teach search techniques and use of the terminal are available free of charge on WESTLAW.

*Tax Highlights*

This special file alerts the tax researcher to cases and developments of interest and significance.

*American Bar Association Summaries*

This database provides a collection of abstracts from the ABA containing information on publications, programs, activities and products of the ABA.

# APPENDIX D

# WESTLAW—Certified Compatible Equipment List

*Note*: Only the specific hardware/software combinations which are shown have been certified. Substitutions will *not* be considered. See page 192 for additional information.

*Word Processors and Micro Computers—Dial–Up*

*ALPHA MICRO*

Hardware: Alpha Micro AM–1010, 1011, 1030, 1031, 1050 or 1051; with Hazeltine 1420 or 1500 CRT

Software: WESTLAW software by STAT Systems

*ARCHIVES I, II, or III*

Hardware: Archives I, II, III

Software: WESTLAW software by Coherent Systems

*ATV JACQUARD J100 or J500*

Hardware: ATV Jacquard J100 or J500; with Communication capabilities

Software: WESTLAW software by Tangent Computing

*BILLINGS*

Hardware: Billings Computer BC–12FD or BC–12DF2M

Software: WESTLAW software by Billings Computer

*COMPUCORP OMEGA*

Hardware: Compucorp Omega 20 Model 655, 665, 675, or 685; with Serial Communication Controller (Option 015)

Hardware Modification: 24 line display required (Option 024)

Software: WESTLAW software by Compucorp

*CPT 8000, 8100, 8510, 8515, 8520, or 8525*

Hardware: CPT 8000 or 8100 (with Communications board); 8510, 8515, 8520, 8525

Software: WESTLAW software by CPT Corporation

*DEC (Digital Equipment Corporation) WS–78 or WD–78*

Hardware: DEC WS–78 or WD–78; with Communications module

Software: "WPS" word processing software by DEC

*IBM DISPLAYWRITER*

Hardware: IBM Displaywriter with 25 line display, 192K of memory, and asynchronous communications board

Software: WESTLAW software by Coherent Systems, Inc. (Requires CP/M–86 operating system)

*IBM PERSONAL COMPUTER (PC)*

Minimum Hardware: IBM PC with 96K, diskette drive(s), Monochrome display and adapter card, serial communications card, printer adapter card

Software: WESTLAW Software by Direct Aide, Inc. (Requires IBM PC DOS)

*LEGAL TALK*

Hardware: Legal Talk, with IBM 3101 (Model 20) Hazeltine 1520, or other terminal subject to WESTLAW approval

Note: This unit is a "talking terminal" designed for use by the visually impaired

*LEXITRON VT1202 or VT1303*

Hardware: Lexitron VT1202 or VT1303; with Communications option

| | |
|---|---|
| Software: | WESTLAW Software by Lexitron Corp. (ASCII ASYNCH VERSION 0106) |

*NORTHSTAR HORIZON*

| | |
|---|---|
| Hardware: | Northstar Horizon; with Hazeltine 1420 CRT |
| Software: | WESTLAW software by Coherent Systems (requires CP/M operating system) |

*ONTEL*

| | |
|---|---|
| Hardware: | Ontel Video Display Terminal OP–1/50 or OP–1/70 with Magnetic storage |
| Software: | WESTLAW software by Graphics Unlimited |

*RADIO SHACK TRS–80 MODEL 2 (64K)*

| | |
|---|---|
| Hardware: | TRS–80 Model 2 (64K) |
| Software: | WESTLAW software by LexIntellect |

*RADIO SHACK TRS–80 MODEL 2 (64K), Model 12, or Model 16*

| | |
|---|---|
| Hardware: | TRS–80 Model 2 (64K), Model 12, or Model 16 |
| Software: | WESTLAW software by Tandy Corporation |

*SCIENTIFIC DATA SYSTEMS (SDS) 420, 421, 422, or 423*

| | |
|---|---|
| Hardware: | SDS 420, 421, 422, or 423 |
| Software: | WESTLAW software by ACET, Inc. |

*XEROX 860 IPS*

| | |
|---|---|
| Hardware: | Xerox 860 IPS (full or partial page display); with 860 Communications Accessory |
| Software: | WESTLAW software by Xerox Corp. |

*COMPUTER TERMINALS—DIAL-UP:*

*Note:* Unless otherwise indicated, the following terminals (hardware) function on WESTLAW without the need for user supplied software or hardware modification.

*BEEHIVE DM310*

| | | |
|---|---|---|
| Firmware Required: | Terminal: | 10–178A |
| | Keyboard: | 10–0151 |

*HAZELTINE 1520*

Hardware
Modification: Insert/Delete Character PROMs

*IBM 3101 (MODELS 20, 22, & 23)*

*TELETYPE DATASPEED 40/2 (Bell Telephone)*

*Word Processors and Micro Computers—Leased Line:*

*LANIER NO PROBLEM LTE–3*

| | |
|---|---|
| Hardware: | Lanier No Problem LTE–3 |
| 3270 | Communications Board |
| Software: | 3270 emulation software (with EBCDIC code) by Lanier |

*Computer Terminals—Leased Line:*

*IBM 3270 Series*

*TELETYPE DATASPEED 40/4 (Bell Telephone)*

*"Character Mode"—Dial-up*

In addition to the foregoing equipment, several hundred models of personal computers permit WESTLAW access using asynchronous teletype communications. The following minimum criteria must be satisfied to allow this form of WESTLAW access:

1. Screen display must be at least 80 characters by 24 lines.
2. Terminal must permit "dial-up" access. (If your terminal currently works with Tymnet, Telenet or Uninet public data networks, it meets this requirement.)
3. The terminal and modem must operate at 120 characters per second (1200 baud).

To fully verify that a specific unit will work adequately, a WESTLAW demonstration should be given. Units may require specific hardware/software configurations to function properly with WESTLAW.

# APPENDIX E

## LEXIS Data Base

*Federal Law Libraries*

*GENERAL*

United States Code

Federal Register beginning in July 1980

Code of Federal Regulations

*Cases*

Supreme Court decisions beginning in 1925

Court of Appeals decisions in 1938

District Courts decisions beginning in 1958

Court of Claims decisions beginning in 1960

*Supreme Court Briefs beginning with the fall term of 1979*

*TAX*

*Internal Revenue Code*

*Regulations* (final, temporary, and proposed)

*The Cumulative Bulletin beginning in 1954*

Rulings under the 1954 Code

Rulings under the 1939 Code

Administrative, procedural, and miscellaneous

Commissioner's acquiescences, technical and other releases

*Private Rulings*

All private rulings released to the public beginning in 1977

Private Rulings from 1954 to 1977 released to the public and classified "reference" by the Internal Revenue Service

*Cases*

Tax cases decided in the Supreme Court beginning in 1913

Tax cases decided in the Court of Appeals beginning in 1938

Tax cases decided in the District Courts beginning in 1958

Tax cases decided in the Court of Claims beginning in 1942

Tax opinions and memorandum decisions from the beginning (1942)

Board of Tax Appeals opinions from the beginning (1924)

*Internal Revenue Manual*

*Legislative History*

Public Laws and House, Senate, and Conference Reports for the 1954 Code and amendments thereto

*SECURITIES*

*Relevant sections of title 15 of the U.S. Code*

*Regulations*

Final and proposed regulations promulgated under the Securities Acts

Final and proposed regulations (G, T, U and X) issued by the Board of Governors of the Federal Reserve System

*Administrative Determinations*

No-action letters beginning in 1971

Selected Securities and Exchange Commission administrative decisions beginning in 1933

Selected interpretive releases of the Securities and Exchange Commission beginning in 1933

*Cases*

Securities cases decided in the Supreme Court beginning in 1933

Securities cases decided in the Court of Appeals beginning in 1933

Securities cases decided in the District Courts beginning in 1933

*Legislative History*

House, Senate and Conference reports associated with the 1933 and 1934 Acts, amendments thereto

*TRADE REGULATION*

*Administrative determinations*

Commissioner's opinions beginning in 1950

Administrative Law Judges' initial decisions beginning in 1950

Administrative Law Judges' procedural orders beginning in 1976

Consent and interlocutory orders beginning in 1970

*Cases*

Trade regulation cases decided in the Supreme Court beginning in 1890

Trade regulation cases decided in the Court of Appeals beginning in 1938

Trade regulation cases decided in the District Courts beginning in 1950

*BANKRUPTCY*

*Cases*

Bankruptcy cases decided in the Supreme Court beginning in 1925

Bankruptcy cases decided in the Courts of Appeals beginning in 1938

Bankruptcy cases decided in the District Courts beginning in 1958

Bankruptcy Judges' decisions beginning in October, 1979

*PATENT, TRADEMARK AND COPYRIGHT*

Patent, trademark and copyright cases decided in the Supreme Court beginning in 1850

Patent and trademark cases decided in Court of Customs and Patent Appeals beginning in 1952

Patent, trademark and copyright cases decided in the Courts of Appeals beginning in 1938

Patent, trademark, and copyright cases decided in the District Courts beginning in 1958

Patent, trademark, and copyright cases decided in the Court of Claims beginning in 1960

*COMMUNICATIONS*

*Administrative determinations*

Federal Communications Commission Reports, Second Series

Federal Communications Commission Reports:

Vol. 39 (frequency allocations) beginning in 1939

Vol. 40 (sponsorship identification, equal time, fairness doctrine, FM frequency allocations) beginning in 1941

Vol. 41 (television matters) beginning in 1950

Vol. 42 (common carrier and safety and special radio services) beginning in 1947

*Cases*

Communication cases decided in the Supreme Court beginning in 1936

Communication cases decided in the Court of Appeals beginning in 1929

Communication cases decided in the District Courts beginning in 1958

*LABOR*

*Administrative determinations*

National Labor Relations Board Reports beginning in 1972

*Cases*

Labor cases decided in the Supreme Court beginning in 1925

Labor cases decided in the Court of Appeals beginning in 1938

Labor cases decided in the District Courts beginning in 1958

*State Law Libraries*

*Alabama*

Alabama Supreme Court decisions beginning in 1965

Alabama Court of Appeals decisions from 1965 to 1969

Alabama Court of Criminal Appeals decisions beginning in 1969

Alabama Court of Civil Appeals decisions beginning in 1969

*Alaska*

Alaska Supreme Court decisions beginning in 1965

Alaska Court of Appeals decisions beginning in 1980

*Arizona*

Arizona Supreme Court decisions beginning in 1965

Arizona Court of Appeals decisions beginning in 1965

*Arkansas*

Arkansas Reports beginning in 1965

Arkansas Court of Appeals decisions beginning in 1979

*California*

California Reports, Second Series, beginning in 1945

California Reports, Third Series

California Appellate Reports, Second Series, beginning in 1955

California Appellate Reports, Third Series

*Colorado*

Colorado Supreme Court decisions beginning in 1965

Colorado Court of Appeals decisions beginning in 1970

*Connecticut*

Connecticut Reports beginning in 1965

Connecticut Supplement beginning in 1965

Connecticut Circuit Court Reports from 1965 to 1974

*Delaware*

Delaware Supreme Court decisions beginning in 1965

Delaware Court of Chancery decisions beginning in 1965

Delaware Superior Court decisions beginning in 1965

*District of Columbia*

District of Columbia Court of Appeals decisions beginning in 1965

*Florida*

Florida Supreme Court decisions beginning in 1955

Florida District Courts of Appeal decisions (excluding memoranda) beginning in 1957

*Georgia*

Georgia Supreme Court decisions beginning in 1955

Georgia Court of Appeals decisions beginning in 1955

*Hawaii*

Hawaii Supreme Court decisions beginning in 1965

Hawaii Intermediate Court of Appeals beginning in 1980

*Idaho*

Idaho Supreme Court decisions beginning in 1965

Court of Appeals, 1982

*Illinois*

Illinois Reports, beginning in 1945

Illinois Reports, Second Series

Illinois Appellate Court Reports, Second Series, beginning in 1955

Illinois Appellate Court Reports, Third Series

*Indiana*

Indiana Reports beginning in 1965

Indiana Court of Appeals (formerly Appellate Court) Reports beginning in 1965

*Iowa*

Iowa Supreme Court decisions beginning in 1960

Iowa Court of Appeals decisions beginning in 1977

*Kansas*

Constitution of Kansas

Kansas Statutes

Kansas Supreme Court decisions beginning in 1963

Kansas Court of Appeals decisions beginning in 1977

*Kentucky*

Kentucky Supreme Court (formerly Court of Appeals) decisions beginning in 1955

Kentucky Court of Appeals decisions beginning in 1976

*Louisiana*

Louisiana Supreme Court decisions beginning in 1945

Louisiana Courts of Appeal decisions beginning in 1965

*Maine*

Maine Supreme Judicial Court decisions beginning in 1965

*Maryland*

Maryland Reports beginning in 1965
Maryland Appellate Reports beginning in 1967

*Massachusetts*

Massachusetts Reports beginning in 1950
Massachusetts Appeals Court decisions beginning in 1972

*Michigan*

Michigan Reports beginning in 1945
Michigan Appeals Reports beginning in 1945

*Minnesota*

Minnesota Reports beginning in 1965

*Mississippi*

Mississippi Supreme Court decisions beginning in 1965

*Missouri*

Constitution of Missouri
Missouri Revised Statutes and Session Laws
Missouri Supreme Court decisions beginning in 1945
Missouri Court of Appeals decisions beginning in 1945

*Montana*

Montana Supreme Court decisions beginning in 1965

*Nebraska*

Nebraska Reports beginning in 1965

*Nevada*

Nevada Supreme Court decisions beginning in 1965

*New Hampshire*

New Hampshire Supreme Court decisions beginning in 1965

*New Jersey*

New Jersey Supreme Court decisions beginning in 1948
New Jersey Superior Court decisions beginning in 1965

*New Mexico*

New Mexico Supreme Court decisions beginning in 1965

New Mexico Court of Appeals decisions beginning in 1966

*New York*

Constitution of New York

Consolidated Laws of New York

New York Reports (excluding memoranda and motion tables) beginning in 1940

New York Reports, Second Series

Appellate Division Reports, Second Series

Miscellaneous Reports, Second Series

*North Carolina*

North Carolina Reports beginning in 1965

North Carolina Court of Appeals Reports beginning in 1968

*North Dakota*

North Dakota Supreme Court decisions beginning in 1965

*Ohio*

Constitution of Ohio

Ohio Revised Code and Rules of Civil Procedure

Ohio Reports beginning in 1821

Ohio State Reports beginning in 1852

Ohio State Reports, Second Series

Ohio Appellate Reports beginning in 1913

Ohio Appellate Reports, Second Series

Ohio Law Abstracts beginning in 1922

Ohio Miscellaneous Reports beginning in 1965

*Oklahoma*

Oklahoma Supreme Court decisions beginning in 1965

Oklahoma Court of Criminal Appeals decisions beginning in 1965

Oklahoma Court of Appeals decisions beginning in 1969

*Oregon*

Oregon Reports beginning in 1965

Oregon Court of Appeals beginning in 1969

*Pennsylvania*

Pennsylvania Supreme Court decisions beginning in 1945
Pennsylvania Superior Court decisions beginning in 1955
Pennsylvania Commonwealth Court decisions beginning in 1970

*Rhode Island*

Rhode Island Supreme Court decisions beginning in 1965

*South Carolina*

South Carolina Supreme Court decisions beginning in 1965

*South Dakota*

South Dakota Supreme Court decisions beginning in 1965

*Tennessee*

Tennessee Supreme Court decisions beginning in 1965
Tennessee Court of Appeals decisions beginning in 1965
Tennessee Court of Criminal Appeals decisions beginning in 1967

*Texas*

Texas Supreme Court decisions beginning in 1955
Texas Court of Criminal Appeals decisions beginning in 1965
Texas Courts of Civil Appeals decisions beginning in 1965

*Utah*

Utah Supreme Court decisions beginning in 1965

*Vermont*

Vermont Reports beginning in 1965

*Virginia*

Virginia Supreme Court decisions beginning in 1925

*Washington*

Washington Reports, Second Series, beginning in 1965
Washington Appellate Reports beginning in 1969

*West Virginia*

West Virginia Supreme Court of Appeals decisions beginning in 1965

*Wisconsin*

Wisconsin Reports, Second Series, beginning in 1965

Wisconsin Court of Appeals decisions beginning in 1978

*Wyoming*

Wyoming Supreme Court decisions beginning in 1965

*Delaware Corporation Law Library*

Delaware cases construing the Delaware General Corporation Law

Reported decisions beginning in 1895

Unreported decisions beginning in 1970

Federal cases construing the Delaware General Corporation Law

Supreme Court decisions beginning in 1925

Court of Appeals decisions beginning in 1938

District Courts decisions beginning in 1960

*United Kingdom Law Libraries*

*English General*

*Statutes*

*Statutory Instruments*

*Cases*

Law Reports beginning in 1945

All England Reports beginning in 1945

Weekly Law Reports beginning in 1945

Lloyds Reports beginning in 1945

Property and Compensation Reports beginning in 1949

Criminal Appeals Reports beginning in 1945

Criminal Appeals Reports (Sentencing) beginning in 1945

Unreported cases beginning in 1980

*TAX*

*Statutes*

*Statutory Instruments*

*Double Taxation Agreements*

*Inland Revenue publications* (press releases, extra-statutory concessions, and other publications)

*Cases*

Report of Tax Cases from 1875 to 1972

Simon's Tax Cases beginning in 1972

Value Added Tax Tribunal Reports beginning in 1973

Unreported cases beginning in 1980

*Industrial Relations*

*Statutes*

*Statutory Instruments*

*Cases*

Industrial Cases Reports beginning in 1972

Industrial Tribunal Reports from 1967 to 1978

Industrial Relations Law Reports beginning in 1974

Reports of Restrictive Practices Cases from 1957 to 1972

All England Reports beginning in 1945

Unreported cases beginning in 1980

*Intellectual Property*

*Statutes*

*Statutory Instruments*

*Cases*

Reports of Patent Design and Trademark cases beginning in 1945

Unreported cases beginning in 1980

*European Communities*

*Cases*

European Communities Reports beginning in 1954

*Local Government*

*Statutes*

*Statutory*

*Cases*

Local Government Reports beginning in 1945

Ryde's Rating Cases beginning in 1956

Unreported cases beginning in 1980

*French Law Libraries*

*Public Law*

Conseil d'Etat general and fiscal cases beginning in October 1964

Tribunal des Conflits cases beginning in October 1964

*Private Law*

Cour de Cassation cases (civil, criminal, labor and commercial) beginning in 1959

*Statutes and Regulations*

Secretariat General du Gouvernement asbstracts

Journal Officiel beginning in 1955

---

*AUTO–CITE*

AUTO–CITE, offered under agreement with The Lawyers Cooperative Publishing Company and its affiliate, Bancroft-Whitney, permits verification of the accuracy of virtually any case-law citation, provides parallel citations, and lists any appellate cases that directly affect the requested case's validity as precedent.

*Shepard's Citations*

Under agreement with the Shepard's Division of McGraw-Hill, Inc. all federal, state and regional case-law citators are offered, giving for each case cited the case history, parallel citations, and a statement of the subsequent history of the case.

*NEXIS*

NEXIS is a full-text library of general and business news and information. The initial NEXIS library comprises a core group of leading publications and wire services and will be significantly enlarged with additional newspapers, magazines, wire services, newsletters and other sources of useful information. The library contains the full text of the listed publications and wire services, except for materials such as advertisements, stock tables, indices, schedules, sports scores and standings, graphics, and the like, and stories and items in which the publication has only first publication rights.

*Newspapers, such as,*

*American Banker* beginning on January 1, 1979

The BBC's *Summary of World Broadcasts and Monitoring Report* beginning in January 1979

*Christian Science Monitor* beginning on January 1, 1980

*Japan Economic Journal* beginning in June 1980

*The Washington Post* beginning on January 1, 1977

*Magazines, such as,*

*ABA Banking Journal* beginning in January 1980

*Aviation Week & Space Technology* beginning in January 1975

*Business Week* beginning in January 1975

*Chemical Engineering* beginning in January 1981

*Chemical Week* beginning in January 1975

*Coal Age* beginning in January 1975

*Congressional Quarterly Weekly Report* and *Editorial Research Reports* beginning in January 1975

*Dun's Business Month* (Dun's Review) beginning in January 1975

*The Economist* beginning in January 1975

*Electronics* beginning in January 1981

*Engineering and Mining Journal* beginning in January 1981

*Engineering News-Record* beginning in January 1981

*Newsweek* beginning in January 1975

*U.S. News & World Report* beginning in January 1975

*Wire Services, such as,*

The Associate Press world, national and business wires beginning on January 1, 1977

Jiji Press Economic News Service beginning on January 4, 1980

Kyodo English Language News Service beginning on December 1, 1980

PR Newswire beginning on January 22, 1980

The Reuters General News Report beginning on April 15, 1979

The Reuters European News Service beginning on September 26, 1980

The United Press International world, national, business and sports wires beginning on September 26, 1980

The United Press International states wires beginning on November 1, 1980

The United Press International biographical data base complete file

States News Service beginning in December 1981

Xinhua News Agency (China) beginning on January 1, 1977

*Newsletters, such as,*

"Latin American Regional Reports" (Andean Group, Caribbean, Southern Cone, Mexico, Central America and Brazil) beginning in 1980

"Latin American Political Report" beginning in 1967

"Latin American Weekly Report" beginning in 1980

"Latin American Commodities Report" beginning in 1967

"Latin American Special Report" (Venezuela, Mexico and Colombia)

"Latin American Book News" beginning in 1979

"Latin American Economic Report" beginning in 1973

"Synfuel Week" beginning on August 1, 1980

"Coal Outlook" beginning in 1975

"Update/American States" beginning in January 1981

---

## *ACCOUNTING INFORMATION LIBRARY*

### *Annual Reports*

Annual reports, selected by the American Institute of Certified Public Accountants (AICPA), of corporations listed on the New York Stock Exchange and the American Stock Exchange and corporations quoted over-the-counter

### *Proxies*

Extracts from proxy statements selected by the AICPA

### *Literature*

Authoritative accounting materials, such as statements of auditing standards, industry accounting guides, and accounting series releases, issued by the AICPA, the Securities and Exchange Commission, the Financial Accounting Standards Board, and other organizations.

*Encyclopedia Britannica*

*Britannica 3,* specifically the 10-volume *Micropaedia,* with important facts in the capsule form, and the *Macropadeia,* 19 volumes of comprehensive information on a wide range of subjects, made available under an agreement with Encyclopedia Britannica, Inc.

# APPENDIX F

# DIALOG Database (File Number(s)) Dates of Coverage

*Chemistry*

CA SEARCH (308, 309, 310, 311, 320) 1967–present

CHEMICAL INDUSTRY NOTES (19) 1974–present

CHEMICAL REGULATIONS AND GUIDELINES SYSTEM (174) Current

CHEMLAW (197) Current

CHEMNAME (301) 1967–present

CHEMSEARCH (30) Current

CHEMSIS (328, 329, 330, 331) 1967–present

CHEMZERO (300) 1965–present

CLAIMS COMPOUND REGISTRY (242) Current

PAPERCHEM (240) 7/68–present

SCISEARCH (34, 94, 186, 187) 1970–present

TSCA INITIAL INVENTORY (52) 1979 edition

*Agriculture and Nutrition*

AGRICOLA (10, 110) 1970–present

BIOSIS PREVIEWS (5, 55) 1969–present

CAB ABSTRACTS (50) 1973–present
CRIS/USDA (60) Current
FOOD SCIENCE AND TECHNOLOGY ABSTRACTS (51) 1969–present
FOODS ADLIBRA (79) 1974–present

*Medicine and Biosciences*

BIOSIS PREVIEWS (5, 55) 1969–present
CA SEARCH (308, 309, 310, 311, 320) 1967–present
CHEMNAME (301) 1967–present
CHEMSEARCH (30) Current
CHEMSIS (328, 329, 330, 331) 1967–present
CHEMZERO (300) 1965–present
EXCERPTA MEDICA (72, 73, 172) 6/74–present
HEALTH PLANNING AND ADMINISTRATION (151) 1975–present
INTERNATIONAL PHARMACEUTICAL ABSTRACTS (74) 1970–present
LIFE SCIENCES COLLECTION (76) 1978–present
MEDLINE (152, 153, 154) 1966–present
MENTAL HEALTH ABSTRACTS * (86) 1969–present
PHARMACEUTICAL NEWS INDEX (42) 1975–present
SCISEARCH (34, 94, 186, 187) 1970–present
TELEGEN (238) 1973–present
ZOOLOGICAL RECORD (185) 1978–present

*Energy and Environment*

APTIC (45) 1966–9/78
AQUACULTURE (112) 1970–present
AQUALINE (116) 1974–present
AQUATIC SCIENCE AND FISHERIES ABSTRACTS (44) 1978–present
BIOSIS PREVIEWS (5, 55) 1969–present
CA SEARCH (308, 309, 310, 311, 320) 1967–present
DOE ENERGY (103) 1974–present
ELECTRIC POWER DATABASE (247) 1972–present
ENERGYLINE (69) 1971–present

* Forthcoming database

ENERGYNET (169) Current
ENVIROLINE (40) 1971–present
ENVIRONMENTAL BIBLIOGRAPHY (68) 1973–present
OCEANIC ABSTRACTS (28) 1964–present
POLLUTION ABSTRACTS (41) 1970–present
WATER RESOURCES ABSTRACTS (117) 1968–present
WATERNET (245) 1971–present

*Science and Technology*

BHRA FLUID ENGINEERING (96) 1974–present
COMPENDEX (8) 1970–present
Ei ENGINEERING MEETINGS (165) 1979–present
GEOARCHIVE (58) 1969–present
GEOREF (89) 1961–present
INSPEC (12, 13) 1969–present
INTERNATIONAL SOFTWARE DATABASE (232) Current offerings
ISMEC (14) 1973–present
MATHFILE (239) 1973–present
METEROLOGICAL AND GEOASTROPHYSICAL ABSTRACTS (29) 1972–present
MICROCOMPUTER INDEX (233) 1980–present
NTIS (6) 1964–present
SCISEARCH (34, 94, 186, 187) 1970–present
SPIN (62) 1975–present
SSIE CURRENT RESEARCH (65) Current
STANDARDS AND SPECIFICATIONS (113) 1950–present
TRIS (63) 1968–present
WELDASEARCH (99) 1967–present

*Materials Sciences*

CA SEARCH (308, 309, 310, 311, 320) 1967–present
CHEMNAME (301) 1967–present
CHEMSEARCH (30) Current
CHEMSIS (328, 329, 330, 331) 1967–present
CHEMZERO (300) 1965–present
METADEX (32) 1966–present
NONFERROUS METALS ABSTRACTS (118) 1961–present

PAPERCHEM (240) 7/68–present
SURFACE COATINGS ABSTRACTS (115) 1976–present
TEXTILE TECHNOLOGY DIGEST (119) 1978–present
WORLD ALUMINUM ABSTRACTS (33) 1968–present
WORLD TEXTILES (67) 1970–present

*Patents*

CA SEARCH (308, 309, 310, 311, 320) 1967–present
CLAIMS/CITATION (220, 221, 222) 1947–present
CLAIMS/CLASS (124) not applicable
CLAIMS COMPOUND REGISTRY (242) Current
CLAIMS/U.S. PATENT ABSTRACTS (23) 1950–1970
CLAIMS/U.S. PATENT ABSTRACTS (24) 1971–1981
CLAIMS/U.S. PATENT ABSTRACTS (25) 1982–present
CLAIMS/U.S. PATENT ABSTRACTS WEEKLY (125) Current month
CLAIMS/UNITERM (223, 224, 225) 1950–present
INPADOC (123) Current six weeks
PATLAW (243) 1970–present

*Business/Economics*

*Bibliographic*

ABI/INFORM (15) 8/71–present
ADTRACK (43) 10/80–present
CHEMICAL INDUSTRY NOTES (19) 1974–present
ECONOMICS ABSTRACTS INTERNATIONAL (90) 1974–present
FIND/SVP REPORTS AND STUDIES INDEX (196) 1979–present
HARFAX INDUSTRY DATA SOURCES (189) 1979–present
HARVARD BUSINESS REVIEW (122) 1971–present
INSURANCE ABSTRACTS (168) 1979–present
JOURNAL OF ECONOMIC LITERATURE (139) 1969–present
MANAGEMENT CONTENTS (75) 1974–present
PHARMACEUTICAL NEWS INDEX (42) 12/75–present
PTS ANNUAL REPORTS ABSTRACTS (17) Current
PTS F & S INDEXES (18, 98) 1972–present
PTS PROMT (16) 1972–present
STANDARD & POOR'S NEWS (132) 9/79–present

STANDARD & POOR'S NEWS DAILY (133) Current

TRADE AND INDUSTRY INDEX (148) 1981–present

*Numeric*

BI/DATA FORECASTS (129) Current

BI/DATA TIME SERIES (128) Varies from record to record

BLS CONSUMER PRICE INDEX (175) Varies from record to record

BLS EMPLOYMENT, HOURS, AND EARNINGS (178) Varies from record to record

BLS LABOR FORCE (177) Varies from record to record

BLS PRODUCER PRICE INDEX (176) Varies from record to record

DISCLOSURE II (100) Current

PTS INTERNATIONAL FORECASTS (83) 1971–present

PTS INTERNATIONAL TIME SERIES (84) 1972–present

PTS U.S. FORECASTS (81) 7/71–present

PTS U.S. TIME SERIES (82) 7/71–present

U.S. EXPORTS (126) 1978–present

*Directories*

CATFAX: DIRECTORY OF MAIL ORDER CATALOGS* (198) Current

COMMERCE BUSINESS DAILY (195) Current

DISCLOSURE II (100) Current

DUNS MARKET IDENTIFIERS 10 + (516) Current

EIS INDUSTRIAL PLANTS (22) Current

EIS NONMANUFACTURING ESTABLISHMENTS (92) Current

ELECTRONIC YELLOW PAGES—CONSTRUCTION DIRECTORY (507) Current

ELECTRONIC YELLOW PAGES—FINANCIAL SERVICES DIRECTORY (501) Current

ELECTRONIC YELLOW PAGES—MANUFACTURERS DIRECTORY (510) Current

ELECTRONIC YELLOW PAGES—PROFESSIONALS DIRECTORY (502) Current

ELECTRONIC YELLOW PAGES—RETAILERS DIRECTORY (504, 505, 506) Current

* Forthcoming database.

ELECTRONIC YELLOW PAGES—SERVICES DIRECTORY (508, 509) Current

ELECTRONIC YELLOW PAGES—WHOLESALERS DIRECTORY (503) Current

FOREIGN TRADERS INDEX (105) Current five years

MILLION DOLLAR DIRECTORY (517) Current

TRADE OPPORTUNITIES (106) 1976–present

TRADE OPPORTUNITIES WEEKLY (107) Current three months

*Industry Specific*

CHEMICAL INDUSTRY NOTES (19) 1974–present

COFFEELINE (164) 1973–present

FOODS ADLIBRA (79) 1974–present

INSURANCE ABSTRACTS (168) 1979–present

PHARMACEUTICAL NEWS INDEX (42) 12/75–present

*Multidisciplinary*

COMPREHENSIVE DISSERTATION INDEX (35) 1861–present

CONFERENCE PAPERS INDEX (77) 1973–present

DIALINDEX (411) Current

NTIS (6) 1964–present

*Education*

AIM/ARM (9) 1967–1976

ERIC (1) 1966–present

EXCEPTIONAL CHILD EDUCATION RESOURCES (54) 1966–present

IRIS (53) 1979–present

NICEM (46) 1979 edition

NICSEM/NIMIS (70) 1978 edition

U.S. PUBLIC SCHOOL DIRECTORY (120) Current

*Online Training and Practice*

ONTAP ABI/INFORM (215)

ONTAP CA SEARCH (204)

ONTAP CHEMNAME (231)

ONTAP COMPENDEX (208)

ONTAP DIALINDEX (290)

ONTAP ERIC (201)
ONTAP INSPEC (213)
ONTAP MAGAZINE INDEX (247)
ONTAP MEDLINE (254)
ONTAP PTS PROMT (216)

*Bibliography-Books and Monographs*

BOOK REVIEW INDEX (137) 1969–present
BOOKS IN PRINT (470) 1900–present
DIALOG PUBLICATIONS (200) Current
GPO MONTHLY CATALOG (66) 7/76–present
GPO PUBLICATIONS REFERENCE FILE (166) 1971–present
LC MARC * (426) 1968–present
REMARC (421–425) 1897–12/31/78

*Foundations and Grants*

FOUNDATION DIRECTORY (26) Current
FOUNDATION GRANTS INDEX (27) 1973–present
GRANTS (85) 1977–present
NATIONAL FOUNDATIONS (78) Current

*Law and Government*

ASI (102) 1973–present
CIS (101) 1970–present
CHEMICAL REGULATIONS AND GUIDELINES SYSTEM (174) Current
CHEMLAW (197) Current
COMMERCE BUSINESS DAILY (194, 195) 1982–present
CONGRESSIONAL RECORD ABSTRACTS * (135) 1976–present
CRIMINAL JUSTICE PERIODICALS INDEX (171) 1975–present
FEDERAL INDEX (20) 10/76–present
FEDERAL REGISTER ABSTRACTS (136) 3/77–present
GPO MONTHLY CATALOG (66) 7/76–present
GPO PUBLICATIONS REFERENCE FILE (166) 1971–present
LABORLAW (244) 1938–present
LEGAL RESOURCE INDEX (150) 1980–present

* Forthcoming database.

NCJRS (21) 1972–present
NTIS (6) 1964–present
PATLAW (243) 1970–present
TSCA 'NITIAL INVENTORY (52) 1979 edition

*Current Affairs*

CHRONOLOG NEWSLETTER (410) 1981–present
MAGAZINE INDEX (47) 1976–present
NATIONAL NEWSPAPER INDEX (111) 1979–present
NEWSEARCH (211) Current month
ONLINE CHRONICLE (170) 10/81–present
PAIS INTERNATIONAL (49) 1976–present
STANDARD AND POOR'S NEWS (132) 9/79–present
STANDARD AND POOR'S NEWS DAILY (133) Current

*Directories*

AMERICAN MEN AND WOMEN OF SCIENCE * (236) Selective living scientists
BIOGRAPHY MASTER INDEX (88) Current edition
CAREER PLACEMENT REGISTRY/EXPERIENCED PERSONNEL (162) Current
CAREER PLACEMENT REGISTRY/STUDENT (163) Current
ENCYCLOPEDIA OF ASSOCIATIONS (114) Current
MARQUIS WHO'S WHO * (234) Current
ULRICH'S INTERNATIONAL PERIODICAL DIRECTORY * (480) Current

*Social Sciences and Humanities*

AMERICA: HISTORY AND LIFE (38) 1964–present
ARTBIBLIOGRAPHIES MODERN (56) 1974–present
CHILD ABUSE AND NEGLECT (64) 1965–present
HISTORICAL ABSTRACTS (39) 1973–present
LANGUAGE AND LANGUAGE BEHAVIOR ABSTRACTS (36) 1973–present
LISA (61) 1969–present
MLA BIBLIOGRAPHY (71) 1970–present
PAIS INTERNATIONAL (49) 1976–present

* Forthcoming database.

PHILOSOPHER'S INDEX (57) 1940–present

POPULATION BIBLIOGRAPHY (91) 1966–present

PSYCINFO (11) 1967–present

RILM ABSTRACTS (97) 1972–present

SOCIAL SCISEARCH (7) 1972–present

SOCIOLOGICAL ABSTRACTS (37) 1963–present

UNITED STATES POLITICAL SCIENCE ABSTRACTS (93) 1975–present

WORLD AFFAIRS REPORT * (167) 1970–present

* Forthcoming database.

# INDEX

**References are to Pages**


## A

ABF processor, 157.
ALU Arithmetic Logic Unit, 8.
Abstracts, 66.
Accounting, 4, 27, 35, 94.
Accounts receivable aging, 93.
American Bar Foundation, 38, 157.
American Legal Systems, 60.
Analog signal, 24.
Analogic legal reasoning systems, 160.
Apple IIe, 34, 77.
Application program, 20.
Artificial intelligence, 6, 38.
Aspen, 60.
Assemblers, 18.
Atlis Systems, 60.
Attorney, 84.
Attorney productivity reports, 93.
Authority lists, 63.
Auto-Cite, 112, 134.
Automated document preparation systems, 155.
Automatic speech recognition, 15.
Auxiliary mass storage, 13.
Auxiliary storage or memory, 10.

## B

BASIC, 20, 31.
BRITANNICA 3, 114.
BRS, 99, 144.
Batched data, 27.
Bibliographic indexes, 66.
Billing, 4, 27, 35.
Bit, binary information digit, 8.
Boolean logic, 68, 107, 111.
Boolean operators, 69.
Buffer, 78.
Business and Finance data bases, 140.
Byte, 8.

## C

CALR computer assisted legal research, 99.

CAT Computer Assisted Transcription, 65.
COBOL, 20.
CONDOR, 61.
CP/M, 19, 33, 35, 47, 78.
CPU, 10.
Center for Computer Assisted Legal Instruction, 165.
Central processing unit, 7.
Check writing, 94.
Chip, 32.
Client collections, 93.
Coaxial cable, 24.
Coding, 63.
Communications, 22, 74.
Communications programs, 18, 21.
Compilers, 18.
Computer aided legal instruction, 164.
Computer assisted conflict systems, 89.
Computer Assisted Litigation Support, 57, 70.
Computer typesetting, 149.
Computerized document preparation systems, 159.
Concordance, 111.
Condor, 35.
Conflict of interest systems, 88.
Congressional and Legislative data bases, 140.
Consultation machines, 159.
Control Data, 60.
Control unit, 7, 10.
Corporate practice, 75.
Customized software, 20.

**D**

DBASE II, 35, 61, 90.
DBMS Data Base Management System, 36.
DCF Document Coding Form, 66.
DIALINDEX, 146.
DIALOG, 2, 22, 36, 99, 114, 144, 166.
DISCLO, 136.
DISCLOSURE II, 2.
Daisy wheel printer, 17, 78.
Data base, 62.
Data base management systems, 35.
Data base publishing, 150.
Data entry, 64.
Data processing, 96.
Data processor, 81.
Dedicated leased line, 25.
Dedicated word processor, 20, 39, 78.
Deposition, 56.
Depositions, 65.
Digest topics, 102, 105.
Digital signal, 24.
Discovery, 70.

Disk, 11.
Disk publication, 152.
Distributed logic, 80.
Docket/calendar control, 74.
Docket control/calendar system, 85.
Dot matrix printer, 78.
Dumb terminal, 14.

**E**

EDUNET, 165.
ELSS, 99.
ELSS Electronic Legislative Search System, 115.
Electronic clock, 32.
Electronic mail, 3, 26.
Electronic publishing, 150.
Employees, 46.
European libraries, 109.
Extracts, 66.

**F**

FLITE, 117.
FORTRAN, 20.
Facsimile equipment, 23.
Family law, 75.
Federal law libraries, 111.
Federal libraries, 108.
Fiber optic transmissions, 24.
Field searches, 114.
Financial management, 91.
Floppy disk, 11.
French Law Libraries, 112.
Full text, 105.
Full-text retrieval, 61.

**G**

General ledger, 93.
General News and Information data bases, 143.
Global search, 74.
Graphics, 52.

**H**

Handwriting recognition, 17.
Hard disk, 11, 36.
Hardware, 4, 45.
Headnotes, 105.

**I**

IBM, 61.
IBM Displaywriter, 79.
IBM PC, 34, 77.
Impact printer, 17.

Informatics, 60.
Infrared transmission, 24.
Ink jet printer, 17.
Input device, 13.
Insta-Cite, 109.
Institute for Computer Science and Technology, 28.
Intelligent terminal, 14.
Interpreters, 18.
Intra-office network, 26.

**J**

JURIS, 116.
Judicial predictors, 161.
Jury predictors, 162.
Jury selection, 163.

**K**

Key numbers, 105.
Key words, 102, 120, 130.
Kilobyte, 9.

**L**

LAWNET, 118.
LEGITECH, 116.
LEXIS, 36, 99, 104, 110.
LEXPAT, 113.
LSI Large Scale Integrated Circuit, 7.
Laser printer, 17, 18.
Law office manager, 84.
Legal data base, 103.
Legal education, 154.
Legal Resource Index, 139.
Legislative drafting, 154.
Legislative tracking systems, 115.
Letter quality printer, 17.
Litigation, 75.
Litigation support, 4, 109, 114.
Litigation support systems, 55.
Litigation vendors, 59.
Local area network, 26.
Lotus I, II, III, 35.

**M**

MOS memory, 9.
MS–DOS, 19, 33, 35, 78.
Machine cycle, 32.
Machine-readable form, 66.
Machine-readable tape, 107.
Magnetic tape, 13.
Main memory, 8.
Mainframe, 42.

Malpractice, 85.
Management, 54.
Management reports, 27, 93.
Math functions, 74.
Mathematical modeling, 153.
Matsco, 60.
Mead Data Central, 104, 110.
Medical and Technical data bases, 143.
Megabyte, 9.
Mellonics, 60.
Memoranda, 75.
Merging, 73.
Microcomputer, 19, 30, 33, 47.
Microcomputer hardware, 30.
Microcomputer software, 33.
Microcomputers, 61, 97.
Microfilm, 12.
Micrographing, 62.
Microprocessor, 32.
Minicomputer, 40, 51.
Minicomputer hardware, 41.
Minicomputer software, 41.
Minicomputers, 60, 97.
Modem, 3, 25.

**N**

NEXIS, 99, 113, 136, 147.
National Bureau of Standards, 28.
National Reporter system, 106.
Networking, 21.
Network, 14, 51, 80.
Networks, 23.
Non-impact printer, 18.
Non-legal data bases, 137.

**O**

OCR, Optical Character Recognition Unit, 14, 15, 65, 76, 80.
OEM, 41.
ORBIT, 36, 99, 144.
On-line, 10.
Operating system, 18, 19, 31.
Optical disk, 12.
Out-of-house computers, 27.
Output device, 13.

**P**

PAI Public Affairs Information, 116.
Packet-switching network, 25.
Paralegal, 4, 51, 83.
Payroll, 27, 94.
Perfect Writer, 34.

Personnel, 82.
Photocomposition interface, 74.
Printers, 17.
Private data bases, 100.
Programmer, 42.
Public data bases, 100.

**R**

RAM, random access memory, 8, 9.
RFP, 59.
RIRA, 118.
ROM, read only memory, 8, 9.
Radio Shack TRS Model II, 34.
Real estate, 75.
Records management, 73.
Remote computers, 27.
Repagination, 74.
Restrictive connectors, 121, 130.
Roots, 121.

**S**

STAIRS, 61.
Scanner, 14.
Search query, 120.
Secretary, 83.
Segment searches, 134.
Service bureau, 27, 38.
Service bureaus, 96.
Shared logic, 79.
Shared resource system, 14.
Shared resources, 80.
Shepard's 134.
Shepard's Citations, 109, 112.
Shepardizing, 124.
Software, 18, 45.
Software house, 20.
Software houses, 41.
Specialized libraries, 135.
Specialized searches, 128.
Specialty Law Libraries, 113, 108.
Speech recognition devices, 15.
Spelling checks, 73.
State law libraries, 112.
State libraries, 108.
Statutes, 125, 135.
Storage, 73.
Substantive systems, 36.
SuperCalc, 35.
Synonyms, 121, 130.
Synopses, 105.

## T

TAXMAN, 160.
TELENET, 2, 25, 104, 166.
TYMNET, 22, 25, 104.
Tape storage, 13.
Tax, 75.
Taxonomies, 64.
Telecommunications, 22, 28, 44.
Telephones, 23.
Telex, 23.
Terminal, 14.
Text editing, 73.
Time keeping, 25.
Time-sharing, 28, 43.
Timekeeper, 93.
Trial, 70.
Trial transcripts, 65.

## U

United Kingdom Law Libraries, 112.
Utility program, 20.
Utility programs, 18.

## V

VisiCalc, 35.

## W

WESTLAW, 2, 22, 36, 99, 104, 166.
West Publishing Co., 104.
Winchester disk, 12, 33.
Witness preparation, 70.
Witnesses, 56.
Word processing, 34, 71.
Word processor, 39.
WordStar, 34, 77.
Work product, 66.

## X

XENIX, 33.

†